MOBFATHER

OTHER BOOKS BY GEORGE ANASTASIA

Blood and Honor
The Goodfella Tapes
The Summer Wind
The Big Hustle
The Last Gangster

MOB FATHER

The Story of a Wife and a Son Caught in the Web of the Mafia

GEORGE ANASTASIA

Camino Books, Inc.
Philadelphia

Published by arrangement with the author.

Manufactured in the United States of America

1 2 3 4 5 6 7   09 08 07 06

Library of Congress Cataloging-in-Publication Data

Anastasia, George.
    Mobfather : the story of a wife and a son caught in the web of the mafia / George Anastasia.
        p. cm.
    Includes index.
    ISBN-13: 978-0-940159-99-0 (alk. paper)
    ISBN-10: 0-940159-99-6 (alk. paper)
    1. Mafia—Pennsylvania—Philadelphia Metropolitan Area—Case studies.
2. DelGiorno, Robert, 1967- 3. Fisher, Maryann DelGiorno. I. Title.

    HV6452.P4M3426 2006
    364.106'092274811—dc22   2006004205

ISBN-13: 978-0-940159-99-0
ISBN-10: 0-940159-99-6

Cover design by Jerilyn Bockorick

This book is available at a special discount on bulk purchases for promotional, business, and educational use. For information write to:

Camino Books, Inc.
P. O. Box 59026
Philadelphia, PA 19102

www.caminobooks.com

Acknowledgments

This book could not have been written without the cooperation and candor of Robert DelGiorno and his mother, Maryann Fisher. Also, a thank you to Joe Fisher and Thomas DelGiorno, Jr., for their support and encouragement.

I would also like to acknowledge the guidance, information and direction provided by dozens of law enforcement officials who, over the years, have been both accessible and willing to share their expertise. These include, but are not limited to, members of the Philadelphia Police Department, the New Jersey State Police, the Pennsylvania Crime Commission, the New Jersey Attorney General's Office, the New Jersey State Commission of Investigation, the FBI and the U.S. Attorney's Offices for the Eastern District of Pennsylvania and for New Jersey. There were also numerous reporters for the *Philadelphia Inquirer* and *Philadelphia Daily News* whose stories over the years helped to accurately sketch the backdrop of events portrayed here.

Special thanks to Alice Alfonsi, whose editing and enthusiasm made this process work, and to Jerome Perles, as always, for his counsel.

Finally, I would like to acknowledge the late Thomas C. Renner, a gracious and unselfish reporter who always had a word of encouragement or advice. Tom was considering this story at the time of his passing. I hope he is pleased with the finished product.

For Angela

Prologue

Whenever anyone asks Bobby DelGiorno what his father, the gangster, is really like, he tells a story about the present he got for his nineteenth birthday.

This was back in September of 1986. At the time, Bobby's father, Thomas DelGiorno, or "Tommy Del," was a major player in the South Philadelphia underworld. He was a man who routinely dealt in extortion, loan-sharking, narcotics and murder as a member of one of the most violent Mafia families in America.

Bobby's birthday was a week away and his father had told him to stop by the clubhouse where he hung out. The building, a tiny storefront that formerly housed a plumbing supply company, was located at Camac and Moore Streets in the heart of South Philadelphia. Two large plate glass windows framed a narrow doorway that opened onto the street. On the wall opposite the doorway hung a collage of photos of Tommy Del and his friends, who were some of the city's most notorious gangsters. Some were dressed in expensive suits and ties as they smiled against the backdrop of a fancy restaurant or nightclub, others wore shorts or bathing suits as they waved from the deck of a cabin cruiser or stood on a sunny Florida beach. There was also a large and surprisingly benign portrait of Tommy Del's mob boss, Little Nicky Scarfo, a violent and arrogant Mafia don who had shot his way to the top of the organization.

Above the pictures were drawings of the American and Italian flags. A coffeepot sat atop a cabinet near the door. Newspapers and magazines were strewn about the room. An ominous printed warning, CLUB MEMBERS ONLY, hung on the wall between the flags and the photos.

Bobby walked in and asked for his dad. He was directed to some tables in the back where Tommy Del was playing cards.

"Heh, Bob, how are ya?" his father said with a smile. "Wait a minute till I'm done this hand."

At the time, Bobby was living with his mother, stepfather and older brother, Tommy junior, in a tiny brick row house on South Philadelphia's Gladstone Street, not far from the warehouses and loading terminals along the Delaware River. Tommy Del, remarried and with two younger sons from his second wife, lived in a much larger home in a classy residential neighborhood a dozen blocks away. He was, however, very much a part of Bobby's life. He provided jobs for both Bobby and Tommy junior while they were growing up. And even though he seldom had much time to spend with his boys, he always had lots of money to spend on them.

Bobby, more than his older brother, was impressed by this. And by almost everything else about his father's lifestyle. He would often stop by the clubhouse or his dad's bar to watch him conduct "business," hoping to be asked to run an errand— to drop off a brown bag full of cash or pick up an envelope. Better still were the times when his dad would ask him to drive him to a meeting or a social gathering. Sometimes they'd head for one of the casinos in Atlantic City. There Bobby would watch in awe as his father pulled a wad of one-hundred-dollar bills out of his pocket, bought a stack of chips and then settled in for a night of blackjack or craps.

On this day, however, there were no meetings, no errands to run, no trips to the casinos.

"Get in the car, Bob," Tommy Del said as they walked out of the clubhouse together after the card game had ended. "Let's go for a ride."

Bobby, who had been itching to go to work full-time for his father, knew better than to ask where or why.

They drove past the neatly kept two-story row houses, corner grocery stores and neighborhood taverns that lined the gridwork of streets in South Philadelphia, heading for Broad Street and the freeway that led to the Walt Whitman Bridge. Tommy Del eased his Cadillac into a line at the tollbooths, threw ninety cents into one of the electronic baskets and drove over the Delaware River toward South Jersey.

Within minutes they pulled into the parking lot of an automobile showroom. Tommy parked the car, got out, walked into the office and began talking to a man who appeared to be in charge. Then he came back and told Bobby, "Pick out whatever you want. This guy owes me a favor."

Bobby's eyes nearly popped out of their sockets.

Whatever I want, he thought as he looked out at rows of gleaming new automobiles.

That afternoon young Bobby DelGiorno returned to South Philadelphia behind the wheel of a brand-new, fully loaded Chrysler Fifth Avenue. "It was white with a blue ragtop roof," he recalls, embarrassed now by both the gaudy gift and his thrill at receiving it.

Later he would ask his father about the man in the showroom. Tommy Del laughed and then proudly explained to his son that the car dealer frequently borrowed money from him and, after paying years of usurious loan shark rates, was deeply in his debt.

"We have an arrangement," Tommy Del said. "Every week he sends me money and every week I let him live."

Bright, shiny and expensive, the Chrysler Fifth Avenue symbolized the grandiose style and the insatiable greed that consumed Tommy DelGiorno. I first heard the story in the summer of 1991 when Bobby showed up at the newspaper office where I work. I had written several stories about his father, then an infamous mob turncoat who testified in a dozen trials that brought down the Scarfo crime family. I had also written a few about Bobby himself. But I had never met either DelGiorno.

Bobby, like his father, was short, about five foot six. But he was stockier than Tommy Del and unlike his father, Bobby had the soft and innocent features of a choirboy. His voice and manner, however, were right off the streets of South Philadelphia. He showed up in a gray designer sweatsuit carrying a three-hundred-page handwritten manuscript. It was, he said, the story of his life. Another ninety pages, more neatly written, had been prepared by his mother, Maryann. Together the documents formed the outline for this book.

It is a tale of murder, money and corruption that unfolds against the backdrop of the rise and fall of Little Nicky Scarfo and Tommy DelGiorno, two of the most ruthless and greedy Mafia figures in America. Scarfo is now in prison. Tommy Del, whose testimony helped put him there, is in the Federal Witness Protection Program. Given a new identity, he disappeared in the late 1980s along with his second wife and their two young sons. He now lives his life under the constant threat of a Mafia murder contract.

But while Scarfo and Tommy Del are key figures in the story, it is Bobby and his mother, Maryann, who play the central roles. Maryann, a feisty, no-nonsense woman with more heart than any of her ex-husband's gangster friends, waged a twenty-year battle—first to break away from Tommy Del and then to protect her sons from him. Her view of the Mafia is unique. It comes from across the kitchen table of a South Philadelphia row home. She knew no "men of honor" in the underworld. Saw no justification for the venal, depraved and greedy lifestyles of those who lived there. And nearly fighting both the mob and a criminal justice system that—oi. it embraced Tommy Del as a witness—seemed to become a. corrupt and petty as the Mafia family it was trying to destroy.

Bobby, on the other hand, had a romanticized view of his father's world. He grew up in the shadow of one of the most notorious gangsters in South Philadelphia and, at first, he loved it. He was amazed by his father's various business interests, by the huge amounts of cash in his pockets, and by the deference shown him by people in the neighborhood. When Bobby was an impressionable teenager in the early 1980s, Tommy Del and a dozen of his cohorts were dominating the headlines in Philadelphia. There was a bloody internecine struggle raging for control of the local branch of the Mafia. Bodies were dropping everywhere. When the shooting stopped, twenty-eight mob figures were dead and Scarfo sat at the top of the heap, controlling a criminal organization whose tentacles stretched from the Boardwalk in Atlantic City to the ski resorts of the Pocono Mountains.

But South Philadelphia was the hub of the Scarfo crime family, and Tommy Del was the man in charge there. He was Scarfo's day-to-day operations chief. Short and thin, with sharp features, DelGiorno was a master of treachery, guile and deceit. He was also, like Little Nicky, a heartless killer.

"My father was the type of person, he'd be laughing one minute, then be shooting you in the back of the head the next," Bobby DelGiorno said soberly several years later.

At the time, however, Bobby gloried in his father's reputation, status and wealth. Largely disregarding the warnings of his mother and stepfather, he danced on the edge of the mob, living an underworld version of *The Wonder Years,* fascinated by what he perceived as his dad's larger-than-life, money's-no-object existence.

That fascination would eventually rip Bobby's life apart, as well as the lives of those closest to him—his older brother, Tommy junior, and his mother, Maryann. But it would be years before he realized the danger, years before the mob lost its mystique. As a teenager, he looked at the Mafia with wide eyes and thought it was wonderful. He saw his father surrounded by guys with nicknames right out of the movies: Joe Chang; Frankie Flowers; Broadway Eddie; Nicky Crow. They seemed like Damon Runyon characters, displaying swagger and style that filled the head of a thirteen-year-old who wanted nothing more than for his father to notice and love him.

"I remember one time down the shore," Bobby said. "My father had a house in Longport [New Jersey] for the summer. And every weekend his friends would come down to play cards. Man, you never saw so much money. More than in a bank. I couldn't believe it. From that point on, I wanted to be like those guys, live like they did, have that kind of money."

––––––––––

Tommy junior was the older, by seventeen months, and the more level-headed of the two brothers. Slightly taller than Bobby, Tommy junior favored his mother's side of the family in both appearance and temperament. He wanted nothing to do with the mob.

Bobby also looked more like his mother than his father. But like Tommy Del, he was volatile and more susceptible to the intoxicating power of the Mafia. Even when the headlines screamed of murder, even when his father was identified as a prime suspect in a shooting, even when some of the same men who had sat around the table playing cards turned up dead in the trunk of a car, Bobby wanted in.

One of his first jobs was at a grocery not far from a neighborhood bar owned by his father. The butcher was a loan shark. The deli man was a bookmaker. Two of the women who worked the cash registers took numbers for his dad. Another employee dealt in stolen goods.

"Nobody really cared how much food we sold," Bobby said.

It was there that he began to appreciate the strength and

influence of the mob; there that he saw the multimillion dollar underground economy it fueled and the fear it instilled. Seduced by Tommy Del's lifestyle, Bobby came to believe that his father was invincible and that he, as his father's son, shared in that invincibility.

As Tommy Del moved up the mob ladder, from gambling and loan-sharking to drug dealing and murder, Bobby dreamed of the day when he'd be old enough to join the organization. Those were heady times for a kid whose father was then a *capodecima*—a "capo," or captain—in one of the most notorious crime families in America. Tommy Del's name was always in the paper and Bobby, like his father, took pride in that fact.

"All I ever wanted to do was quit school and be a gangster like my dad," he said.

But then a million-dollar extortion scam turned sour, a drug deal went bad and a lucrative gambling and loan-sharking ring was exposed. Suddenly, the mob was under attack. Indictments were coming from all directions. Scarfo held Tommy Del accountable. And the world turned upside down for Bobby Del-Giorno.

In November of 1986, fearing he would be murdered, Tommy Del agreed to become a cooperating witness for the New Jersey State Police and the FBI. Bobby and his brother—surrogate targets for mob retribution once Tommy Del began to sing—were forced to go into hiding with their father, stepmother and two young half brothers.

It was while living on the run in government "safe houses" between 1986 and 1988 that Bobby's fascination with the mob and with his father ended. And it was there that his fight to survive—and his mother's final valiant struggle to win back her sons—began.

Today Bobby and his brother are back in South Philadelphia. Both are married and each lives within blocks of their mother's home on Gladstone Street. They have cut all ties with their mobster-turned-informant father and with the law enforcement community that provides for his safety. They are once again a part of the community where they were born and raised and where they intend to spend the rest of their lives. They have negotiated "an understanding" with the mob that once wanted them dead.

"We don't bother them, they don't bother us," Bobby says. "All we want is to be left alone."

Conversations recounted here are based on the recollections of at least one person involved, usually Bobby or Maryann. Nothing has been fabricated, but the timing of some events has been consolidated in order to enhance the story's flow. The identities of some minor figures and the descriptions of some businesses have been altered in order to protect the privacy rights of those inadvertently affected by the criminal conduct of others. The book's narrative is based on a dozen years of reporting on the events recounted here and on a review of thousands of pages of court testimony. The comments of mobster Tommy DelGiorno are culled from those court records and from never-before-published FBI and New Jersey State Police debriefing reports in which DelGiorno detailed his life inside the Mafia.

—George Anastasia
March 1993

Chapter One

Shortly after midnight on April 17, 1988, in an alley behind Eddie's Lounge on O'Donnell Street in Baltimore, a man named Stephen Hemerlein was shot in the face with a .357 Magnum.

He died instantly.

Less than an hour later, Robert DelGiorno and Anthony Forline, two young South Philadelphians, surrendered to a surprised Pinkerton security guard at the gates of a Bethlehem Steel plant about ten miles from the murder scene.

"We just shot someone," DelGiorno shouted as he jumped out of the passenger side of the car Forline was driving. "I think he's dead."

The front of DelGiorno's shirt and pants were soaked in blood as he stood in the gravel driveway leading to the plant gate. The security guard pulled his gun and pointed it at the car as DelGiorno tried desperately to explain the situation. The guard asked if they had any weapons and then told Forline, who had the Magnum stuffed in his waistband, to throw the gun out the window with his left hand. Then he ordered Forline to step slowly out of the car.

"Now both of you put your hands on the hood where I can see them," he said nervously.

Within minutes two police cars and a paddy wagon, their sirens wailing and their red lights flashing, pulled up to the plant's entrance. One cop approached DelGiorno and Forline, while at least four others, their weapons drawn, took up positions behind their vehicles. By Bobby DelGiorno's count there were now five guns pointing at his head. For a brief instant, the thought of running flashed through his mind. It would be quick and easy. And in an instant it would be all over.

DelGiorno was twenty years old, and for most of his young life he had considered himself invincible. But in the past year, he had come to realize how vulnerable he was, how little control he really had over the circumstances surrounding his life and over those, like his father, who seemed to be dictating how he should live. Dying on the gravel driveway of a steel plant might be preferable to going back to the life he had been living. What he wanted more than anything else was to go home to South Philadelphia. Baltimore, he had thought, was merely a stop on the way back. Now it looked like a dead end.

Bobby stood perfectly still as one of the cops approached and told him to put his hands behind his back. He felt handcuffs being snapped on both his wrists. In a daze, he watched as his friend Anthony was handcuffed. Then the other cops, their guns still drawn, closed in. One grabbed Bobby high on the arm. Another did the same with Anthony. Together they were hustled to one of the police cars, pushed into the back seat and driven off.

Neither said a word.

Bobby DelGiorno and Anthony Forline had grown up together in the same tough, blue-collar neighborhood around Second Street in South Philadelphia. For most of their lives they had been inseparable, sharing each rite of passage in the slow and steady progression from childhood. They had spent hours sitting on the stoops in front of their row homes or hanging in the neighborhood schoolyard talking about sports, sex, money and clothes. They had chased girls together and fought guys from other corners. They got drunk for the first time when Bobby was fourteen, bribing a neighborhood rummy to buy them takeout quarts of beer from a local taproom. In junior high they organized their own weekly football pool, running off betting sheets in the school library each week, collecting bets on Fridays, making payouts on Mondays and stuffing their winnings in a shoebox that Bobby kept hidden under a floorboard in his bedroom. By the end of the football season, they each had several hundred dollars.

"It was easy," Bobby said years later. "We never spent any of the money during the season, in case we had a bad week and we needed to make a big payout. And we always, always paid the winners on time. You build up trust and confidence. People know they can depend on you. Who's it hurt? People bet all the time. What's the difference? To this day, I still don't see what's wrong with betting. All the states do it. The lotteries. The casinos. The racetracks."

Bobby and Anthony shared one other fascination while growing up. Indirectly, this obsession led them to Baltimore and the shooting of Stephen Hemerlein. As kids, both had been intrigued with stories about the Mafia. Each had bragged to the other about his own "connections."

Anthony had an uncle, Frank "J. R." Forline, who was described by law enforcement types as a known mob associate. Frank Forline was in the construction business but, according to some sources, he supplemented his income by serving as a collector and an enforcer for a mob loan-sharking operation. In 1985 he turned up dead, shot in the back of the head. Police found his body slumped behind the wheel of his pickup truck in suburban Delaware County just outside of Philadelphia. The murder has never been solved.

Bobby's line to the mob was even more direct. His father, Tommy DelGiorno, was a "made"—formally initiated—member of the Philadelphia crime family headed by Little Nicky Scarfo, arguably the most violent Mafia boss in America. In the early 1980s, Scarfo was to Philadelphia and South Jersey what John Gotti was soon to become to New York—a bold, ruthless and flamboyant mob boss who ruled through fear and intimidation.

Tommy Del had been Scarfo's right-hand man in Philadelphia, rising to the rank of capo in the sixty-man organization. But late in 1986 the two had a falling out and Tommy, fearing that he was about to be killed, turned informant and agreed to cooperate with state and federal prosecutors in a series of cases that would eventually bring down the Scarfo mob. In fact, Tommy Del was about to take the witness stand in Philadelphia in a mob murder trial when news broke about his son's arrest in Baltimore.

MOB INFORMANT'S SON HELD IN MD. SLAYING read a headline in the *Philadelphia Daily News* when word of the arrest finally filtered up to the City of Brotherly Love. For those unfamiliar with the latest circumstances in Bobby DelGiorno's life, it was a simple case. Like father, like son, they said. People knew that as a kid Bobby used to brag that he wanted to be just like his father. Now, it seemed, he had succeeded. Those who remembered a cocky little twelve-year-old sitting on a row house stoop talking about how he hoped to become a Mafia hitman shook their heads in pity and disgust. The murder in Baltimore seemed to be the fulfillment of that twisted aspiration.

In fact, that was not the case. Although few people knew it at the time, Bobby was in Baltimore because he had broken away from his father. Tired of his dad's macho posturing and disgusted with law enforcement's willingness to do almost anything to keep Tommy Del happy and on the witness stand, Bobby had set out on his own, hoping to start a new life. Instead, twenty-four hours after arriving in Baltimore, he was facing a murder charge.

As he sat in the police car, his hands cuffed behind his back, Bobby tried to clear his head and stay focused. There were people he knew he should call: the FBI; the U.S. Attorney's

Office; the New Jersey State Police. Bobby wasn't sure what, if anything, they could do for him, but he knew they had to be notified. There was, however, only one person he *wanted* to call.

He just didn't know what he would say to her.

Chapter Two

Maryann DelGiorno Fisher despised her ex-husband for many reasons. Ticking them off on the fingers of one hand, she would mention his greed, his arrogance, his macho bravado, his hair-trigger temper and his cowardice.

But these character flaws were secondary issues when she stacked them against what he had done to her and to her two sons. For that, she despised him most of all. Many women say they would like to see their former husbands dead. Maryann Fisher meant it. There had been times when the South Philadelphia housewife, who is barely five feet tall, knew that if Tommy DelGiorno were in her presence, she would simply kill him. Somehow, some way, she would end his life. A gun, a knife, a hammer, a baseball bat. It wouldn't matter. She would do it and gladly suffer the consequences. She would forever wipe the smirk off Tommy Del's face, freeing herself and her sons from the web of deceit, treachery and murder that was her ex-husband's legacy.

The day she learned of Bobby's arrest in Baltimore she once again felt that cold, murderous rage. To her, it was simple. Her former husband, the big shot mobster, was the reason her son was in jail. It was his fault. Mister tough guy, who used to shoot people in the back and then brag about it to his boys, had destroyed his own life. Now he was wrecking Bobby's as well. Bobby and his older brother, Tommy, had gone into hiding with their father after he began cooperating with the law in November 1986. Maryann was sick about it, but had no choice. According to law enforcement authorities, both of her sons' lives were in danger. There was a murder contract out on her ex-husband. And if the mob couldn't get to him, Maryann was told, then his two sons were logical proxy targets. To stay in South Philadelphia was insane. They would be gunned down on the street.

More than a year had passed since the boys were whisked away, and now they were secretly working out a deal that would allow them to come back. Tommy was living in Lancaster, Pennsylvania, with his fiancée. Bobby had just moved to Baltimore. Both had broken with their father. Both wanted to come home. Maryann had been patient. She had prayed, and her prayers were being answered. Then the phone call came.

"He's really done it this time," said her ex-husband's sister.

And that's how Maryann learned that her youngest son was in jail for murder.

Maryann didn't remember much else about the conversation—something about a bar; a fight in an alley; a gun. She was standing in the kitchen of the row house she had lived in for most of her adult life. It was a small, neatly kept two-story brick house in the three-hundred block of Gladstone Street, the house where the boys had grown up. Her house. Their house. The parish church where they were baptized, where they received their First Communion, where they were confirmed, was around the corner. So was the Catholic grammar school they had attended. Their grandparents—her mother and father—lived just two blocks away. Family and friends were everywhere. Everything she needed, everything they wanted, was right here.

Maryann's head was pounding. Her eyes filled with tears. She heard herself scream. Then she was standing in the middle of the kitchen, sobbing as her husband, Joe Fisher, wrapped his arms around her. She had thrown the phone across the room and then ripped a thick, wooden decorative spoke off the dividing shelf that separated the kitchen from the living room. When Joe rushed downstairs, he found his wife slamming the three-foot-long wooden pole against the kitchen table—again and again and again.

Maryann met Tommy DelGiorno in 1964.

It was not a good year.

She was working in a wholesale jewelry store on Chestnut Street in Center City and had just broken up with a guy she had dated steadily since high school. Everyone thought they would marry, but it didn't work out. She was twenty years old, living at home with her parents on Snyder Avenue in what was considered a mixed neighborhood in 1960s South Philadelphia. This, in fact, meant that there were Irish, Polish and Italian residents. Racial integration was a long way off in the working-class sections of the city.

Maryann's father, George Welch, was a truck driver. Her mother, Katherine, took care of the house. Their neighborhood, known as Pennsport, revolved around the parish church and the corner tavern. Social life consisted of beef-and-beer nights, parish bingo games, charity fundraisers and excursions to see the Phillies and the Eagles play. The neighborhood sprang from the industries that once dominated the Delaware River waterfront, which was just two blocks from the Welch home. Most of the men of her father's generation had worked either on the docks or in the factories and warehouses that once flourished along the river. Almost all of those jobs were gone by the time Maryann graduated from Saint Maria Goretti High School in 1962, but the neighborhood had remained solidly blue-collar. The men drove trucks or worked at the navy yard.

A few of the lucky ones still found work as longshoremen. Occasionally someone really hit it big and got a job with the city, usually as a cop or fireman. The women, for the most part, stayed home to raise families.

In 1964 Tommy DelGiorno was driving a truck for United Parcel Service. His route included the jewelry store where Maryann worked. He recognized her before she recognized him. About a year earlier he had been dating a friend of hers and they had been in each other's company at a few parties. He was friendly, always joking. Charming in a streetwise sort of way. He asked her out several times before she finally accepted.

Coming out of a broken romance, she welcomed his attention.

"He boosted my ego, which was something I really needed," she said years later in trying to explain the strange and nearly fatal attraction. "From the beginning he doted on me, smothering me with attention, almost gallant behavior. I began to relax and enjoy all the fancy places he took me to. He was very romantic."

It would be a whirlwind courtship. For three weeks they dated steadily. Every Friday, Saturday and Sunday night they would go out. Shows at swank nightclubs all over the city. Dinners at the best restaurants. Movies and late-night drinks in posh cocktail lounges. Money didn't seem to matter to Tommy Del. He drove a truck—which, in 1964, meant that he was making maybe $250 a week. Maryann didn't know much else about him, except that he lived in St. Gabe's parish on the other side of Broad Street, a neighborhood not unlike her own. He had one sister, Loretta, and his parents were, like hers, working-class.

Although his given name was Andrew, he preferred his middle name, Thomas. He was twenty-four but seemed older and wiser; at ease on the streets and in the clubs and bars that defined South Philadelphia's nightlife. Everywhere they went, they'd run into someone who knew "Tommy Del." Maryann, caught up in the romance and the excitement of the early stages of their relationship, didn't ask too many questions. She was out, having a good time with a guy who seemed to want nothing more than to be with her. To her mind, there was no better cure for a broken heart.

Three weeks after their first date, Tommy proposed. He was drunk at the time, and Maryann dismissed the offer with a laugh, telling him that he was "being irrational" and that they'd talk about it some other time. The proposal came while they were on a double date. Tommy had been boisterous and-full of swagger all night, playing the role of the tough guy, which she found somewhat humorous since he stood about five foot seven and weighed no more than 130 pounds. Nevertheless, Maryann had been surprised, even a little scared at his behavior. She didn't know how to take him. It was a side that she had never seen before and she wasn't sure she wanted to see it again.

Later that night, after he had taken her home, Maryann tossed and turned in bed, thinking about their relationship and where it was heading. Was it going too fast? How did she really feel about him? Was this a romance, or was she grabbing for attention on the rebound? Had he been serious when he asked her to marry him? Did she *want* to marry him? Was he a decent guy or was he really an obnoxious bore?

Maybe, she thought, he had been loud-mouthed and arrogant because he was trying to hide his nervousness. Maybe he had to get drunk in order to work up the courage to pop the question. The next day Tommy called and acted as if nothing had happened. He said they ought to go "someplace quiet" that night, like a drive-in movie. Maryann said fine.

That night he was so timid, so unsteady, Maryann couldn't believe he was the same guy who had so boldly proposed to her the night before. As they sat watching the movie play across the big outdoor screen, Tommy turned, put his arm around her shoulder and looked directly into her eyes.

"I'm sober and I'm rational," he said in a soft, gentle voice. "Will you marry me?"

They had been dating for less than a month. Was it possible he had fallen for her so quickly? Did she love him?

Deep inside, Maryann knew what her answer *should* be.

Instead, she said, "Yes."

As they kissed, a part of her filled with anxiety. If he really loved her, she wasn't being fair to him. She knew she didn't feel the same way. But hell, they were young. And at times he was so charming. I'll learn to love him, she thought.

———

Andrew Thomas DelGiorno and Maryann Theresa Welch were married on November 21, 1964. Maryann chose red and white as her colors, a Sacred Heart wedding. She had four bridesmaids and a maid of honor, all dressed in red velvet. Four hundred people—friends and family—sang and danced and drank at the reception that followed. Then the young couple departed for a week-long honeymoon at Cove Haven, a resort that had just opened in the Poconos. Only Maryann's maid of honor knew how close she had come to calling the whole thing off.

The morning of her wedding Maryann burst into tears, confiding to her best friend that she wasn't sure about the marriage. During their four-month engagement she had seen more and more about Tommy that bothered her. He was pensive and brooding, always at odds with his sister and parents, especially his mother, Veronica.

Maryann herself was less than charmed by the DelGiornos. Her family was warm, open and loving. They hugged and kissed whenever they met. Her older brother, a grown man, still kissed his father hello and goodbye, but she found the DelGiornos cold and aloof. Maryann, for example, wasn't at all sure that her future mother-in-law was happy about her son's marriage. She believed Mrs. DelGiorno had deliberately spoiled a surprise wedding shower by getting into an argument with Tommy in front of her and then letting the information about the party "slip out."

On another occasion, while they were at Tommy's house, someone knocked a box off an end table and hundreds of what Maryann would later recognize as football betting pools spilled out onto the floor. Tommy went into a rage as he gathered the slips up, yelling at both his mother and father as if it were their fault. Tommy's father, who Maryann considered a quiet, gentle man, didn't say a word. But his mother shouted right back at him. Maryann couldn't make sense of everything that was said. She clearly got the impression, however, that her future mother-in-law welcomed the confrontation.

Nodding toward Maryann, she said to her son, "Well, she ought to know what you're into. Stop hiding everything from her."

Later, after they had left the house, Tommy explained that the slips were football betting pools that he was holding "for a friend." He said people tried to pick winners in the college and pro games each week. It was, he said, "all for fun." Years later Maryann wondered at her own naivete. She wasn't sure if she really believed his explanation, or just wanted to accept it.

All of her doubts came out as tears on the morning of her wedding.

"If that's the way you feel, just call it off," her maid of honor said as they sat in her bedroom dressing.

"My parents would kill me," Maryann said. "They've put out so much money, I couldn't do that to them."

"You'll pay it back," her friend replied. "Don't ruin the rest of your life."

It was the best advice Maryann got that day. And for years she would regret not taking it.

———

The wedding night was a disaster. Tommy was quick, rough, and disappointed. He said he couldn't believe she was still a virgin. He knew she had dated the same guy for nearly four years before they had met, and he found it inconceivable that they hadn't slept together. For Maryann, it was as if he had stuck a knife in her heart and twisted it. She turned over and pretended to sleep, quietly sobbing to herself.

None of this was the way it was supposed to be, she thought. A wedding night is supposed to be "bells and fireworks and dreams come true." That's what she and her girlfriends had laughed and joked about. This was nothing like that. She felt guilt and shame. She felt dirty. Was this God's way of punishing her for marrying somebody she didn't love? What am I doing here, she asked herself? And who is this man lying in bed with me?

It was a question that would come back again and again over the eight stormy years of their marriage. But it was driven home with shocking emphasis less than an hour after they first made love.

Tommy had gone out for a drink after he thought Maryann had fallen asleep. When he returned, he smiled and threw the bag of wedding cards on the bed.

"Let's see how much we got," he said.

Maryann, relieved that he wasn't interested in sex again, readily agreed. And so for the next hour they opened the cards and stacked the cash, tens, twenties and an occasional fifty-dollar bill, into a neat pile. When they were finished they counted out three thousand dollars. Maryann immediately thought about a down payment on a row house in her old neighborhood. Three thousand dollars would be more than enough. Houses at the time were selling for from eight thousand to ten thousand dollars. They'd mortgage the rest. Tommy certainly made enough that they could afford it.

But Tommy DelGiorno had other ideas.

"Maryann, we can't spend this money," he said. "I owe it."

"What do you mean?" she asked.

"I owe it. I lost money gambling and I had to borrow money to pay the debt and now I gotta pay this money back. I promise you, it won't happen again. Never."

For twenty minutes Tommy begged and pleaded for Maryann to forgive him. He said he'd never gamble again. He said he was through with all that. He said he'd make it up to her. Maryann listened, but said nothing. Then she turned over and pretended to sleep.

She never saw the three thousand dollars again. When they returned from their honeymoon Tommy happily bragged to her mother and father about how much they had gotten. But he never mentioned what he did with the cash. To this day, Maryann still isn't sure if Tommy was telling her the truth, or if he just wanted to get his hands on the money.

―――――

Tommy DelGiorno was a tenth-grade dropout but a first-rate hustler. Almost everything he did was motivated by greed—by an insatiable desire for money. This would eventually make him a major earner and valuable asset for the mob. It was understood in underworld circles that Tommy Del would do just about anything, if there was a payoff at the end.

When he married in 1964, Tommy was still operating on the very fringes of the South Philadelphia underworld, and he remained there for the first five years that he and Maryann lived together. He drove a truck for United Parcel and ran a small bookmaking and numbers business at nights and on weekends. Eventually he set up a phone line and hired a girl to take calls during the day while he worked his legitimate job. It was all very low-key, a way to earn a couple hundred extra bucks a week. His sports book got its heaviest play during the football season. People loved to bet the college and the pro games.

Numbers, on the other hand, were consistent year round. This was before the state lottery and at a time when it seemed every bar and candy store in South Philly was linked to a numbers writer. People bet from five cents to five dollars. They played for weeks at a time on credit before settling up. Tommy DelGiorno was just one of the hundreds of numbers writers out there chasing after that action. At the same time he began hanging out in the bars, taverns and after-hours private clubs that were the underworld's social centers and began to frequent mob-run card and dice games.

"I liked to gamble," Tommy DelGiorno told the New Jersey State Police in explaining how he hooked up with the mob. "I used to play cards a lot . . . I did any form of gambling. So one time I was out in West Philly and I met this guy, John Bastione, who was a pretty big numbers writer out in Delaware County.

"Me and him became friendly, you know. I was young. He was an older guy, I think he might have been in his sixties at the time. . . . He helped me out a lot. Like when I used to go broke with gambling, he would always lend me money and stuff like that. So as the years went by, he was gettin' older and he got out of the numbers business. Well, he had a pretty half decent numbers business. He gave it to me. He even lent me some money to back the work.

"So now you're talking about where numbers was big. Like, I used to keep two thousand to three thousand numbers [a week]. Now I went to twenty thousand or thirty thousand, which now I couldn't handle these numbers. . . . And the sports betting business had started to grow."

It was a classic story of an underworld entrepreneur and the problems of expansion. Tommy needed partners, backers, financiers. He needed someone who could cover his action in the event a heavily played number came out or an underdog parlay came in during a football weekend. He needed someone to help him take the edge off the big money bets.

In short, Tommy needed the mob.

In South Philadelphia in the 1960s and 1970s, the best "edge-off" houses were run by the Mafia. This was because mob boss Angelo Bruno had come up through the underworld as a bookmaker, numbers writer and loan shark. In fact Bruno, who many believed was a millionaire several times over as a result of a series of smart real estate and legitimate business investments, never got away from the rackets that had brought him his first serious money. Up to the day he died in 1980,

Bruno was still actively involved in loan-sharking and gambling, the two businesses that were the financial lifeblood of his organization.

Bruno brought a laissez-faire approach to the business. He was not interested in controlling all the gambling and loan-sharking that went on in the city—or in South Philadelphia, for that matter. Independent operators like DelGiorno did their business with relative impunity, provided they didn't try to steal customers or stake out territories where a mob-backed operator was already in business.

Bruno, whose nickname, the "Docile Don," stood in stark contrast to the wanton violence that engulfed his organization after his death, was in fact a rather gentle mob boss by Mafia standards. He was content to make money at a slow and steady pace. He abhorred unnecessary violence. Shied away from all publicity. And frowned on flash and glitter. He drove a Buick. Lived in a South Philadelphia row house near the corner of Tenth and Snyder. Dressed in suits that he bought off the rack. And, when he dined out, usually chose an unassuming neighborhood restaurant.

Bruno never forced his way into any business venture. He seldom found the need to call upon the mob muscle that was readily available to him. He continued to expand his gambling and loan-sharking network because bookmakers, gamblers and numbers writers would voluntarily come to him or his associates for help. They'd need a loan to get them over a bad week. Or they'd need a bigger operator who could take some of their action. Bruno was only too happy to oblige. And when they'd fall behind on their loan payments or when too many gamblers hit big on the same number or game, they'd offer Bruno a share of their business in exchange for forgiving the debt or covering their losses. Angelo Bruno was a master businessman, an underworld entrepreneur who understood the economic dynamics of the illegal gambling business better than almost anyone in the city. It could be said without question that the Bruno organization only went where it was invited.

It would be several years after his marriage to Maryann before Tommy DelGiorno would seek out the Bruno organization. But when that time arrived, when his business had gotten so big that he needed a place to edge off some of his bets, Tommy was introduced to a guy named Broadway Eddie Colcher. Broadway Eddie was partners with Frankie Flowers D'Alfonso, one of the biggest bookies in the city. D'Alfonso, in turn, was a close personal friend and longtime business associate of Angelo Bruno.

Chapter Three

In 1964, the same year that Tommy and Maryann were married, Nicodemo "Little Nicky" Scarfo was released from jail after serving less than a year on a manslaughter charge.

Scarfo, a made member of the Bruno crime family, had stabbed a longshoreman to death during an argument over a seat in a South Philadelphia diner. It was a stupid, senseless killing, the kind of act that Angelo Bruno could neither condone nor tolerate. It was also the latest in a series of altercations, some within the organization and some without, for which the thirty-five-year-old Scarfo was to blame.

A few older mob members who were close to Bruno advised him to have Scarfo killed. They said that he was loud, arrogant and disrespectful and that he brought nothing but trouble to the organization. What's more, they pointed out, he wasn't much of a moneymaker.

But Bruno chose to ignore their advice. Some thought it was because Scarfo was the nephew of Nicholas "Nicky Buck" Piccolo, a highly regarded capo in the organization. Others attributed the decision to Bruno's laid-back, conciliatory style.

Whatever the reason, Scarfo's life was spared and the future of the Philadelphia crime family was set on a course that would eventually lead to its destruction. Instead of a bullet, Scarfo got banishment. He was sent to Atlantic City, at the time a seedy, down-at-the-heels South Jersey resort. For the next twelve years, Nicodemo Scarfo, bitter, angry and resentful, struggled to survive.

Although she didn't know it at the time, Maryann DelGiorno was watching her husband embark on a career that would eventually lead him to Scarfo and a violent but highly lucrative run at the top of the Philadelphia mob. Had she known, it's doubtful their marriage would have lasted more than a few months. As it was, the eight years they stayed together provided bits and pieces of information about what was to come. Slowly, almost imperceptibly, Maryann felt herself being sucked into a life she did not understand.

The DelGiornos had rented a two-bedroom row house in Maryann's old neighborhood, a few blocks from her mother and father. While Maryann went about the business of turning the house into a home, Tommy Del went about the business of writing numbers, making book and hanging out.

Along the way, there were occasional flashes of romance, brief periods when Tommy Del really seemed to care, when he once again became the gallant, almost shy truck driver who had courted her so intently. During one of those periods, Maryann became pregnant. Their first son, Thomas George DelGiorno, was born April 26, 1966.

———————

"It was like a whole new world for me. My son was the light of my life. After he came along, I didn't care what Tom did or where he went. I'd be lying if I didn't admit that things got a little better after the baby. For a while, anyway. Tom was elated with the birth of his first son. He wanted to name him Tommy from the moment he was born. After him, he said, which was strange because my husband's real name was Andrew Thomas. But everyone called him Tom.

"My son was a wiry little guy, active from the first moment. Not a sleeper. It seemed like he was up every two hours. And we were always taking him to the doctor's. He had to be put on a special formula because he couldn't keep the regular one down. I had many, many sleepless days and nights, but he was worth it. Sometimes I would catch Tom, out of the corner of my eye, being very loving and affectionate with the baby. But as soon as he saw me looking, he would put him down. . . . It was like he thought he was being a sissy by being affectionate. I thought this was sad, not being able to show his own feelings, afraid he'd be caught."

Tommy Del played the role of devoted husband and father for about three months. Then he returned to his old ways, staying out late at night and sometimes disappearing on weekends. His numbers and bookmaking operations continued to expand. He was meeting more and more influential people "in the business" and he was also making connections with some of the leaders of Teamsters Local 107, one of the most powerful and notorious labor organizations in the city.

Occasionally he would take Maryann out on a Saturday night, usually to one of the after-hours clubs where everyone seemed to know his name. One of his favorites was in his old neighborhood, around Twenty-sixth and Tasker. The club was owned by Joey McGreal, a tough-talking Local 107 organizer. Tommy belonged to the union and, on the surface at least, had begun to take a more active role in the labor movement. In 1967, when the Teamsters struck United Parcel, Tommy was quick to volunteer for picket duty and spent a part of each day down at union headquarters. It was obvious to Maryann that he didn't mind being out of work. In fact, he seemed to relish the freedom, the less structured daily routine. And the strike didn't seem to be having much of an impact on Tommy's wallet. He still had the money to pay the rent, buy the groceries and finance his nightlife.

One night while they were drinking in McGreal's place, Maryann overheard someone refer to Joey and her husband as union "goons." A few days later she asked her father, who had been a truck driver all his life, what that meant. "He told me a goon was a guy who beats up and breaks arms and legs on people who interfere with the union," Maryann said. "I couldn't believe Tom would do such a thing."

Tommy DelGiorno was twenty-seven, a short, skinny hustler with a wise mouth, but not much muscle. McGreal, on the other hand, was a former middleweight Golden Glove's boxer, a savvy street fighter who had grown up in the rough, working-class Grays Ferry section of South Philadelphia. Quick and fearless, McGreal was willing to take on anyone. Few were up to the challenge. He was also smarter than most of the other union goons then laboring for Local 107 and quickly moved to the top of the organization, earning both the respect and the plum assignments handed out by union leaders. Whenever national teamster boss Jimmy Hoffa visited Philadelphia, for example, McGreal was tapped to serve as his chauffeur and bodyguard.

Although he was just thirty years old at the time, McGreal was already something of an underworld legend when he and Tommy Del crossed paths. His associates came from various rackets and union organizations. In the early 1960s he had been linked with a hijacking ring controlled by a notorious South Jersey mobster known as Cherry Hill Fats. A few years later, McGreal was one of several underworld figures, including mob soldier Frank "Chickie" Narducci, brought in for questioning during a highly publicized medical examiner's inquest into what the newspapers were calling "Philadelphia's murder mystery of the decade."

This was the June 19, 1964, double murder of a café owner and his partner's beautiful young wife. Both were found shot to death in the basement of Dante's Inferno, a popular but financially troubled Center City restaurant. The woman's husband was eventually convicted, along with the triggerman he had hired to carry out the contract killings. McGreal was called in for questioning because he had been spotted riding in a car with the hitman shortly after the slayings and because investigators learned of a cryptic phone call to Local 107 headquarters the day of the shootings warning Joey to stay away from Dante's that night. Nothing ever came of the medical examiner's investigation, but the notoriety added to McGreal's reputation and enhanced his stature in the underworld.

While Tommy Del had begun to frequent McGreal's club shortly after he and Maryann married, it wasn't until 1967 and the strike that eventually forced United Parcel to close that he and Joey became close friends and "business associates." During the strike, Maryann noticed, a day did not pass without Tommy either stopping by the club or talking with McGreal on the phone. Most of those conversations, however, had little to do with the American labor movement. Tommy's gambling operations—his bookmaking and numbers writing—appeared to be at the core of his relationship with McGreal. That summer, when police raided her home, Maryann was sure of it.

"At the time, I didn't know what was going on. I just knew that Tommy and Joey McGreal were involved with the [betting] pools and also with betting on games. The day they raided our house, I didn't know what to think. I was scared. All I knew was what I had seen on television, cops ripping apart your house looking for stuff. I didn't want that. So what do I do? I hand them everything. Betting slips, pools, everything that Tom had in the house. He wanted to kill me, but I figured the police would find the stuff anyway.

"They took him out in handcuffs and as they're leaving, he looks at me and says, 'Now, you know who to call.' All I could think of was calling my dad. But then one of the cops says, 'Yeah, Joey will be waiting for the call.' So it clicks. Joey McGreal. That's who I'm supposed to call.

"Tommy made bail the next day. Joey or somebody put it

up. And when he got home, we had a battle royal. . . . I was pregnant again. It had happened that Christmas. Tom was being nice. He had turned the house into a toy store for little Tommy. It was his first Christmas. I had had a little too much to drink and one thing led to another. Two months later, I realized I was pregnant. The baby was due in September. . . . Anyway, after Tom makes bail and comes home, I'm screaming at him, 'How can you raise two babies in a home and have no respect for it.' I called him an asshole and blurted out everything I knew or suspected about what he was doing. Of course, he denied it. And, of course, he was lying. His one eyebrow used to twitch whenever he lied. I had learned this. And he would lie over the most meaningless things. It didn't make sense."

Maryann, however, managed to extract a promise from her husband. No more gambling operations out of the house. It turned out to be a temporary concession; but for the moment, at least, she felt she had reestablished some control over her home. Tommy continued to make book and write numbers. Nothing much came from the raid and arrest, just a small fine and a suspended sentence for illegal bookmaking. In the world Tommy Del operated in it was simply the cost of doing business. When in July of 1967 United Parcel closed as a result of the long and bitter strike, 1,150 truck drivers and warehousemen were left without jobs. Tommy DelGiorno was one of them, but the loss of permanent employment had little effect on his lifestyle. He found work with Highway Express, another local trucking firm. He was "on call," which meant that he was part-time. And this, Maryann said, suited him just fine. He was out of the house all the time now, devoting both days and nights to his numbers and bookmaking. A compulsive gambler himself, he would go to all-night card games on most weekends, winning and losing thousands of dollars.

"I never saw any of the big money," Maryann said. "Where it went, I don't know. But I have to say, he never touched the house money [to support his gambling]. He always used his paycheck to pay the bills."

It was a pattern that would continue throughout the 1970s and 1980s. Tommy DelGiorno wasn't much of a husband or a father to Maryann and the boys. He seldom showed affection and, in fact, was often cold and aloof. But he thought because he provided the money, he was fulfilling his end of the bargain. Paying the bills was what a husband did. Buying toys was what a father did. The other stuff wasn't important. It didn't matter if he missed a birthday party, forgot an anniversary or skipped out on an eighth-grade graduation. Money would make everything all right. So in the early days, Tommy Del always made sure that Maryann had the rent and grocery money. And later, after they were divorced, he might balk at and ignore orders to make support payments, but he'd always be ready to peel twenty-dollar bills off a wad he carried in his pocket and order some flunky to take the boys to Toys R Us and buy them anything they wanted.

Whether Tommy ever really loved Maryann and his two sons is a question that his former wife still wrestles with today. Maybe, in a strange and twisted way, he did. What she is certain of is that before, during and after their marriage, Tommy DelGiorno had one true love. Tommy Del loved money.

Maryann's second pregnancy was problem-plagued from the start. Unhappy in her marriage and already saddled with one baby in diapers, she wasn't sure she could cope with another. Her husband was seldom home and when he was around he was no help. He showed little sympathy or understanding for what his wife was going through. Maryann suffered from constant nausea and, with young Tommy still on a bottle, felt like she spent half her day caring for her son and the other half throwing up in the bathroom. She was desperate for sleep and found peace only during the few hours she could steal when the baby took his nap.

Still, she looked forward to having another child. She wanted another boy, a playmate and best friend for young Tommy. She realized early on that her children wouldn't get much love from their father. But she knew they would always have her love. And she hoped they would always have each other. A week past her due date, bloated, uncomfortable and in pain, she visited her doctor. He decided to induce her labor and scheduled her for admittance to the hospital the next day. That night, scared and anxious, she asked Tom to stay home to help her with the baby and with preparations for the next morning.

"Of course, he had made important plans and couldn't change them. A big card game with big money. That night we had a battle. I screamed at him. I cried. I told him to go and stay there, not to bother coming home. And that's what he did. My brother took me to the hospital the next morning, September 21, 1967. That's when my Bobby was born. He was a chubby little thing, perfectly round and so beautiful. I was ecstatic. Another son. Now I would make my whole world my children.

"Tom showed up at the hospital that night, all happy and apologetic. 'Two sons,' he kept saying. 'Two sons.' He went on and on about how they would carry on his name. Little did anybody know how much of a joke that would turn out to be."

———————

With the birth of her second son, Maryann had more than enough to occupy her time. Tommy Del, as he had been seventeen months earlier, was an attentive father and doting husband when she first returned from the hospital, but that only lasted a few weeks. Then he was back into his routine: days were spent driving a truck or hanging out with Joey McGreal; nights were filled with card games and after-hours clubs.

Within a year, Maryann felt her family was outgrowing their small rented house. By 1969 she began pressuring Tommy to find them a new home. She, naturally, wanted something near her parents, something down around Second Street where her friends and family were. He talked about a house around Twenty-ninth and Tasker, not far from where he had grown up. They argued for months over this and over whether they could afford the money for a down payment. Maryann pointed out that their rent was going up each year and that they had nothing to show for nearly five years of monthly payments. Tommy hemmed and hawed about finances; but Maryann was certain that if she had agreed to move into his old neighborhood, he would have come up with the cash in a minute. She, however, remained adamant about staying close to her roots.

"I know he hated it down here," she said. "But if I was going to be left alone with my two sons all the time, I wanted to be near my family."

Maryann began looking for a house in typical South Philadelphia fashion. She picked the parish, Our Lady of Mount Carmel, that she had always wanted to belong to and started scouring the neighborhood around the church.

Less than a block away, on Gladstone Street, she spotted a small row house for sale. Maryann fell in love with the house and the neighborhood. It was perfect. Just what she wanted. She then arranged to borrow enough money for the down payment from her grandmother, thus removing any financial objection her husband might throw at her. With that, the deal was done. In April of 1970, with one thousand dollars to cover a down payment and closing costs, the DelGiornos negotiated a twenty-year, eight-thousand-dollar mortgage and moved in. Maryann set about turning the house into a home and was already talking about the improvements she wanted to make, especially a new, modern kitchen off the small dining room. Tommy Del was indifferent, but by that point it didn't matter. His likes and dislikes were no longer important to Maryann. Nearly six years into a loveless and steadily deteriorating marriage, she realized she was just going through the motions as a wife. The only love she felt was for her two sons. Tommy was four years old when they moved. Bobby was two and a half.

The row house on Gladstone Street was everything Maryann wanted. It was just around the corner from Our Lady of Mount Carmel and only a short walk from her parents' home on Snyder Avenue. Many of the people she grew up with lived in the area and there were plenty of children on the block for the boys to play with. Maryann knew she could spend the rest of her life there. The grocery stores, taverns, barbershops and beauty parlors that marked each corner were all familiar to her—and so were the social clubs. Scattered throughout the neighborhood were nearly a dozen Mummers organizations, unique Philadelphia clubs whose members dressed up in plumes and feathers each New Year's Day to parade along Broad Street. While the costumes and string bands were a one-day phenomenon to millions of Philadelphia area residents, to the people from Two Street, the clubs were year-round social and community institutions. Like the parish churches, the Mummers organizations defined the neighborhood.

For Maryann, the move to Gladstone Street was wonderfully reassuring. She now had something else to hold onto. Tommy, on the other hand, had more important business to attend to. His relationship with Joey McGreal had begun to sour. Maryann wasn't sure just what had happened, but she knew he was spending less and less time with the union organizer. In fact, McGreal had some problems of his own within Local 107. Another faction had taken control and Joey was on the outs. A year earlier he had moved with his family to the Cherry Hill, New Jersey, area where he was now running with the leaders of the Camden County bartenders union. The talk on the street was that McGreal, while not an elected officer, was the real power in that organization.

The federal government helped confirm this when, in March of 1970, McGreal and two union officials were indicted on labor racketeering and extortion charges. The indictment alleged the three men sought one hundred thousand dollars in payoffs from nine restaurants being struck by the bartenders union. In exchange for the payoffs, the government charged, McGreal and the others promised to settle the strike. In September, McGreal and his codefendants pleaded guilty. In December, Joey McGreal began serving an eight-year sentence in the federal prison at Lewisburg, Pennsylvania. There he was assigned to the same cell block as his old friend Teamster boss Jimmy Hoffa, who was also a guest at the federal facility.

By the time McGreal went to prison, Tommy Del had already found other backers for his bookmaking and numbers business. He first hooked up with John Bastione, the well-connected Delaware County gambler who had befriended him. Maryann remembers Bastione and some of Tommy's other "new friends" coming to the house for all-night card games. Tommy had long since forgotten his promise to keep his gambling out of the house. Maryann, tired of fighting that battle, would take the boys and stay at her mother's while Tommy Del and his friends turned her kitchen and dining room into a clubhouse. Tommy served drinks and had sandwiches delivered from a local deli, and seven or eight guys would spend the night playing high-stakes poker around the kitchen table. Occasionally, Maryann would meet some of the players. She was struck by her husband's clientele. These were not low-life gamblers. The group included doctors and lawyers. They'd be gone by the time Maryann returned in the morning, and she'd be left to clean up the mess while Tommy Del counted his money.

It was nothing for Tommy to "clear" a thousand dollars as the house's cut. And when he played, he would usually win several thousand more. Maryann wondered whether Tommy was running a legitimate game or hustling a bunch of suckers. Knowing her husband, she figured the house cut wasn't enough to satisfy him. If he could cheat and get away with it, she knew that he would. But Maryann had no desire to discuss Tommy's business. A part of her didn't want to know. And a part of her simply didn't care. She saw what her husband was becoming and she hated it. Soon, she would hate him as well.

"He was a big shot, something he always wanted to be. Nothing else seemed to matter. Not me. Not the kids. Tommy and Bobby were getting older, and I wanted to go on picnics and to the movies with them. Family things. Tom had no time for that. So I would take them myself. He'd play with them when he was home, but that wasn't very often. And he'd buy them all kinds of toys. Any new toy that came out, the boys would be the first ones on the block to have it. I'd tell him those things weren't important, that the boys needed his time and his love. But he thought buying was a sign of love. I look back on it now and I pity him his values.

"I really don't know how much money he was making, but it had to be a lot because he never stopped buying. He was generous, I can't deny that. He bought me a large diamond, a fur coat and several new outfits. He was a fanatic when it came to clothes, always meticulous about the way he dressed, which was strange because he was such a slob to live with, never picking up after himself."

Tommy was on the way up and trying to make the right impression. He was meeting and working with people from "downtown," which in Philadelphia argot meant South Philadelphia mobsters and those connected with them. This is when Maryann first heard the names Broadway Eddie and Frankie Flowers. Tommy seemed excited and proud to be on a first-name basis with them.

Likewise, he made it clear to Maryann that it was important for her to fit in. She found this amusing and used it to deliberately get under her husband's skin. Whenever she had the opportunity, she would brag to Tommy's friends about her neighborhood, going on at length about "Two Street" and how she loved it there. She knew this upset Tommy, whose new associates were from around Ninth Street, the heart of South Philadelphia's Italian community. Maryann would make it a point to bring up Tommy Del's Polish heritage. Proud of his Italian surname, Tommy Del would bristle whenever Maryann mentioned the fact that his mother was Polish.

"He didn't want anyone to know," she said. "He would get furious if I told anyone. He really had a problem with that. If he could, he would have made me Italian. But I made it a point to tell everybody, I'm Irish-Polish from Two Street and proud of it. He said this used to embarrass him. I said, 'Who cares.' I didn't care about impressing anyone, especially these new friends of his."

So when Tommy Del bought her a pile of new outfits, said they'd be going out a lot more together and told her she had to "dress the part," Maryann didn't miss the chance to tweak her husband yet again.

"What part?" she asked.

Chapter Four

On any given weekend during the football season hundreds of thousands of otherwise law-abiding American citizens wager millions of dollars at gambling establishments run by the mob. Most of these bets are made with guys who work out of taprooms, grocery stores, or candy shops in urban neighborhoods that look the same today as they did twenty or thirty years ago.

There is a similar rush to place bets before nearly every heavyweight title fight. And for the Superbowl. And the World Series. And the NCAA Finals. Just about any major sporting event, in fact, brings a run of action. This is done with a wink and a nod and with the acquiescence of the sports establishment and the media. Why else, for example, are injury and player availability reports made public by the National Football League each week? And why, other than as a gambling aid, do newspapers post odds, over-and-unders and various other handicapping tips?

In Philadelphia, sports betting is as pervasive as soft pretzels and, in most circles, is considered as harmless as bingo. The attitude of the populace was described at a 1991 federal sentencing hearing for six South Philadelphia bookmakers who had pleaded guilty to gambling charges. The feds, who contend that illegal gambling generates forty billion dollars a year for the mob, said the bookmakers were organized crime associates who helped run a gambling ring that averaged about two thousand dollars a day in action and that, on some weekends during the football season, did as much as four hundred thousand dollars in business. This, of course, was serious money. But there were few, other than the prosecutors involved in the case, who argued that this was a serious crime. Most of those who bet and all of those who book consider it a victimless offense. Lawyers for the six bookies took that argument one step further. Bookmaking and betting, said one of the attorneys, "is part of the culture of the community" in South Philadelphia. Local residents, argued another, have "a more blasé attitude toward gambling." And according to a third attorney, mobsters and their associates are looked upon in certain circles as "prominent fellows, deities if you will."

In the early 1970s Tommy DelGiorno was on his way to becoming one of those "prominent fellows." Eventually, according to what he told authorities, his bookmaking and numbers operations generated millions of dollars in action each year. Back when he split with Joey McGreal, however, DelGiorno measured his weekly gambling income in hundreds rather than thousands of dollars. It was just a way, he said, to "supplement my income fairly decent." But things were about to change. With both his numbers and bookmaking businesses growing, Tommy Del began to look for someone to cover his action, someone to whom he could unload heavy bets in order to keep his books balanced.

One of the keys to a successful bookmaking or numbers operation is to avoid getting hit big. The idea is to keep the bets fairly balanced so that, worst case scenario, one negates the other—the losers' bets cover the payouts to the winners. Factor in odds, parlays, long shots, combinations and the general stupidity of most gamblers and, in almost all cases, a numbers writer or bookmaker walks away with money in his pocket. But on those days when the action is especially heavy on a particular number or a specific team, the smart move is to "edge off" to a bigger operator. You give up some potential profits that way, but you also avoid catastrophic payoffs.

When Tommy Del needed someone to cover his action, Broadway Eddie Colcher was happy to accommodate him.

"I got into the sports business, which started to grow," DelGiorno told the New Jersey State Police. "I met Broadway Eddie and through Eddie, I met Frankie D'Alfonso. He used to, like, edge my sports. . . . And, as time went by, I went from edging to 'em, to becoming him and Frankie's partner."

While not members of the Mafia, D'Alfonso and Colcher were highly regarded and well connected in the Philadelphia underworld. They were, in street terms, "mobbed up." And, over the years, they were able to open the door into Philadelphia's tightly knit organized crime family for Tommy Del. He took it from there.

Frankie Flowers was one of the premier bookmakers in the city. He operated a major edge-off house, providing dozens of local bookies with a place to unload chunks of their action. Federal authorities estimated that at its peak, D'Alfonso's gambling book was doing about twenty thousand dollars a day. Sharp featured, with a high forehead and a large nose, D'Alfonso was a fixture along the Ninth Street open-air Italian Market where his family had owned a florist shop for years. In addition to his gambling, he dabbled in local politics, community and church activities and any number of legitimate and quasi-legitimate business ventures. Many of these he ran in partnership with Angelo Bruno, Philadelphia's shrewd and low-key Mafia boss.

"He was a businessman more than a gangster," one long-time Philadelphia law enforcement investigator said of Frankie

Flowers. "He was an ambassador for the mob, a neighborhood guy who made a lot of money in a lot of different ways."

D'Alfonso had a knack for earning money and a reputation for being fair with his partners, most of whom were mobsters or their associates. But Frankie Flowers would do business with just about anybody if the money was right. On at least one occasion, his "partner" was his parish church. For several years D'Alfonso ran the weekly bingo game at St. Paul's near Ninth and Christian Streets. Years later the Pennsylvania Crime Commission would decry the lack of control the state exercised over bingo operations, documenting dozens of instances where racketeers had used charitable organizations as fronts for six-figure bingo games. The charities would get a few thousand dollars a week while the racketeers charged exorbitant operational fees in order to siphon off the bulk of the profits. The commission report also detailed how mob-dominated companies monopolized the industry by controlling the sale and distribution of bingo supplies and by threatening and extorting legitimate bingo operators. Churches, synagogues, veterans' groups and service clubs were all victimized by what the commission described as a "pattern of racketeering" within the state's bingo industry.

Frankie Flowers was long gone by the time the report was issued in 1992. But those familiar with the way he ran the bingo games at St. Paul's in the 1970s doubt he was scamming the church. That wasn't his style. He might take advantage of a situation, grab at an opportunity, but he'd never cheat a partner. So it was that the pastor of St. Paul's and officials of the Archdiocese of Philadelphia expressed shock and surprise—and pleaded complete ignorance—after police raided their bingo hall one Tuesday night. Frankie Flowers was running the game. There were more than four hundred people in the smoke-filled room, hovering intently over bingo cards that covered rows and rows of tables. But off to one side Frankie's eighteen-year-old daughter was running a change booth. And along the walls were eighteen slot machines, jangling merrily in the background as gamblers took a break from their table games to attack the one-armed bandits. D'Alfonso was arrested and later paid a fine for a gambling violation. The machines were confiscated and carted out of the hall. But the bingo game continued. And the fact that a well-known gambler and convicted bookmaker was running a church-sponsored game of chance was greeted in the community with a shrug and a typical South Philadelphia response. "So what's your point?" neighbors would ask.

Who better to run a bingo game than a guy who knows gambling. The slot machines, however, were another story. Even in South Philadelphia, they were illegal.

D'Alfonso's "work" for the church gave him access to one of the three major institutions that dominated the neighborhood. His friendship with politicians provided him with entrée into another. But it was his relationship with Angelo Bruno that gave him the most clout and stature. Their association was so close and so well known that many people in law enforcement, and even some in the underworld, assumed that D'Alfonso was a made member of the Bruno crime family. This was not the case. Frankie Flowers did a lot of business with and for the Bruno mob, but was never more than an associate of the organization. And that association was more a product of his close personal ties and friendship with Don Angelo than of any deep-seated connection with the Mafia.

Bruno trusted D'Alfonso. What's more, he genuinely liked him. They were kindred spirits who shared the same philosophy. Both were interested in making money, not headlines. Both took the broad view when it came to business, each realizing that the world was not defined by the borders of South Philadelphia. Surprisingly, many other members of the mob lacked that perspective and were constantly at each others' throats as a result.

Police got a glimpse of just how sophisticated and cosmopolitan Bruno and D'Alfonso had become when they raided a private meeting at D'Alfonso's flower shop in 1968. A few years earlier D'Alfonso had opened a travel agency in South Philadelphia called the Victoria Coach Society. Among other things, the agency arranged junkets to a London casino called the Victoria Sporting Club. Law enforcement sources found this interesting; they believed the casino was secretly controlled by Bruno and New England mob boss Raymond Patriarca. When police popped into the flower shop unannounced one night in September 1968, they found the manager of the sporting club sitting at a table with D'Alfonso, Bruno, Bruno's underboss, Philip "Chicken Man" Testa, and Joe Napolitano and Ted Fucillo, two Boston-area men described as lieutenants in the Patriarca organization. The raid made headlines, but not much else. There was nothing illegal about six men sitting around a flower shop. Police later learned that the casino manager had come to Philadelphia seeking Bruno's help in collecting debts from several of the gamblers who had taken Victoria Coach Society junkets to London. The fact that Frankie Flowers was present at such a meeting added to his status in the underworld and reinforced the misconception that he was a member of the Bruno mob. And a year later, when he was sentenced to six months in prison for refusing to answer questions posed by a grand jury investigating the meeting, there was little doubt that Frankie was "connected," as they liked to say downtown. D'Alfonso, establishing a pattern that he would follow all his life, had nothing to say to the grand jury, or to the cops and FBI agents investigating the case, or to the reporters who were writing about it.

Those looking for quips and quotes went, instead, to Broadway Eddie, a South Philadelphia bon vivant who was more D'Alfonso's sidekick than partner. Colcher, who turned up in various newspaper columns and stories over the years, was a character right out of *Guys and Dolls,* a happy-go-lucky gambler with a heart of gold. Built like a small refrigerator—a household appliance to which he was no stranger—Eddie craved good food, good friends and a good cigar. Anything else was a bonus. He had been on the street since the age of thirteen when he started shining shoes outside a popular Center City nightclub called The Click. A few years later, he moved up to waiting tables. This eventually led him to jobs at places like the Latin Casino in Cherry Hill, the 500 Club in Atlantic City and Old Original Bookbinders in Philadelphia. There he met the well heeled and the well connected. Soon he was a minor player in the underworld, running a small book and numbers operation. His interest in gambling, as both a player and operator, led him to Frankie Flowers. They had been associates for several years when their paths crossed with DelGiorno's.

Tommy Del jumped at the chance to use Colcher and D'Alfonso as backers for his ever-expanding gambling operations. They were, after all, the best in town. DelGiorno saw all kinds of possibilities opening up before him. Frank D'Alfonso was where Tommy wanted to be. In many ways, he was *who* Tommy wanted to be. DelGiorno never hesitated; when the chance to become a partner was offered, it took him less than a minute to sign on. Like Broadway Eddie, he became one of D'Alfonso's "associates." But while Broadway Eddie was clearly just along for the ride, Tommy Del was interested in reaching the top.

Maryann DelGiorno found Frankie Flowers to be polite, businesslike, and rather aloof. Broadway Eddie she loved like a brother.

In fact, he was the only business associate of her husband's that she ever cared about. He started showing up at the house on a daily basis once he and Tommy Del became partners. His arrival each day usually coincided with a meal. Sometimes it was breakfast, sometimes it was lunch, sometimes it was dinner. Maryann and the boys didn't care. They loved the company. He took the time to talk to her and would do anything for the kids. And he always had a funny story to tell. With no family of his own, he simply adopted Maryann and her two sons as a sister and nephews. No matter what kind of business he and Tommy were involved in, no matter how pressing a meeting or appointment, he always spent time with them. He'd sit around the kitchen table keeping Maryann company, drinking a cup of coffee and puffing on a cigar. Or he'd roughhouse with the boys, bouncing off the couch and chairs as little Tommy and Bobby wrestled his rotund form to the ground, laughing and squealing till their stomachs hurt.

Shortly after becoming gambling partners, Frankie Flowers offered Tommy Del a piece of a small, private club he planned to open in the basement of a bar-restaurant near Second and Market Streets in Center City. It was one of several buildings that D'Alfonso owned, part of a small and profitable real estate empire that was included in his financial portfolio. Maryann heard about it first from Broadway Eddie, who swore her to secrecy. A few weeks later she got the word officially from her husband. The place was going to be called The Gru. Tommy wanted Maryann there for the grand opening.

"Wear something chic," he said.

She was less than thrilled at the prospect, but eventually gave in to his badgering.

Marriages break up over time. Couples drift apart, find out they have other interests. In most cases, it isn't one incident that drives a spouse out the door, but a series of minor clashes; nagging and sometimes picayune problems that build up and mushroom over time. God knows, Maryann and Tommy Del had had their share of problems. Anyone who knew the couple could tell their marriage was in trouble. But the grand opening of The Gru became the point of no return for Maryann. After that night, she knew her marriage was over and that she wanted no part of Tommy Del, not as a husband, not as a father for her sons.

———————

"Tommy was all excited about this place, but frankly it didn't impress me. It was in a cellar, very dark with candles at each table for lighting. They served pieces of filet mignon, shrimp and crabmeat as hors d'oeuvres. Tommy was being a big shot greeter, rubbing elbows with everyone. I had too much champagne and ended up going upstairs to the bar at the legitimate restaurant. I sat there the rest of the night, in a corner. And every once in a while, I'd see Tom come up, look around, and go back down. He didn't see me. I knew he was looking for me, but I was too drunk to care. In fact, I started to giggle. It all seemed so funny to me.

"A little while later, Eddie comes up and looks around. He doesn't see me either and he looks real nervous. He's also puffing and out of breath because he was so heavy. He was like four-by-four and he always smoked a cigar and going up and down steps was an effort. The second time Eddie came up, all panting and out of breath, I felt sorry for him. I called him over. His face was all flushed, but all I could do was giggle.

"He told me Tom was going wild. He thought I had left with somebody else. He said I was in real trouble. This made me laugh even more. I couldn't believe somebody like Eddie, as big as he was, was terrified of Tom. Now, I look up to order another drink and the bartender has this frightened expression on his face. I said, 'What's the matter? Give me another drink.' The bartender just stood there."

———

Then Maryann turned around and saw an angry and red-faced Tommy Del standing behind her. She laughed. He reached up, grabbed her arm and yanked her off the bar stool. Then, with one hand pressed tightly on the back of her neck, he led her out the back door of the restaurant to an alleyway where he had parked his car. He opened the door and shoved her in. Then he got into the driver's side, looked over at her in a rage, and slapped her hard across the face.

Maryann was stunned. Through all their arguments and shouting matches, Tommy Del had never raised a hand to her before. Her cheek burned red and the slap echoed in her ear. She reacted instinctively.

"I punched him in the mouth. I hit him so hard my knuckles hurt. I looked up and saw blood. I think my ring cut his lip. The blood made me nervous and, for the first time, I started to get scared. He didn't say another word. He just drove home in silence. I was still pretty drunk so he had to help me up the stairs and into bed. Then he tried to make love to me. I couldn't believe it. I said this man is nuts, out of violence he wants love? I shoved him off of me. He tried again, and I screamed at him to get out and to leave me alone. I wanted no part of him.

"He left, probably to go back to the club. I never asked. I didn't care. But I vowed that I would never let him hit me again. I would kill him first.

"The next day, he acted like nothing had happened. His lip was swollen, but I never mentioned a word about it and neither did he. But he seemed more attentive. It was crazy. It was as if the violence excited him and made me more attractive. I didn't want anything to do with it or with his club. A few months later, it closed."

But Tommy Del's gambling operations and business ventures with Frankie Flowers and Broadway Eddie continued. One day early in the summer of 1972 a beaming Broadway Eddie stopped by the house and happily confided in Maryann that he was opening a restaurant.

"I'm finally gonna have my own joint," is the way he put it.

The restaurant, called Broadway Eddie's, opened in July of 1972 in a building owned by Frankie Flowers on the corner of Ninth and Catharine. A huge bar dominated the room. A portrait of Frank Sinatra hung on the wall over the coat rack just off the entrance. Along one wall were photographs of such South Philadelphia entertainment luminaries as Buddy Greco, Frankie Avalon, Al Martino and Fabian. The jukebox was stocked with standards by Old Blue Eyes and by many of his contemporaries. And off to one side was a dining area with seating for about thirty. The menu, to no one's great surprise, was southern Italian, pastas and red sauces, veal dishes and seven kinds of steak. Tommy and Maryann stopped in for dinner every Saturday night. Then they'd go to the bar for a few drinks and Tommy would disappear downstairs for a "business meeting." Eddie would keep Maryann company, smiling, laughing and trying to make small talk. One night, however, when Maryann asked just what it was Tommy was doing downstairs and who it was he was meeting with, the smile disappeared from Broadway Eddie's face. Maryann knew that he was aware of her marital problems, that there was, in fact, no love left between her and Tommy. And she also knew that he cared deeply for her and her sons.

"Maryann, you don't know?" he asked.

"Know what?" she said.

Eddie looked around the bar and then lowered his voice to a whisper.

"Maryann, if Tommy knew I was saying this, he'd kill me. But my advice is for you to take the kids and get away from all this. Tommy's working for the Mafia. These are mob meetings."

Years later, Maryann would wonder about her own naivete during her first marriage. Did she really not know who it was that Tommy Del was dealing with, or did she simply not want to know. Hearing the words from Broadway Eddie, however, brought everything to a head. She felt dizzy even though she had had very little to drink. Eddie continued to talk, but Maryann couldn't make out much of what he said. The room seemed to be buzzing. She kept hearing the word "Mafia" over and over. Her mind began to race. She thought about her boys and her home and her family. She knew Eddie was right. She had to get away.

"Take me home, Eddie," she said finally. "I feel sick."

Maryann immediately began to plan her divorce, Mafia-style. One of the first things she did was steal some papers and documents Tommy kept hidden under a floorboard in the bed-room. She had no idea what they were—gambling records, she suspected—but she figured she could use the information to blackmail her way out of the marriage if Tommy balked at granting a divorce. While it never came to that, the breakup was less than amicable. That summer a contractor was supposed to begin work on renovating the kitchen in the home on Gladstone Street. It was a seven-thousand-dollar job. Tommy paid two thousand up front and owed the rest at the end of the project. Maryann used the construction as an excuse to temporarily get away and sort things out. She told Tommy that since the contractor would be disrupting the house for at least three weeks, she would take the boys and visit her aunt and uncle in Oregon. Tommy went along with the idea without a second thought. He called a couple of times each week while they were gone and picked them up at Philadelphia International Airport when they returned. And there, at the airport, before they had even gotten the suitcases into the trunk of the car, Maryann told him she wanted a divorce.

"I don't want to be married to you anymore," she said. She then insisted that he drive her and the boys back to her parents' home, where she remained for more than a week until Tommy Del moved out of the house on Gladstone Street. He was livid, but Maryann was sure it had nothing to do with love. "He was upset because he was losing a possession. Me. And more important, his sons."

It took nearly a year to finalize the divorce and even longer for Tommy Del to face up to the fact. He tried to make Maryann's life as miserable as possible. He refused to pay the contractor for the work done on the kitchen. He reneged on a promise to pay for the household expenses during the separation. He would flash wads of hundred-dollar bills whenever he came to pick up the boys on Sunday afternoons—the day he had visitation rights—but would cry poverty whenever Maryann asked for help with the bills.

Tommy Del moved back with his parents for awhile, then got his own apartment. He drove a brand-new Cadillac, wore expensive clothes and was always reaching to pick up a restaurant tab or bar bill while out with his friends and associates. Maryann borrowed money from her grandmother again to pay off the contractor, then got a job as a waitress in a neighborhood restaurant and struggled to make ends meet. The place was called Walt's Crab House, just off the corner of Second and Catharine Streets in South Philadelphia. It was a two-story brown brick building with a large front window made of thick glass blocks. There was a long bar on one side of the room, and a dining area crowded with tables on the other. The restaurant sat in the middle of a residential neighborhood, sandwiched by row houses on either side.

Like clockwork, Broadway Eddie would stop by once a week for a late dinner. He'd come in after the rush so that Maryann would have time to talk and socialize. He repeatedly offered to help her out financially and always asked how the boys were doing. Maryann never took any money from him, but was always grateful for the generous tip he would leave. Waitressing work was hard, but she liked it because it was honest and clean. She brought home between two hundred and three hundred dollars a week, most of it in tips.

Tommy Del made fun of her efforts, predicting she'd never last a month in the job. He scoffed at her income, bragging that he won and lost more in one hand of poker than she earned in a week. Maryann ignored his taunts and asides. She knew he wanted her to fail, that he wanted her to beg him to take her back. She didn't know if she could make it financially, but she was determined to go through with the divorce.

A month after she started waitressing, Frank D'Alfonso and two men she had never seen before showed up at the restaurant and asked to be seated at one of her tables. When she came to take their orders, the impeccably dressed D'Alfonso stood up to greet her and kissed her on the check. In the very next breath, he asked her to quit her job. Maryann ignored the comment and asked what they wanted to eat. They chose one of the house specialties, heaping plates of sautéed and seasoned crabs. After she served them she steered clear of their table until it was time to bring the check and clear away the dishes.

Frankie Flowers watched her work and then in a calm, quiet voice, said, "Maryann, what do you need this for? Only a low-class person does this. What do you want, money from Tom? I'll make sure he gives you two, three hundred a week. You don't have to work. You make him look small and cheap."

For a month Maryann had been holding it all in. She never responded to her husband's taunts. She never gave in to self-pity when Broadway Eddie offered her a shoulder to cry on. But this was too much. She was struggling to make an honest living while her husband and his gangster friends were throwing around thousands of dollars. And *she* was making *him* look cheap?

"Who the fuck do you think you are?" Maryann said, the words escaping in a low, controlled fury before she even realized what she was saying. "You may be his boss, but you're nothing to me. Take your dirty money and stick it up your ass. What I do with my life and my children's lives is my business. Tom decided long ago what came first. Now I decide what's best for me and my sons. Stay the fuck away from us."

With that, Maryann slammed the plates back down on the table and a pile of greasy, highly seasoned crab shells cascaded onto the front of Frank D'Alfonso's tailored, five-hundred-dollar tan suit. The two men with Flowers jumped up as if he had been shot. D'Alfonso, ever the gentleman, quietly wiped himself off, got up and left. Maryann never said another word to Frankie Flowers in her life.

She got home from work that night at two in the morning. When she walked in the door, the phone was ringing. She rushed to pick it up and was greeted with a stream of obscenities from her estranged husband. She hung up. Seconds later, the phone rang again. This time he tried to reason with her. He asked if she had gone mad. He asked if she knew what she had done. Did she know who she was talking to? Did she realize she was lucky she didn't wind up at the bottom of the Delaware River?

Maryann held the phone away from her ear for three or four minutes until Tommy Del had finished his tirade. Then, in a quiet but firm voice, she said, "Tell your boss to keep out of my life. And you go to hell."

At the time, Tommy Del was still very much in awe of Frankie Flowers and his ties to Angelo Bruno and was happy to consider him his boss. Over the next ten years, however, his opinion and view of D'Alfonso would change dramatically. DelGiorno used his connections to Frankie Flowers to horn his way into more serious and more lucrative mob gambits. Then, when the connection became a liability rather than an asset, he wiped his hands clean and walked away from the man without a second glance. When D'Alfonso was brutally beaten in 1981 by two local mobsters, Tommy Del didn't raise a finger to stop the attack. And in 1985, when a mob murder contract was placed on D'Alfonso's head, Tommy Del helped carry it out.

Years later, while testifying for the government, DelGiorno offered a rather derisive and condescending description of the man who, quite literally, had shown him the way into the Philadelphia mob.

"Are you familiar with an individual named Frank D'Alfonso?" he was asked.

"Yes, I am," Tommy Del replied.

"And what is his nickname?"

"Frankie Flowers."

"And who did you know him to be?"

"He was just a guy hanging around the neighborhood, pretending he was a gangster."

Chapter Five

The domestic problems that destroyed the DelGiorno marriage in the early 1970s were nothing when compared to the "family" problems Angelo Bruno faced just a few years later. Unfortunately for Bruno, divorce was not an option.

The Docile Don had been sitting peacefully atop the Philadelphia mob since 1959. But in the mid-1970s, things began to change. Simmering resentment and internal bickering threatened the future of the organization. The cause of the unrest was, not surprisingly, money. Bruno had plenty. But some of his crime family soldiers were barely earning a living off the rackets they were operating.

Many of these struggling mafiosi considered Bruno a hypocrite. They pointed out, for example, that while he was adamant about enforcing the American Mafia's ban on dealing narcotics, he himself had business associates who made small fortunes dealing drugs. Many of Bruno's soldiers suspected these drug dealers were kicking back a share of their profits to "the old man."

Most members of Bruno's organization thought the narcotics ban was ludicrous and that Bruno used it as a way to keep them down. They also knew that wiseguys in New York, Chicago and Boston were dealing and making tons of money, despite the supposed prohibition. But Bruno wouldn't bend. His underboss, Phillip "Chicken Man" Testa, dabbled in narcotics, but kept the deals secret because he knew Bruno would tell him to stop. Antonio "Tony Bananas" Caponigro, a highly regarded soldier in the small Newark, New Jersey, branch of the Bruno family, also was trafficking. Like Testa, he did it quietly and out of view of his mob boss.

Both knew they could be killed for dealing. That was the ultimate penalty. And while Bruno had a reputation for nonviolence, underworld members also knew that the mob boss had, on more than one occasion, approved a murder contract to settle a dispute or to make an example of someone who refused to comply with his wishes. Later, murder would become the calling card of the Philadelphia mob, but during Bruno's reign, that was not the case. Bullets and blood made headlines and Bruno wanted no part of that. So in most cases, murder contracts carried out during his tenure were what the Sicilians liked to call "white death." Gangsters were not shot down on the street and left bleeding in the gutter, they just disappeared. As a result, there were no blaring newspaper headlines, no lead stories on the six o'clock news. Murders during the Bruno era were relegated to the bottom of page three in the newspapers; two or three paragraphs, if that, about the "disappearance" of a bookmaker or drug dealer. No one, other than the victim's immediate family, cared. And few, other than Bruno's hitmen, ever knew what became of the bodies.

"They used to bury guys in the woods," said one former member of the organization. "They had a couple of spots in South Jersey. And that was the end of it."

One of the more gruesome hits during this period was carried out by Little Nicky Scarfo, the hothead Bruno had banished to Atlantic City. The victim was a South Philadelphia gambler and loan shark named Reds, who had crossed the mob one time too many. Bruno ordered the killing and designated Santo Idone, who ran the mob's rackets in Chester, Pennsylvania, the hit man. In this way Idone, a Bruno favorite, would be eligible for initiation into the mob. It was standard procedure, part of the Mafia's bloody protocol. No one could become a member without taking part in a murder. Scarfo, who had already been involved in several mob hits, was assigned to lure Reds to a bar in the Vineland, New Jersey, area where two other mob associates were waiting. There, the three mobsters were supposed to tie the victim up and call Idone, who was waiting nearby. Bruno, for reasons perhaps only he knew, wanted Reds strangled, not shot. And then, he told Scarfo, he wanted the body buried deep in the woods.

But Scarfo, who many in law enforcement considered a psychopath, couldn't wait. His blood lust boiling, he pumped three bullets into Reds as soon as he and the victim walked into the empty bar. Then he and the others set about the business of disposing of the body, wrapping it in plastic and tying up the arms and legs. At that point, Reds opened his eyes, looked at Scarfo and blurted out, "Ya got me, Nick." This set Scarfo off all over again. Enraged, he grabbed an ice pick and plunged it repeatedly into Reds's chest. Once he was sure Reds was dead, Scarfo called Idone, the supposed hit man. And in a macabre attempt to go along with Bruno's orders, Idone then strangled the already expired victim. The body was then covered in a plastic sheet, thrown into the trunk of a car and driven into the woods where the four men dug a hole, dumped the bloody remains and covered it over. Those who knew the story would smile cynically whenever they read about Angelo Bruno, the Docile Don of South Philadelphia. Those who considered crossing Bruno, men like Testa and Caponigro, moved cautiously as a result.

One man who threw caution to the wind, however, was Tommy DelGiorno's old union buddy, Joey McGreal. McGreal was released from prison in October of 1973 after doing just under three years of an eight-year sentence in the labor racketeering–extortion case involving the Camden County bartenders union. When McGreal returned to South Jersey he expected to once again assume his role as union power broker. McGreal saw no problem since the union was under the control of Ralph Natale, a former bartender and mob associate whom he had helped rise through the ranks of the union. McGreal, in fact, had backed Natale for a leadership position in 1970. As a result, Natale was appointed secretary-treasurer, the union's most powerful post, when the former occupant of that office pleaded guilty along with McGreal and another union official in the extortion-racketeering case. Two years later, Natale was elected to a full three-year term and set about solidifying his hold on the organization. By the time McGreal returned, Natale was firmly in charge.

The new union boss, however, had neither the time, nor a place in his organization, for Joey McGreal.

As Christmas approached in 1973, Maryann DelGiorno agonized over how she could make the holiday the best ever for her two sons. Little Tommy was seven and a half. Bobby had just turned five. They were still too young to understand completely about the divorce, which was finalized that June. They just knew that their father didn't live with them anymore. But Tommy Del still was a part of their lives, stopping by unannounced whenever he felt like it to "see how everybody was doing." Maryann wasn't sure if he did this because he was really interested, or because he wanted to throw his good fortune in her face. He drove a brand-new Cadillac, wore only the best clothes and always brought the boys a present. Maryann, still struggling as a waitress, couldn't compete. But she wasn't about to be shown up by her ex-husband at Christmas. She pawned her diamond ring for a thousand dollars and blew it all on gifts. Tommy, as she knew he would, responded in kind.

"On Christmas Day, the house looked like a toy store," she said.

Ironically, after opening all the gifts, the boys spent most of the day playing with an air hockey set that had come from neither Maryann nor Tommy. Broadway Eddie stopped over that day with the game. It was so big, it looked like a piece of furniture. The boys loved it. Eddie beamed. For Maryann, he had a huge basket filled with flowers, cheeses, meats and wines. Maryann reached up and gave him a big kiss on the cheek. Eddie's eyes filled with tears.

It was a bittersweet moment. The cigar-chomping, larger-than-life South Philadelphia hustler had stopped coming over the house months earlier. He no longer had dinner at the restaurant where Maryann worked. He had told her, sheepishly, that Frankie Flowers and some of the others said it "looked bad," that it seemed like he was "making a play" for her. Maryann knew that wasn't the case, but Eddie could do nothing about it. He had to stay away. It was one more example of the small-mindedness of her ex-husband and his associates. To them, a wife or a girlfriend was a possession, like a car or a fancy suit, and once a member of the organization had staked his claim, no one else could show any interest. Maryann had argued with Tommy Del about this, claiming that he had broken up her friendship with Broadway Eddie in a stupid and unfounded fit of jealousy. He, of course, denied it. She took particular pleasure, therefore, when the boys—her husband's pride and joy—went wild over just one gift in a room filled with toys, the air hockey game from Broadway Eddie.

Tommy Del spent most of Christmas Day at the house on Gladstone Street. He and Maryann had negotiated an uneasy peace, for the boys' sake. That night, when Tommy got a phone call, Maryann was pleasantly surprised to hear him beg off on attending a "business meeting." What kind of people, she thought, did business on Christmas night? Tommy told her the call was from Joey McGreal, that he had been out of prison for about two months and that they might be doing some business together again. Maryann didn't know what that meant, nor did she care. In the spirit of the day, she listened politely, pleased that on at least this one occasion, Tommy Del chose to be with his sons rather than his hoodlum friends.

No one knows for sure who it was that Joey McGreal was supposed to meet that night. McGreal's wife later told investigators that her husband had not been feeling well and that she had urged him to cancel out. But Joey had told her it was an appointment that he "had to keep."

In December of 1973, Alex Gzawkewski was living in an apartment on top of DiAngelo's Country House, a moderately priced restaurant in Chesilhurst, New Jersey, not far from Cherry Hill. Around 8:30 on Christmas night Gzawkewski heard and felt a thump, as if something had rammed into the building. DiAngelo's was closed for the holiday and so he went downstairs to investigate. What he found was a late-model Cadillac smashed into the side of the restaurant. On closer examination, he saw a man slumped over the steering wheel. Gzawkewski called the police.

Joey McGreal was pronounced dead at the scene. He had been shot three times in the back of the head with a .38 caliber pistol. Police ruled out robbery, noting that McGreal had three hundred dollars in his wallet and was wearing a watch and a ring with a combined value of about five hundred dollars. The newspapers heralded the murder. EX-TEAMSTER FIGURE FOUND SLAIN read the *Philadelphia Inquirer*. "DON'T GO" WIFE WARNED DOOMED McGREAL said the *Philadelphia Daily News.* Maryann DelGiorno felt sick when she read the stories. McGreal had been out of prison for just ten weeks. Now he was dead. He left behind a wife, two young sons, and dozens of unanswered questions. The McGreal murder has never been solved. No one has ever been charged with the slaying.

Originally, investigators speculated that the shooting was an outgrowth of lingering resentment within Philadelphia Teamsters Local 107 where, in the 1960s, different factions routinely took potshots at one another as a means of settling labor disputes. McGreal had been part of a faction suspected of several murders within the local. Some investigators thought his belated killing was an attempt to even an old score. Nearly twenty years after the fact, however, Philadelphia mob informants pointed to the real motive. McGreal was killed on Angelo Bruno's orders, they said, because the mob had big plans for the South Jersey bartenders union, and McGreal—a tough, independent Irishman—could not be depended on to go along with those plans. Seven years later John McCullough, another strong-willed Philadelphia union boss, would also run afoul of the Philadelphia mob in another dispute over the bartenders union. Like McGreal, McCullough would discover that Bruno and those who came after him brought their guns to the bargaining table.

None of that, of course, mattered to Maryann DelGiorno. She just knew that a man a lot like her former husband was dead. And that a woman a lot like herself was left alone with two young boys to care for. She also knew that on the night that Joey McGreal died, her ex-husband was supposed to be with him. For a moment she felt relief. It would have been tragic, she thought, for her boys to lose their father, no matter how much she, herself, despised him. But then she thought of the phone call Tommy Del had gotten Christmas night, and of his out-of-character reponse. Since when did he put his own family before business? she wondered. Then Maryann went cold with the realization that maybe her ex-husband had known what was going to happen to Joey McGreal. Maybe he had been part of the plot to kill him.

The McGreal murder was a piece of Mafia business, a message killing that both removed a problem—McGreal—and let everyone in the underworld know who was in charge. Ralph Natale would maintain control of Local 170 of the Camden County bartenders union until he, himself, ran afoul of the law. Convicted of both arson and drug dealing, he was forced to relinquish power in 1979. But by that point, the union was dominated by the mob and anyone in a position of power had to answer to the organization. Eventually, in a cosmetic attempt to improve its image, it changed its name to Local 33. The players, however, remained the same. Albert Daidone, a mob associate from Camden County, assumed a leadership position within the local. And Daidone's close friend and partner, Raymond "Long John" Martorano, became a power behind the scenes. Martorano was heavily involved in gambling, the vending machine business and drug dealing. For years he was considered one of Angelo Bruno's closest associates and top money earners. And so his sub-rosa connections to the bartenders union solidified the perception that Local 170, and later Local 33, were mobbed up. First through Natale, then through Martorano, Bruno attempted to exert his control and influence over the labor organization. Why Bruno, or any mob boss, wanted control of a union was explained rather succinctly by New York mob figure Vincent "Fish" Cafaro in testimony before a U.S. Senate subcommittee in 1990.

"We got our money from gambling, but our real power, our real strength, came from the unions," said Cafaro, a turncoat member of New York's powerful Genovese organized crime family. "With the unions behind us, we could shut down the city, or the country for that matter, if we needed to get our way. . . . In some cases, we got money from our dealings with the unions, in some cases we got favors such as jobs for friends and relatives, but most importantly, in all cases, we got power."

The importance of the New Jersey bartenders union came into sharp focus in 1976—three years after McGreal was killed. It was a year of momentous developments for the Bruno crime family, a period when events that would dramatically alter the future of the Philadelphia–South Jersey mob were set in motion. These same developments would open the way for Tommy DelGiorno's rise to the top of the organization, turn Maryann DelGiorno's life upside down, and transform Angelo

Bruno from a boss who was feared and respected to one who was mocked and belittled.

In October of 1976, Carlo Gambino died of natural causes at his home on Long Island, New York. The American Mafia's last true boss of bosses was fighting attempts by the government to deport him to Italy as an undesirable at the time of his death. Plagued with heart problems for several years, the seventy-five-year-old mob kingpin passed away in his sleep, a peaceful death for a man who headed one of the most violent and powerful Mafia families in America.

Gambino's death saddened Angelo Bruno. The two Sicilian-born mob leaders were friends as well as allies. Both sat on the Mafia's national commission, a group made up of the leaders of New York's five crime families along with the bosses of mob families from several other cities, including Philadelphia and Chicago. The commission was set up in the late 1930s to settle internal disputes and territorial claims within the underworld.

So close was the relationship between Bruno and Gambino that the New York mob chief had the right to exercise Bruno's proxy vote at emergency commission meetings if Bruno was unable to attend. With Gambino removed from the scene, Bruno lost not only an important *amico nostra,* but also the unquestioned backing and support of the strongest and largest of New York's five families.

Ironically, at about the same time as Gambino's death, two distant cousins, Giuseppe and Rosario Gambino, opened a posh restaurant and supper club called Valentino's near the Garden State Racetrack in Cherry Hill, New Jersey. The trendy club quickly became South Jersey's version of *Saturday Night Fever.* It featured a light show and pulsating disco music on a dance floor that drew capacity crowds most Friday and Saturday nights. The dimly lit dining room, done in a Mediterranean aqua and white (as were the uniforms of the waiters and waitresses), boasted an elaborate and expensive menu. Every item, from the antipasto and minestrone to the espresso and zabagl-

ione, was à la carte. Steaks and pasta dishes were the specialties, including "steak alla Sinatra," a ten-ounce sirloin strip
stuffed with prosciutto and topped with mozzarella and a spicy
red tomato sauce.

Because of the Gambino family connections, the restaurant's opening attracted the attention of several law enforcement agencies, including the FBI and the New Jersey State
Police. Giuseppe and Rosario Gambino were Sicilian immi-
grants whose ties ran to both the New York mob family that
bore their name and to a Mafia clan in Sicily from which they
derived their real power. Bruno, according to investigative reports, welcomed the two young restaurateurs with open arms.
As one sign of respect, he invited them to his Snyder Avenue
home in South Philadelphia for Easter dinner. On a more mun-
dane level, he encouraged members of his organization to stop
by Valentino's when they were in the area to give the boys some
business. Bruno himself was spotted having dinner there once.
His table guest was Paul Castellano, Carlo Gambino's brother-
in-law and the man who succeeded Gambino as boss of the
New York family.

Older members of Bruno's organization, like Phil Testa and
Antonio Caponigro, suspected the young Gambinos were
heavily involved in the Sicilian heroin trade and found Bruno's
posturing hypocritical. Once again, they perceived the old man
as two-faced. While he railed against drug dealing for his own
members, he permitted two greenhorns just off the boat from
Palermo to open a beachhead in his own territory for the highly
lucrative heroin business. While they had no proof, mobsters
like Testa and Caponigro suspected Bruno was getting a cut
from the Gambinos. This, of course, would not be drug money
in the strictest sense, but rather a "tribute payment" from the
two young entrepreneurs, a financial acknowledgement that
they operated in South Jersey under Bruno's auspices and because of his largess. Members of Bruno's organization, who
knew of the astronomical amounts of money that could be
made moving heroin, bristled at the presence of the young

Gambinos in their midst and wondered about a mob boss who would let an economic opportunity like that pass his organization by.

Both the death of Carlo Gambino and the emergence of Giuseppe and Rosario Gambino in South Jersey served to undermine Angelo Bruno within his own organization. Then, on November 2, 1976, voters in New Jersey approved a constitutional amendment permitting casino gambling in Atlantic City. While it would be nearly two years before the first casino opened, jockeying began immediately for control of the service industries, construction companies and ancillary services that were positioned to cash in on what would become a multibillion dollar casino gambling boom.

Amazingly, Bruno said he was not interested. Called before the New Jersey State Commission of Investigation, he said his intentions were to stay clear of Atlantic City, that he wanted no part of any casino or any business connected with it. Again, members of his organization boiled over his posturing. They knew, for example, that a vending machine company controlled by Long John Martorano had already begun to tie up service contracts in the area. And they knew that Bruno had approved a move by Philadelphia union leader John McCullough and leaders of the Camden County bartenders union to take over the organized labor movement in and around the casino industry. The prize possession there was the small but strategically positioned Atlantic City bartenders union, Local 54. Long the poor cousin to Camden County's Local 170, the Atlantic City union suddenly found itself poised to become one of the biggest labor organizations in all of South Jersey. Bartenders, waitresses, bellhops, doormen, maids and janitors— virtually every service employee of any casino-hotel—would have to be a member of Local 54. Union dues alone would amount to millions of dollars a year. The medical, health and welfare and severance funds would account for millions more. It was a honey pot, a once-in-a-lifetime payday. And Little Nicky Scarfo, banished to Atlantic City when there was nothing there but seagulls and saltwater taffy, was ready to cash in.

Scarfo moved quickly after the casino gambling referendum to get his own hooks into Local 54. He had struggled to survive the hard times that enveloped the Boardwalk during the 1960s and early 1970s. He had no intention of stepping aside now that spinning roulette wheels and jangling slot machines were about to turn New Jersey's faded Queen of Resorts into an East Coast gambling mecca. He didn't care what McCullough, Martorano, or even Bruno, said. The bartenders union was his.

Maryann DelGiorno was unaware of the events unfolding in the underworld that would shape her life for the next fifteen years—events that would deepen her hatred of her ex-husband; put the lives of both of her sons in jeopardy; batter her resolve; and lead her to question whether her own life was worth living.

By the time casino gambling was approved for Atlantic City, she and Tommy DelGiorno had gone their separate ways. They both had remarried. Tommy's new wife was named Roseanne. She came from an Italian family in the heart of South Philadelphia—a wife, Maryann thought, more suited to the lifestyle her ex-husband craved. They moved into a stately two-story home in the twenty-nine-hundred block of South Broad Street, within walking distance of Columbus Park and the city's stadium complex. The houses in that section of the city were large, with stone fronts and terraced lawns. Another luxury, by South Philadelphia standards, was almost guaranteed curbside parking. When the homes were built, the city had cut out a small, semiprivate blacktop street, separated by trees and curbing, that ran parallel to Broad Street between that main thoroughfare and the homes in the twenty-nine-hundred block. While parking was at a premium in most of South Philadelphia and while disputes over parking spots often led to acrimonious and longstanding neighborhood feuds, Tommy Del and his new wife were spared that petty hassle. There is no greater definition of living in the lap of luxury in South Philadelphia than the ability to park your car in front of your home each night.

Maryann's home life was much more modest. Parking had always been a problem at the house on Gladstone Street, where she now lived with her new husband, Joe Fisher. So was paying the bills each week. But Maryann didn't care. Joe was a hard-working longshoreman who was also divorced. He had three children from his first marriage, but he treated her sons like they were his own, taking them on fishing and camping trips, to ball games and to ice hockey matches. He was there to help with their homework and to celebrate birthdays and graduations. He offered love and support and encouragement, all the things their real father didn't, or couldn't, provide.

"It felt good to have a man who was there when you needed him and I thought my love from my new husband and our family would get us through anything," Maryann said. "Tom would throw digs at us, making fun of the fact that Joe didn't earn a lot of money. One time he told the boys, 'I don't know how the poor man lives.' I knew he said that so it would get back to me, but I just brushed it off . . . I loved my ordinary life."

But Maryann knew the boys, who spent each Sunday with their father, looked at life through different eyes. She was confident that young Tommy, the more level-headed of her two sons, would have the good sense to recognize his father for what he was. Tommy, she was sure, would see through his father's bluster. Bobby was a different matter. Like any second child, he was more of a risk-taker, more likely to act before thinking a situation through. He depended on his guile and charm to get him out of tough spots. And, Maryann knew, Bobby was easily impressed by flash and glitter.

In the late 1970s, Tommy DelGiorno's star was on the rise in the Philadelphia underworld. And his youngest son, Bobby, was blinded by the light. "Bobby was impressed by everything his father said or did," Maryann recalled. "He swallowed every story he told him, word for word. Then he would come home and repeat them to his boy friends on the block."

It was around this time that Bobby started bragging to his friends about his future. His father, he would say knowingly, "was connected" and would help him up the ladder.

"When I grow up," Bobby said. "I'm gonna be a hit man for the mob."

Chapter Six

It wasn't always guns and money. Bobby DelGiorno still remembers moments when Tommy Del was more a father than a gangster, moments when he seemed to love and care about his sons.

He can still picture the family trip to Disney World in the early 1970s, before his parents separated. Bobby remembers how his mother and father smiled and laughed and how he and his brother felt warm and secure in the Florida sunshine, basking in the glow of cartoon characters come to life, amusement rides unlike any they'd ever seen before and parents who seemed happy and in love.

And then there was the time his father stopped the ice cream truck on Gladstone Street. Bobby was just four years old. But even now, he tells the story with a broad smile.

Every summer day the truck would come through the neighborhood, its canned music blaring from a loudspeaker. This would send kids scrambling. First they would run home to beg for money, and then they would fly back out onto the sidewalk to scream for the truck to stop. Maybe Gladstone Street was too narrow. Maybe it was too short. Whatever the reason, Bobby remembers that the truck would just keep on going. One night at dinner he complained to his father.

"Tomorrow," Tommy Del said, "we'll see what happens."

"Back then my father was funny, down to earth," Bobby recalled. "He was driving a truck and doing a little bookmaking on the side, but he wasn't no gangster. He was just an average guy. So the next day, he stays home from work. And when the ice cream truck comes around, he runs out in the street and lays down. Right in front of the truck. It had to stop."

Every kid in the neighborhood came running. They cheered and hollered. Tommy Del laughed. He bought ice cream for everybody on the block. Bobby and young Tommy grinned with pride. Their dad had stopped the ice cream truck. He was a hero.

"He used to do things like that," Bobby said. "I remember. But then he got too busy and he started making a lot of money and he never had no time for us no more."

Bobby was nearly six years old when his parents' divorce was finalized. The details were imprecise and obscure. He can recall some of the fights and the shouting. He remembers his mother crying. And then he realized that his father was no longer living in the house on Gladstone Street.

More sharply focused are the Sunday afternoon excursions to the heart of South Philadelphia. As part of the divorce settlement, Tommy Del had weekly visitation rights. He was supposed to pick his sons up late each Sunday morning, usually after they'd gone to mass, and return them after dinner. There were Sundays when Bobby and his brother would sit on the couch until midafternoon waiting. Sometimes Tommy Del would call ahead and beg off. More often than not, however, he'd come by for them. They'd pile into his car and he'd drive them over to his mother's house for Sunday dinner. Usually they'd make three or four stops along the way where Tommy Del would pick up the proceeds from his bookmaking and numbers operations. Occasionally their grandmother would scold Tommy Del for bringing the boys along while he conducted his gambling business, but neither Bobby nor Tommy junior complained. They were just happy that their father was showing some interest in them, happy to be a part of his life.

Later the Sunday trips would include a stop at an office on Ninth Street near the Italian Market where Frank D'Alfonso was running a ticket and travel agency in what used to be his family's flower shop. This was actually the nerve center for one of the biggest bookmaking operations in the city. Tommy Del was now a full-fledged partner of D'Alfonso, effectively usurping the role played by Broadway Eddie, who was still a part of the operation, but now even further in the background. D'Alfonso moved his gambling business to the ticket agency after the FBI raided Broadway Eddie's restaurant in 1972. Using information obtained from a series of wiretaps, the feds arrested Eddie, Frankie Flowers, Tommy Del and four other associates and charged them with running a major organized crime–linked gambling ring that was said to be doing about twenty thousand dollars a day in action. In fact, on a good football weekend, the number was about ten times that amount.

The raid led to probation and suspended sentences for all seven defendants. It had no impact on the gambling operation. The only difference was that now the bets were being taken at the ticket agency instead of Broadway Eddie's restaurant.

Bobby remembers desks and telephones ringing off the hook at his father's "office." Business, he figured, was great. His dad always had plenty of money. So did Frank D'Alfonso. Bobby and Tommy junior would spend an hour or so hanging around the ticket agency and then Tommy Del or Frankie Flowers would peel off some bills, hand them to D'Alfonso's eighteen-year-old son and tell him to take the boys to a video arcade or a toy store. There they'd spend the rest of their Sunday visit with their dad. It was not what the sociologists refer to as quality time. But neither Bobby nor Tommy junior knew any better. Bobby, especially, couldn't get enough of his father's world and the men who populated it.

"From the time I started going around Frankie Flowers's place, I admired all those guys," Bobby said. "They all wore expensive clothes, nice sports jackets and slacks. They drove Caddies, LTDs, big, expensive cars. And the thing I remember most is, they were always flashing cash. They used to call it their 'walking money.' These guys had anywhere from five hundred to two thousand dollars in their pocket. I loved being around them. For me it was exciting. And they'd always give us money or buy us toys. Then I'd go home and brag about it to all my friends, tell them how rich my father was.

"I used to think my mother was stupid for divorcing my father because he had all this money and she could have had anything she wanted and never would have had to work a day in her life. . . . What did I know? I was eight years old."

In 1976, while many other mobsters were looking toward Atlantic City for new business opportunities, Tommy Del stayed focused on South Philadelphia. Flush with the success of his gambling business and making more money than even he had hoped for, DelGiorno jumped at the chance to join Frank D'Alfonso in a new and "legitimate" business venture. Together they bought a restaurant at Eleventh and Christian Streets from the Piccolo brothers, three made members of the Angelo Bruno crime family. The restaurant, known as Piccolo's 500, had been a mob hangout for years. It was a neighborhood joint where wiseguys and wannabe wiseguys would go to see and be seen. Nothing fancy. Little Nicky Scarfo, who was a nephew of the three Piccolos, used to tend bar there before he was banished to Atlantic City.

Nicholas Piccolo, the oldest brother, was a capo in the Bruno organization. His brothers, Joseph and Michael, were crime family soldiers. They were known as the Buck Brothers, as in "Nicky Buck," "Joey Buck" and "Mike Buck." Like most

South Philadelphia nicknames, this one's origin was hazy. More than a few people who knew the Piccolos, however, suspected that it came from their tightfisted, penny-pinching personalities. None of the brothers were quick to spend a buck.

Tommy DelGiorno used to joke about Nicky Buck and his cheapskate personality. Whenever he had the chance, he would tell a story about an encounter he had with the oldest Piccolo brother a few years after buying the restaurant.

"My dad said he was walking down Christian Street one day when he ran into Nicky Buck," Bobby DelGiorno recalled. "The old man says to him, 'Where ya goin'?' and my Dad says he's going to the store to buy a newspaper. And Nicky Buck tells him, 'Wait. I got one in the house I'm done with. I'll go get it for you.'

"Now Nicky Buck lived about two blocks away and the store was right around the corner. And my Dad laughs and tells him, 'Forget about it. I can afford it.' My father would always tell that story and then he'd say, 'What kind of fuckin' gangster was he, worried about saving twenty-five cents.' "

Although Tommy Del and Frankie Flowers had put up the money to purchase Piccolo's 500, the owners of record were their wives, Roseanne DelGiorno and Micheline D'Alfonso. This arrangement was an attempt to avoid any problems in obtaining a liquor license. While the Pennsylvania Liquor Control Board was notoriously lax in its enforcement of liquor control laws, even the LCB might have raised a red flag at a license application from the likes of Tommy Del and Frankie Flowers. Their wives, however, were approved without question.

While Tommy Del's name did not appear on any of the legal papers connected to the operation of the restaurant, he was in charge of the day-to-day business. Years later he told New Jersey authorities his intention was to use the place as a meeting spot and office from which he would continue to operate his ever-expanding gambling and loan-sharking ventures. He said he didn't really care about its business potential. But he and D'Alfonso's next move defied that notion. They hired a notable Philadelphia chef, Vincent "Cous" (pronounced "kuz") Pilla, who happened to be one of Frankie Flowers's better gambling customers, to run the kitchen. As an inducement to lure Pilla from the popular Villa Di Roma on Ninth Street where he was then working, DelGiorno and D'Alfonso agreed to change the name of their establishment.

And that's how Piccolo's 500 became Cous' Little Italy. Within weeks, customers were jamming the place for dinner. Its "shady connections" added a sense of excitement for couples who drove in from New Jersey or the Pennsylvania suburbs, but the real draw was Cous Pilla and his fabulous food.

Pilla was a happy-go-lucky South Philadelphia personality whose passion for pasta was matched by his penchant for gambling. He loved to bet nearly as much as he loved to cook. But his connection to the wiseguys was strictly culinary. "His only crime," a popular newspaper columnist noted at the time, "is that he makes the best pasta in South Philadelphia."

"When I first bought Cous'," Tommy Del told the New Jersey State Commission of Investigation in 1992, "I bought it only for—it was a little place at the time and I bought it only for a place to—like an office where I could hang out, a place where people could come and meet me and a place where I could get messages.

"As time went on it became so successful that it—you know, it made money in spite of me, actually. It just took off because of the chef and because of the location. It just made money. I didn't—I never dreamt it was going to make that much money."

Tommy went on to explain the ins and outs of the business, from a wiseguy's perspective. A bar or a restaurant, in addition to serving as a secure meeting spot, offered the opportunity to either launder money or hide money. Some guys, he said, liked to run their illegitimate income (from things like bookmaking, loan-sharking and drug dealing) through the books of their bar or restaurant, thereby legitimizing the money and allowing them to use it to buy homes and cars, or make investments in other legal businesses. Others went in the opposite direction, skimming profits from their bar to finance drug dealing and loan-sharking ventures. At different times and at different locations—after Cous' he would own two other bars in South Philadelphia—Tommy Del used his business to clean money and to hide money.

"There's a lot of things you can do," he explained. "I mean, a lot of things. It's an office. It's a place for people to meet you. It's a place where people can locate you, to meet new people, funnel money. It's a place where you can hide money, steal money. . . . It depends on the individual and how he wants to use it."

A few years after DelGiorno opened Cous' Little Italy, the Pennsylvania Crime Commission investigated the mob's control of certain liquor licenses and restaurants. Among other things, the commission report cited the findings of an audit of Cous' for a twelve-month period beginning in November of 1979. The commission pointed out that during this period "organized crime associate and convicted gambler Thomas DelGiorno called the shots at Cous' with respect to all major business decisions."

The audit showed that Cous' listed bank deposits of $454,964 during the twelve months in question. Yet the total cash on hand, based on an analysis of the restaurant's receipts and expenses, was only $303,879. In fact, Cous' Little Italy deposited $151,085 more in revenue than it generated.

Vincent Pilla's pasta was good, but not that good.

One other benefit to owning a legitimate business, Tommy Del said, was the opportunity to provide jobs for friends and associates. Cous' had a staff of forty to fifty employees, including two part-time dishwashers who had the same last name as the owner.

"My father gave me and my brother our first real jobs, washing dishes at Cous'," Bobby said. "I would work Friday and my brother would work Saturday. We worked different nights because my father knew if we were together we'd either start fooling around or fighting. We made twenty dollars a week.

"I worked for about two hours, but most of the time I was either eating or running around talking to all the people in the restaurant. . . . It was great. All kinds of people would come in. Ballplayers. Gangsters. Celebrities. One time Jay Johnstone, who was an outfielder with the Phillies, was there having dinner and talking to my father. It was getting late and I had to be home, but my father had to go somewhere, so he asked Jay to drive me. I couldn't believe it, being driven home by a real ballplayer. He had a Thunderbird with a see-through glass T-top. We talked about baseball, and I told him how much I admired him. This was in the late 1970s. He was one of the Phillies' best hitters. When we got to the front of my house, he gave me two baseballs with his autograph on them, one for me and one for my brother, Tommy. I ran into the house yelling and screaming. I couldn't believe it.

"A lot of Phillies stopped in to Cous'. My father said they respected him for what he did for a living and he respected what they did for a living and that's why he never asked them to fix a game or do anything illegal for him. But he told me that one time he was out with another Phillies player drinking until three or four in the morning. He said the guy was really drunk. So my dad figured he'd be in no shape to play the next day. This was on a Saturday. My dad goes and bets a ton of money against the Phillies, figuring he had an edge. . . . That night the guy goes four-for-six with a triple, double and two singles and the Phillies win big. My dad laughed about it, 'It was worth a try,' he said."

Tommy Del's ability to rub elbows with ballplayers and

with the entertainers and movie stars who occasionally stopped by the restaurant further enhanced his standing with his young son. Bobby simply turned a deaf ear to his mother's warnings about his father and "the company he keeps." He saw nothing wrong with his father's friends. He liked the way they carried themselves and the fact that other people treated them with respect. He liked the way they dressed and the way they talked. None of these guys were worried about their next paycheck. In fact, most of them didn't even have jobs. But they all had plenty of cash and Bobby liked the way they threw their money around.

Once a woman customer at Cous' complained to his father that an expensive camera had been stolen off the seat of her car, which had been parked on the street while she was in the restaurant. Tommy Del asked the woman how much the camera was worth, then he peeled off four one-hundred-dollar bills from the wad in his pocket and handed them to her. Bobby's stepfather, Joe Fisher, would work all week to make that much money. And here was his father handing a total stranger four bills.

To thirteen-year-old Bobby, that was class. That was style. That was what he wanted. Despite what his mother said, Bobby took pride in the fact that his father was "Tommy Del," a man of influence and respect, a man clearly moving up the underworld ladder. Bobby's dream was to climb right along with him.

Tommy Del's ownership of Cous' Little Italy and his association with Frankie Flowers brought him in closer contact with more members of the Bruno crime family. Frank Sindone, who headed Bruno's multimillion dollar loan-sharking operation, became a regular at the restaurant. He was usually accompanied by Joseph "Chickie" Ciancaglini, a hard-as-nails soldier in the organization who served as Sindone's bodyguard and driver. Bruno himself would stop by on occasion, usually ordering one of Vince Pilla's specialties. Despite sometimes severe gastrointestinal problems, Bruno liked the rich dishes that Pilla served up—especially the Chicken Sicilian, boneless chunks of chicken prepared in a rich butter sauce with olives, capers and pimento.

On one occasion in late 1979 or early 1980, Tommy Del was sitting at a table with Bruno, Sindone and Ciancaglini when Bobby showed up at the restaurant looking for something to eat. Tommy Del made a point of calling his son over to the table.

"This is my youngest son, Bobby," DelGiorno said to Bruno in a respectful tone that Bobby had seldom heard his father use around any of his other associates. "Bobby, this is Mr. Bruno."

Bobby eyed the elder Mafia boss cautiously. He had heard a lot about the man, but had never seen him. This was more important, he knew, than meeting any professional baseball player or movie star. In his father's world, Angelo Bruno was king. Bruno was in his sixties, slightly balding, with a round face and surprisingly soft features. He reminded Bobby more of Broadway Eddie than of any of the really hard-nosed characters who hung around his dad.

Bobby held out his hand and Angelo Bruno took it.

"It's a pleasure to meet you, Bobby," the head of the Philadelphia underworld said as they shook hands.

"Nice to meet you, Mr. Bruno," Bobby replied.

Then Tommy Del told him to go over to the bar and get a soda and something to eat. From there Bobby watched his father huddle for more than an hour in conversation with three of the top mob figures in the city. Although he was unaware of it at the time, Bobby learned later that Frank Sindone had replaced Frankie Flowers as his father's partner in the restaurant. Tommy Del would say that D'Alfonso balked at an expensive remodeling and expansion plan for Cous' and was happy to sell out. In fact, while there might have been some truth to that explanation, Tommy Del had decided that he had gone as far as he could with D'Alfonso. Sindone, a made member of the organization, had more clout and could open the final door for Tommy Del. Ever conscious of the fact that in the underworld *who* you're with is as important as what you do, Tommy decided that hooking up with Sindone and Ciancaglini was the right career move.

It was a gamble that nearly cost him his life.

The unrest that had been simmering in the underworld since 1976 began to surface in late 1979 and early 1980. One FBI informant, a mob hit man named Charlie Allen, told authorities a remarkable tale about how he had been ordered by Bruno to stockpile weapons in anticipation of a potential mob war. According to Allen, Bruno was concerned about his underboss, Philip "Chicken Man" Testa. Other sources said that Testa had boldly asked Bruno's permission to start a new family. While New York had five mob families, no other city in America had more than one. Testa's request was insulting if not seditious.

"Right then Testa shoulda been whacked," said another informant familiar with the maneuverings that were taking place at the time. But Bruno, perhaps out of a sense of loyalty to a man who had served him for nearly twenty years, hesitated. Antonio "Tony Bananas" Caponigro, Bruno's *consiglière*— crime family counselor—was ready to move on Testa. All that he wanted was Don Angelo's okay. Instead, Bruno took off for a vacation in Italy. And when he returned, he appeared even more indecisive.

Several mob informants have since detailed to state and federal investigators the Machiavellian intrigue that brought Angelo Bruno down. All put Caponigro at the center of the plot.

Tony Bananas, whose unspoken ambitions rivaled those of Testa, had been named consiglière in 1978, shortly after he completed a two-year prison term for assaulting a federal agent. The "consig" is the number-three man in the organization. The job is usually given to a veteran member of the family whose loyalty is beyond question. In that regard, Tony Bananas did not fit the bill. In fact, the Pennsylvania Crime Commission later noted, Bruno's decision to name Caponigro consi-glière was a misguided attempt to ensure his loyalty.

What's more, it proved to be a fatal mistake for nearly everyone involved.

As consiglière, Caponigro was supposed to mediate dis-putes between crime family members and to be a court of last appeal whenever a murder contract was discussed. Instead, he fanned the flames of discontent, pitting members against one another and undermining Bruno's authority whenever he could.

Now Bruno's reluctance to move against Testa provided Caponigro with the chance he had been waiting for. He decided to act on his own. But instead of pointing his gun at Testa, he aimed higher. In private conversations with a few close associ-ates, Caponigro argued that the crime family—faced with the opportunities offered in Atlantic City and in the mushrooming drug trade—needed strong leadership. Bruno, he said, was weak.

Caponigro cleared his plan with a faction of the Genovese organization in New York who assured him that neither they nor any of the other families had an interest in an internal dispute in Philadelphia. He was then told to "do what you gotta do," says a mob informant who was involved in the machinations.

On March 21, 1980, Angelo Bruno had dinner at Tommy DelGiorno's restaurant. Appearing casual and relaxed follow-ing his recent vacation in Italy, Bruno dined on the Chicken Sicilian and lingered over coffee and drinks with several associ-ates who stopped by his table. When it was time to leave, Bruno looked for Raymond "Long John" Martorano, a friend and business partner who usually drove him home each night.

But Martorano had been called away. Someone suggested that John Stanfa, a low-key mob associate who operated a small construction company in South Philadelphia and hap-pened to be in the restaurant that night, could drive the mob boss home. Stanfa lived on Passyunk Avenue, just a few blocks from Bruno's Snyder Avenue home.

They left Cous' Little Italy around 9:30 P.M. and fifteen minutes later pulled up in front of Bruno's home, a two-story, brick row house just off the corner of Tenth Street and Snyder Avenue. Stanfa drove a late-model maroon Chevrolet Caprice. Bruno sat in the passenger seat beside him smoking a cigarette and talking. It was a Friday night. A light rain had slicked the streets. As the car sat idling in front of the house, Stanfa pushed a button on the door panel and the window next to Bruno lowered. At the same time a man wearing a raincoat walked out of the shadows toward the car, pulled out a twelve-gauge shotgun and blew a hole in the back of Angelo Bruno's head. The gunman then turned and ran to the corner where a car was waiting.

The reverberations from that shotgun blast would be felt through the Philadelphia underworld for the next ten years. Angelo Bruno died instantly. By the time his wife ran screaming into the street moments after hearing the shot, he was already a corpse. Stanfa, struck in the arm and shoulder by the spray of shotgun pellets, was rushed to the hospital by police, who were on the scene within minutes.

Despite an intense investigation, no one has ever been charged with the Bruno killing. There is little doubt in the underworld or within the law enforcement community, however, that Caponigro set the assassination in motion. And there are those who knew Tony Bananas who say without equivocation that he was the man with the shotgun.

"Tony would never ask you to do something he wouldn't do himself," said one longtime friend. "Plus, in this case, there weren't that many people he could trust or who even knew what was going on."

"He was a stone cold killer," said another. "The last of the real gangsters."

Bruno's murder, the first significant mob hit in more than a decade in Philadelphia, dominated the headlines and television news in the days following the shooting. There was some speculation that the murder was part of a push by the New York families to take control of Atlantic City, where three casinos were now up and running. There were also hints of an internal dispute and reports that Bruno had been killed by some of his most trusted allies. Events over the next several months would confirm this.

———————

Bobby couldn't make sense of it all, but knew that it was exciting. For the first time he saw his father's name in the paper, identified as a gambler and mob associate who owned the restaurant where Bruno had had his last meal. Subsequent stories mentioned Sindone, Phil Testa, Frankie Flowers, Ciancaglini and dozens of others. It was like reading the box scores and game reports after a Phillies game. Bobby knew many of the men identified as major figures in the Philadelphia underworld. Those he didn't know, he had heard of.

The fact that one of them was now dead, brutally blown away with a shotgun, seemed immaterial. The quiet, soft-spoken man who had shook his hand in the restaurant months earlier had been murdered, but Bobby was focused on other things. Shooting one another was what these guys did. That, he thought, was what the mob was all about. He didn't yet know about the smell of a quick, violent death. Of a face frozen in a voiceless scream. Of blood, thick and sticky, rushing from a wound and then drying stiffly, as it turned from bright red to dark brown. Eventually, Bobby would come to learn all of this. And death would take on a new and more somber meaning for him. But in 1980, reading about the mob was like reading about baseball. He was a fan. And he knew many of the players.

"From that day, when I saw my dad's name in the paper, I wanted to be just like him," Bobby said. "I wanted to be in the Mafia and drive expensive cars and have lots of money in my pocket, just like my father and his friends. I was still a kid, but I knew what I wanted. Some kids wanted to be policemen or firemen or lawyers. Not me. I wanted to be in the Mafia. No matter how bad people talked about it, my mind was made up and nobody could change it.

"Some people would have been embarrassed if their father was in the mob. But I was so proud of my father. I thought it took courage and guts to do what he had to do."

It was about that time that thirteen-year-old Robert DelGiorno, much to his mother's anguish and dismay, started referring to himself around the neighborhood as "Bobby Del."

Chapter Seven

Bobby's job at Cous' Little Italy lasted a little more than a year. He and his brother were sacked after they started an egg fight in the restaurant kitchen one busy Saturday night. Several other workers joined in—hell, they figured, if the owner's sons were involved, why not? But Vince Pilla, who liked to cook almost as much as he liked to gamble—and who approached both endeavors with equal dedication—was outraged. Throwing eggs around his kitchen was unacceptable. He knew he couldn't reprimand Bobby or Tommy junior, so he vented his rage at the other workers.

A few days later, Tommy Del called his sons and told them not to bother coming around to work at the restaurant anymore. He said he'd still pay them each twenty dollars a week and that they could always stop in for food or a soda, but that their services as dishwashers were no longer required.

Tommy junior, who was then enrolled in Saint John Neumann High School in South Philadelphia, had more than enough to occupy his time.

Bobby, in a public junior high school and taking vocational

training courses, also had other—although less academic—interests. He and his best friend, Anthony Forline, who lived two doors away on Gladstone Street, were developing independent sources of income. Bobby was fourteen now. Anthony was thirteen. And on Friday nights they used to hang out in the schoolyard at Second and Ritner with a dozen other guys from the neighborhood talking about sports, sex, gambling and girls. Occasionally someone would get up the nerve to approach the bartender at one of the corner taprooms and try to buy a few quarts of beer. None of them looked old enough, and the gambit rarely worked.

Then Bobby and Anthony came up with a different plan. There were several drunks in the neighborhood; older men who would go on a binge each weekend, moving from taproom to taproom. Bobby and Anthony would hang out on a corner near one of the bars and when one of the drunks approached, they'd offer him two dollars if he'd buy them a dollar quart of beer. The one-hundred-percent markup worked every time. Bobby and Anthony were chugging quarts most Friday and Saturday nights. Soon, however, they got tired of the added cost and developed a scheme that would allow them to drink and earn a little pocket change for themselves.

Both Bobby's mother and stepfather, Maryann and Joe, worked during the day, so the boys used Bobby's house rather than Anthony's. They set the plan in motion for the first time one Friday afternoon. Anthony, whose voice was much deeper than Bobby's, called a local beer distributor and ordered a case of quarts to be delivered to the house on Gladstone Street. When the deliveryman arrived, Bobby answered the door. Anthony was upstairs, running the shower.

"Is your father home?" the deliveryman asked.

"Yeah, he's upstairs," Bobby said.

Then, on cue, Anthony hollered down, "Who is it?"

"It's the beer man, Dad," Bobby replied.

"Tell him the money's on the kitchen table," Anthony shouted back.

The boys had already put fifteen dollars on the table. A case cost twelve bucks. Bobby made sure to tip the deliveryman a dollar. More would be too obvious. He and Anthony then took the beer and hid it in the back yard, stashing it under a trash bag. That night, on the corner, they offered to make the beer run, collecting two dollars from each of their friends. But instead of paying a drunk, they pocketed the extra money, returning to the corner with the quarts they had purchased earlier in the day.

This went on for about a month. After the first week, the deliveryman didn't even ask any questions. The money was always on the table. So was his tip. And Bobby and Anthony were in business. It wasn't big bucks. In fact, between the beer they drank themselves and the tip for the deliveryman, the boys barely broke even. But when you're fourteen years old, the game's the thing.

"Our luck ran out when one of the kids who bought beer from us got caught coming home drunk one Friday night by his mother," Bobby said. "He ratted on me and Anthony. So the boy's mother comes over my house and tells my mother."

Bobby, who had been paying close attention to his father, did the logical thing. He lied.

"When my mother asked me if I was getting the kid beer, I said no. I told her he was just saying that to try to get himself out of trouble. Then I asked her if she ever saw me coming home drunk. She hadda say no, because she hadn't. So then I say, 'So why would I get the kid beer and not me?' "

It was a typical mother-teenager standoff. Maryann questioned her son's innocence, but couldn't prove anything. Bobby knew that and wouldn't budge. Maryann did what mothers always do in that situation. She threatened.

The one thing she knew Bobby couldn't stand was being told he couldn't go out. Having to sit in the house, confined, was the only punishment that had ever had any effect on her youngest son. From the time he was old enough to play outside, Bobby loved the streets, loved moving around, loved the freedom. When he was six or seven, being grounded and housebound for a week was far worse than a spanking. Being grounded for a month was capital punishment. The neighborhood was his playground. He knew everyone, and everyone knew him. As he got older, that particular corner of South Philadelphia became the center of his universe.

"Never mind," Maryann said as Bobby continued to protest his innocence. "Just don't let me find you drinking beer or you'll be in *for a year!*"

With that, Bobby's bootlegging days ended. He continued to drink. He knew he could hold his own and his mother would never find out. But selling to others offered too many potential problems. Why get in trouble because some other guy was a sloppy drunk? The few bucks he was earning just weren't worth the risk. Besides, he and Anthony had hit on a far more lucrative enterprise. Pro football pools were big with the older guys and could be found in almost any bar or corner grocery store. Each week Bobby or Anthony would grab a betting form, take it to their school library and make about fifty copies. By Tuesday they were distributing them in their junior high school. On Friday they'd collect the bets. Most guys went for fifty cents or a dollar. And while the best bet usually involved picking just four teams—with a payout of ten to one—the majority of their customers would try to pick seven, eight, nine or even ten winners.

"We would collect about forty dollars in bets each week," Bobby said. "And usually we'd only have to pay out twelve, fourteen, maybe twenty bucks to winners. We used to keep the money in a box in my bedroom. Just let it pile up in case we got hit with a big win. But that never happened."

By the end of the football season, the two young bookies split their earnings fifty-fifty.

"It was a couple hundred dollars," Bobby said. "When you're fourteen, that's a lot of money."

What's more, it was easy.

Bobby had watched his father earn money this way for

years. And while he and Anthony were hardly in the same league as Tommy Del, he saw the cash from the football pools as a first step. Now he was doing more than just talking about becoming a mobster like his dad.

Tommy Del also was moving toward a rite of passage. This one, however, would be far less innocent than his son's. The March 1980 murder of Angelo Bruno had brought chaos to the once stable Philadelphia underworld. Over the next two years, sixteen members and associates of the crime family would be killed, including another mob boss. Tommy DelGiorno, drifting ever closer to the center of power, was now a "proposed member" of the organization, meaning that he was in line to be formally initiated. There was just one more test that he had to pass. He had to "do some work" or "make his bones," as they said in the underworld. In other words, he had to take part in a mob murder.

His victim would be one of the more daring loan sharks, gamblers and drug dealers in the Philadelphia–South Jersey area, a man named Johnny Calabrese. Like Bruno, Calabrese would spend his last night at Cous' Little Italy. And like Bruno, Calabrese would never know what hit him.

But before Tommy Del could take aim at Calabrese, ten others would have to die. Greed, envy and a blatant grab for power propelled events. Former friends and associates turned on one another. A bullet to the back of the head became the solution to every and any problem. In rapid succession, three of the men suspected of being behind the Bruno killing turned up dead.

The first to go were Tony Bananas Caponigro and his brother-in-law, Alfred Salerno. A month after Bruno was shot the two were summoned to New York for a meeting with the heads of the five families. Caponigro had told associates not to worry.

"The night before he got killed he was in my bar," Tommy

Del later told authorities. "And he was, you know, he was saying—you know, he was sittin' at the bar, now I ain't gonna say he directed it right to me, which he may have, but he said, 'Everything's gonna be all right. I'm gonna be the boss'. . . . He had this meeting in New York."

The meeting was set for April 18, 1980. Caponigro and Salerno were picked up by a crew from the Genovese crime family near the Diamond Exchange on Forty-seventh Street and Seventh Avenue. Salerno had a wholesale jewelry business there. The Genovese crew was headed by Vincent "Chin" Gigante and included John DiGilio, a onetime professional boxer who worked the Bayonne waterfront for the New York mob.

Instead of a meeting, however, Caponigro and Salerno were driven to a warehouse where they were brutally beaten, stabbed, shot and strangled. A week later their bodies were discovered in the trunks of two cars parked a few blocks apart and abandoned in the South Bronx. Caponigro had been shot thirteen times. Strewn about his body and stuffed in his mouth and anus were ripped twenty-dollar bills.

The message was clear to everyone in the underworld: Tony Bananas had gotten too greedy.

Caponigro had been betrayed by the Genovese organization, whose leaders had led him to believe the Bruno killing had been sanctioned by the mob's national commission. Then, to cover up the treachery, those same leaders took out Caponigro. On the surface, it appeared that they were avenging the Bruno murder. In fact, they were cleaning up the loose ends of a bloody double-cross rooted in an internal mob dispute nearly two years old.

Late in 1978, Caponigro had clashed with members of the Genovese family over control of a two-million-dollar book-making operation in Jersey City. Tony Bananas said the operation belonged to the Bruno crime family but the Genoveses said Jersey City fell under their sphere of influence. A sitdown was scheduled in New York to work out the problem. Bruno and the New York bosses attended the meeting and, after much haggling, the dispute was settled in Caponigro's favor. Everyone shook hands, embraced and went about their business.

But the leaders of the Genovese organization never forgot. Now both Bruno and Caponigro were dead. Within months, the Jersey City bookmaking operation was in the hands of the Genovese crime family.

Meanwhile, in Philadelphia, Phil Testa—who had the support of the five New York families—was named to succeed Angelo Bruno. In one of his first moves, he named Little Nicky Scarfo the new family consiglière. Scarfo's stature in the mob was increasing with each new casino that opened in Atlantic City. His elevation to crime family counselor was a reflection of both his increasing power in the casino city and his long-standing friendship with Testa. Pete Casella, an old-time Philadelphia mob soldier who had done time in a federal prison in Atlanta for heroin trafficking, was named underboss.

Testa wanted an infusion of new blood after years of stagnation during the Bruno era. Hoping to stock the mob with members whose loyalty would be beyond question, he initiated several new members into the organization. Among those who took the bloody oath were Testa's own son, Salvatore, the brothers Salvatore and Lawrence Merlino and Philip Leonetti. The Merlinos were close friends of Little Nicky Scarfo. Leonetti was Scarfo's nephew.

Five months after the discovery of the bodies of Caponigro and Salerno, another mobster suspected of plotting Bruno's murder turned up dead. John "Johnny Keyes" Simone was found shot three times in the back of the head. His body was dumped along the side of the road near a landfill in Staten Island.

Bobby read the stories in the paper and was fascinated by the developments. Tommy Del, who didn't need the media to tell him what was going on, had a much closer view and was troubled by what he saw.

In the months following Bruno's murder, DelGiorno began to suspect that Frank Sindone—his new partner in Cous' Little

Italy and the man he hoped would pave his way into the mob—had been involved in the plot. In fact, several members of the organization knew that Caponigro had planned to make Sindone his underboss once he took over. This meant that Phil Testa, a natural rival for power, would have had no place in Caponigro's planned crime family. Now, with Caponigro gone, DelGiorno and the others wanted to know if there was a place for Sindone in Testa's crime family.

The answer would be delivered shortly.

Sindone, a dour-faced man with a receding hairline who always wore thick, horn-rimmed glasses, was considered the premier loan shark in the city. Although he had replaced Frankie Flowers as DelGiorno's partner in Cous', his base of operation was a small steak shop called Frank's Cabana at Tenth and Moyamensing in South Philadelphia.

Sindone, who had never married, was one of the wealthier members of the Bruno organization. Like Caponigro and Testa, he was fed up with Bruno's conservative style. In 1976 the FBI had managed to plant an electronic bug in Frank's Cabana and had picked up several conversations in which Sindone complained to other mobsters about Bruno. What good was having all this money, Sindone asked, if you couldn't spend it.

"I didn't have nothing," he said in one rambling monologue later played in court. "My mother and father wasn't rich people. Whatever I have, I had to steal. I had to make it on my own. My father used to sell fish, like a fuckin' Indian. So now I got money. I'm getting old fast. I'm almost fifty. I want to enjoy the fuckin' money."

Sindone said he wanted to leave South Philadelphia and move out west to California or Nevada. His dream, he said, was to buy a ranch, own a few horses and raise grapes and oranges. But Bruno, he said, wouldn't let him leave.

"If I don't make no money for the rest of my fuckin' life I'd never be broke," he said. "I can't spend what I've got . . . I got a right to enjoy myself. I've lived my fuckin' life in one lousy place."

But, he said, Bruno had "them old fuckin' ways. He ain't getting out of them, you know what I mean? Those guys, I don't know. I don't understand them. It's just 'Get the money. Get the money.' Don't spend it. What the fuck good is it?"

Sindone may have seen Caponigro's move on Bruno as his way out. Or, despite what he said on the FBI bug, by 1980 he may have gotten caught up in the grab for power and wealth. Whatever the motivation, once Caponigro was killed and the plot began to unravel, Sindone was in a precarious situation. Testa and Scarfo were determined to clean house. Anyone whose loyalty might be questioned or whose strength might present a challenge was targeted. Sindone was marked on both counts.

One Saturday morning early in October of 1980, Bobby was having breakfast with his brother and two of their friends in the Oregon Diner when Sindone walked in. Bobby recognized him right away and waved hello.

Sindone, who was accompanied by another man, was standing near the entrance looking out into the parking lot, as if he were waiting to meet someone. But when he saw Bobby, he walked over to the booth where the boys were sitting and shook hands.

"What are you guys doing here?" Sindone joked. "You look like you're getting ready to knock over the joint."

Bobby and the others just laughed.

"Stay out of trouble, you little hoods," he said. Then Sindone walked over to the cashier, put a twenty-dollar bill on the counter and told her he was picking up the breakfast tab for Bobby and his friends. A few minutes later, he and his companion left.

"Who was that?" one of the boys asked.

"His name's Frank Sindone," Bobby said knowingly. "He's my dad's partner. He owns half of Cous' Little Italy. He's loaded with money. They say he's in the Mafia."

Two weeks later, Frank Sindone's membership was abruptly terminated.

"Sindone, principal loan shark for the Philadelphia family, was found dumped behind a variety store in South Philadelphia," said a law enforcement report of the October 29, 1980, murder. "He . . . had been shot three times in the head. The body was bound with rope, his hands tied behind his back, and stuffed inside two green plastic trash bags. One bag had been pulled down over his head, the other up over his legs. A few hours later, police located Sindone's car, wiped clean of fingerprints, parked near Frank's Cabana Steaks, a business Sindone owned."

Sindone was wearing a gold watch and had five hundred dollars in cash in his pocket. His body was dumped behind a store in the two-thousand block of Oregon Avenue, less than a five-minute drive from the diner where, a few weeks earlier, he had joked with Bobby and his friends.

To this day, mobsters and law enforcement authorities continue to speculate about the motive for the Sindone shooting. Some say it was because he was involved in the assassination of Angelo Bruno. But others, including Tommy Del, believe Sindone was whacked because Testa feared a power struggle. DelGiorno, for example, knew that before the New York families interceded and ordered that Testa take over the Bruno family, the members were split over who should be the new boss.

"Actually, Sindone had more votes than Phil for boss," Tommy Del said. "Sindone actually won the vote from the captains. . . . But New York turned it down . . . beings that Tony [Caponigro] got whacked and they felt that Sindone was with Tony."

Once Testa became boss, he had the only vote that mattered. The result was a forgone conclusion. Sindone had nowhere to hide and no one to whom he could appeal.

"Naturally, Phil had him killed," said Tommy Del.

Bruno had been blown away in March. By the end of October the four men suspected of plotting his death were murdered. Five mobsters killed brutally in the span of eight months. And Bobby had known two of them. Had shaken hands with them, in fact. Had sat down and talked with them. Both men had impressed him. Bruno was soft-spoken but self-assured, a man clearly in charge. Sindone was a little rough around the edges, hiding a friendly manner behind a tough exterior, a man who acted as if he didn't have a care in the world. But, Bobby would learn, things were seldom as they seemed in the mob, especially in Philadelphia in the early 1980s.

Sindone was killed on a Wednesday. The following Sunday, when Tommy Del went to Gladstone Street to pick up Bobby and Tommy junior, the boys mentioned the murder.

"Dad, that was a shame what happened to Frank Sindone, wasn't it?" Bobby asked.

"Listen, he was no good, so forget about him," Tommy Del said. "He was messing with the wrong people. And I don't want to talk about it no more, you hear?"

End of conversation.

Tommy Del considered himself lucky. He had not been around Sindone long enough to become part of his inner circle. If he had, he might have been drawn into the Bruno assassination plot. And that, he realized, could have been his death sentence. As it was, Joseph "Chickie" Ciancaglini, Sindone's driver and bodyguard, narrowly escaped death. Testa and Scarfo, in solidifying their hold on the mob, considered taking Ciancaglini out with Sindone. But they decided instead to test his loyalty to the new regime. According to several mob members who subsequently became cooperating witnesses, Ciancaglini helped set Sindone up, luring him to a meeting where he was killed.

No one ever told Tommy Del this, but there were enough other signs for him to know that Ciancaglini had made his peace with Testa and Scarfo. Shortly after Sindone was killed, Testa sent word to DelGiorno: Sindone's interest in Cous'

Little Italy would now be shared by Frank Monte, a capo in the organization, and Ciancaglini. Tommy Del was also told that Ciancaglini had been promoted to the rank of capo and that DelGiorno—now a proposed member of the organization— would report to him.

The murders of the Bruno conspirators, carried out in conjunction with the New York families, were just the first phase of a bloody reorganization instituted by Testa and Scarfo. While Bruno had frowned on the use of violence and abhorred public executions, Testa and Scarfo seemed to enjoy the public spectacle of a mob rubout: the newspaper headlines, the television cameras, the gory pictures of a body stuffed inside a trash bag or left bleeding in the gutter. There was nothing subtle about the new regime as it sent out its message to the rest of the underworld. The Bruno era of compromise and conciliation was over.

Wallace P. Hay, executive director of the Pennsylvania Crime Commission during the carnage, said the power struggle that followed Bruno's death was a war motivated by greed and marked by a brutality rivaling the mob killings of the Prohibition era.

"I think it goes back to the 'haves and have nots,' " Hay said in a report issued at the time. "The oldsters are always conservative, the young ones, the hungry ones, are progressive, or aggressive. Angelo [Bruno] had his pile made and wouldn't share it downward.

"There's an old saying that applies to business as it does to the mob. When you're Number One you can afford to be pure. When you're Number Two you got to work harder."

As 1980 drew to a close, there was still plenty of work to be done.

Scarfo, especially, was concerned about his hold on Atlantic City. He knew he'd have to make accommodations with the New York families, particularly the Genovese and Gambino organizations. In many ways, Atlantic City would become like Las Vegas, an open city where any mob family could operate. As a courtesy, however, most checked with Philadelphia first to clear their action and to avoid stumbling on or over any other mob operation.

As a result, various mob families from New York, New Jersey and even Boston, Chicago and Los Angeles got involved in the junket business, in the service industries and in the fight game, which had taken off once the casinos got going. While sports betting was prohibited, boxing matches became part of the draw on the Boardwalk. Several heavyweight championship matches were fought in Convention Hall. And many casinos staged their own fight cards in smaller auditoriums or theaters converted for the occasion. Tommy Del, among others, developed a small stable of fighters and became a frequent ringside habitué. Scarfo, himself a former amateur boxer, was also an avid fan of the sweet science and, until being barred from the casinos as an undesirable, attended most of the big matches in town.

Through his friend Lawrence Merlino and his nephew Phil Leonetti, Scarfo also had established a foothold in the construction industry. Both Merlino and Leonetti owned companies involved in the concrete and steel business and became subcontractors on a half dozen casino-hotel projects.

But it was the ever-expanding bartenders union that was Scarfo's prime concern. Local 54 of the International Restaurant Employees and Hotel Employees Union (commonly known as Bartenders Local 54) would eventually represent more than twenty thousand casino-hotel workers. Scarfo had been jockeying for control of the local since the 1976 casino gambling referendum, ignoring Bruno's orders to back off and maneuvering to ensure that neither Camden County Local 33 nor Philadelphia union boss John McCullough was able to wrest control.

Local 33, where Joey McGreal had once held sway, was now firmly in the hands of Albert Daidone and Raymond

"Long John" Martorano, both of whom had quickly fallen in line behind Testa. Scarfo knew those two would not be a problem. But Philadelphia roofers union boss Johnny McCullough was another story. The tough-talking Irishman was the business agent for one of the roughest trade union groups in the area.

With Angelo Bruno's support, McCullough had moved in 1979 to set up a rival bartenders union in Atlantic City. But now, with Bruno out of the picture, McCullough was exposed. Called to a meeting with Testa and Scarfo, he failed to show up. Summoned again, he sent a terse, no nonsense message.

"Fuck you," John McCullough said.

Testa and Scarfo replied by sending him flowers. Bright red poinsettia plants. They were delivered to McCullough's home in Northeast Philadelphia on the night of December 16, 1980, by a hit man who later confessed that he was working for Martorano and Daidone. After placing the flowers on the kitchen table, and with McCullough's wife Audrey standing nearby, the deliveryman pulled out a gun and pumped six bullets into McCullough's head and neck.

The roofers union boss died in a heap on his own kitchen floor.

After McCullough's murder, Scarfo reestablished complete control over the Atlantic City bartenders. Little Nicky, banished from Philadelphia in 1964, was now one of the most powerful figures in New Jersey's booming casino city. Within months, as violence continued to rip through the underworld, Scarfo would succeed Testa as boss.

At that point, the Mafia family that Angelo Bruno had nurtured and guided for more than twenty years was on its way to self-destruction.

Chapter Eight

In the underworld, murder is not a crime of passion, it is a piece of business. For the Scarfo crime family, it was also a negotiating tool, a way to send a message and, sometimes, the final payment on a debt. In Philadelphia they called it "doing some work" and no one got to be an initiated or "made" member of the family without taking part.

Scarfo's nephew, Philip Leonetti, who was involved in ten gangland slayings before the age of thirty-five, once was asked if he considered himself ruthless. "I know what it is to be ruthless," Leonetti replied. "But I don't remember ever doing anything, as a matter of fact I know for sure, I never did nothin' ruthless besides, well I would kill people. But that's our life. That what we do."

Tommy DelGiorno displayed the same cold and cavalier attitude when a defense attorney asked him about the murder of Johnny Calabrese.

"You are the kind of man who would take a loaded gun and point it to the back of the head of John Calabrese and not have a second thought about shooting him twice, aren't you?" the lawyer asked.

"I shot him in the back *four* times," DelGiorno corrected.

"Pardon me," the lawyer said sarcastically.

———

John Calabrese was killed on October 6, 1981. He died because he refused to fall in line with the new regime. Independent and with enough money and influence to call his own shots, Calabrese's final act of defiance was an attempt late in 1980 to set up his own loan-sharking operation out of several pawnshops in Atlantic City, literally in Nicky Scarfo's back yard.

Scarfo marked Calabrese for death from the moment he showed up in town, but it would be months before "the work" was assigned to Tommy Del. There was other, more important, business to attend to first.

Early in 1981, as a favor to the Gambino organization, Scarfo—with mob boss Phil Testa's approval—arranged the murder of Frank "Frankie Stale" Stillitano. Stillitano was a Trenton, New Jersey, gangster who had gone into hiding in 1978 after shooting two members of the Gambino organization in a gambling dispute outside a bar in the Chambersburg section of Trenton. After the shootings, which left one Gambino member dead and the other wounded, Stillitano disappeared. For nearly two years, members of the New York family searched for him in vain. Finally, Salvatore "Sammy the Bull" Gravano, then a Gambino soldier, came to Atlantic City to meet with Scarfo and Leonetti. While sharing drinks in a lounge at Bally's Park Place Casino-Hotel, Gravano said that he believed Stillitano was hiding in Philadelphia. He said the Gambino organization would be indebted if Scarfo could locate him. Scarfo said he would go one better, promising to take care of the matter.

Using information provided by several mob associates who were involved in gambling and loan-sharking in Northeast Philadelphia, Scarfo quickly found out where Stillitano was living. He then had three of those associates set a trap, luring

Stillitano to what he thought was a meeting to discuss a planned burglary. Stillitano left for that meeting on the night of February 14. Two weeks later his body was found in the trunk of a car parked in a garage at the Philadelphia International Airport. He had been shot once behind the left ear with a .38 caliber pistol.

Disposing of Stillitano solidified Scarfo's standing with the Gambino organization and with the other New York families. He had acted quickly and decisively and had murdered without compunction, character traits that were valued in the underworld. A month later, Scarfo would go to New York to ask a favor in return.

On March 15, 1981, Scarfo's closest friend and ally, mob boss Philip Testa, was blown away. Literally. A bomb, packed with roofing nails and explosives and hidden under the porch of his South Philadelphia duplex did the trick. It was around 3:00 A.M. Testa was just returning home. As he walked up his front steps, the bomb was detonated by a remote control device. The blast, felt throughout the neighborhood, sent the Mafia chief through the front door, ripped apart the bottom half of his body and left him bleeding to death in the rubble of his own home.

Pete Casella, Testa's underboss, and Frank Narducci, a capo and South Philadelphia gambling czar, immediately pointed a finger at the Philadelphia roofers union, calling the murder retaliation for the poinsettia-plant slaying of John McCullough. The nails in the bomb, they said, were an obvious message. At a hastily convened meeting on the night of Testa's wake, Casella said he would be taking charge of the organization. He told Scarfo he had cleared it with New York.

Several years later, Tommy DelGiorno told authorities that Casella and Narducci were behind the Testa murder.

"They put the nails in the bomb to make it look like it came from the roofers or the IRA [Irish Republican Army]," said

DelGiorno. "Johnny McCullough was very close to the IRA. . . . He used to help them. He used to send them money and he used to get them guns, somehow. He had a lot of benefits for them. He was very, very friendly with them. Big supporter of theirs . . . Johnny was a roofer guy, okay. The IRA always used bombs. So it's a combination of both of them . . . [and] It looks like [Testa] got killed because he killed McCullough."

At the time, Scarfo, a master of treachery in his own right, sensed that something was wrong with the story Casella was trying to sell. He didn't buy the old mobster's version of events. Nor did he believe Casella had the backing of the New York families. The next day, instead of joining the hundreds of mourners who crowded into Saint Monica's Church to hear Testa eulogized, Scarfo went to New York to meet with the leaders of the Gambino and Genovese organizations. There he learned that no one had approved Casella's ascension. And there, with Testa's remains barely in the ground, Scarfo was crowned the new mob king of Philadelphia.

Casella was banished to Florida rather than killed, perhaps because he had built up enough IOUs over the years. There he would die of natural causes. But Narducci, like Frank Sindone a year earlier, became a man living on borrowed time. Scarfo was now in charge. The hothead who had been banished to Atlantic City in disgrace almost twenty years earlier was now the boss of a mob family that, with the coming of casino gambling, was positioned to exert its influence throughout the American underworld. Little Nicky, who stood just five foot five and weighed about 130 pounds, was now the biggest mobster in town. And he wasted little time setting the tone for what would prove to be one of the most violent Mafia regimes in the country. While Testa's reign had been bloody, Scarfo's would be marked by a wanton and indiscriminate use of violence that—even by mob standards—was excessive. Ordinarily, mob hits were carried out in the shadows. Bodies would turn up in the trunks of cars or decomposing in some shallow grave in the woods. Scarfo, who proudly boasted that he was a "real gangster," preferred public executions.

On May 25, 1981, Harry Peetros, a member of Philadelphia's Greek mob, was found shot to death. Police speculated that the killing was part of an armed robbery. Peetros, a well-known loan shark who always carried thousands of dollars in cash and wore a six-carat-diamond ring, was found without any money or identification and without his trademark ring. While the Peetros murder was not connected to the Scarfo organization, it helped to cloud and deflect suspicion two nights later when two Scarfo gunmen entered a small restaurant in South Philadelphia and opened fire on Greek mob boss Chelsais "Stevie" Bouras. Bouras died in a hail of bullets. His dinner companion, Jeannette Curro, was also fatally wounded in the ambush, which took place in a crowded restaurant in the middle of the dinner hour.

Initially investigators thought that Bouras had been killed either in retaliation for the Peetros murder or as part of an internal dispute within the small, loosely knit Greek mob. Years later, investigators learned that Scarfo had ordered the hit because Bouras was horning in on the methamphetamine trade, actively competing with mobster Raymond "Long John" Martorano for multimillion-dollar distribution deals. Bouras had helped finance several Atlantic City real estate transactions in which Scarfo associates had an interest. With Bouras out of the way, nearly $350,000 that he had loaned a mob associate would not have to be repaid.

From Scarfo's point of view, the ruthless and coldly calculated Bouras murder was simply an aggressive piece of business. The fact that an innocent woman was killed did not matter at all.

"The gunmen opened fire from a range of three feet or less, striking Bouras four times in the head," read a Pennsylvania Crime Commission report of the killings. "He died shortly before 11:30 P.M. in a hospital. Bouras's woman companion also was shot once in the head and died at 10:07 P.M. It appears she was hit by mistake."

Tommy DelGiorno, who had been standing on the sidelines making money for the mob, got tapped to carry out the next hit. This time there would be no mistake. Johnny Calabrese was the target. He was dispatched gangster-style.

DelGiorno had gotten the assignment to kill Calabrese in the spring of 1981, about the time that Bouras was killed. DelGiorno was told to "get close to the guy" in order to set up the murder. Calabrese, however, did not make himself an easy target. He was aware of the unrest within the organization. He had been a friend of Tony Bananas Caponigro and knew, on that count alone, that he was viewed suspiciously by Scarfo and those sitting atop the mob with him.

Calabrese also had serious legal problems. The feds had begun to unravel his criminal organization. Operating out of a tavern he owned on the White Horse Pike in Gloucester Township, New Jersey, Calabrese had coordinated a series of burglaries, arsons, truck hijackings and armed robberies that had made him rich and independent. Among other things, he was suspected of having his own mother's house torched in order to collect five hundred thousand dollars in insurance. His group of thugs was also under investigation for a series of Post Office robberies and the murder of a federal witness who was to testify against Calabrese in a pending tax evasion case.

In the underworld, no one operates in a vacuum. Johnny Calabrese thought he could. For years he had been "with" Tony Bananas and had conducted his business under Caponigro's protection. In all probability he had shared his profits with the mobster. This, in effect, was his underworld insurance, his protection from any other mob member who might want to grab a piece of his action. If another member of the Bruno family tried to shake Calabrese down, he'd simply say, "Go see Tony. I'm with him." And that would be the end of it.

With Caponigro gone, Calabrese needed another patron. The problem was, he didn't want one. He ignored Scarfo's offers to form a business alliance and then openly defied the new mob boss by setting up a loan-sharking operation in Atlantic City.

Through the summer and early fall of 1981, DelGiorno and Frank "Faffy" Iannarella, another proposed member, stalked Calabrese. They tried to get a line on his daily comings and goings to determine if there was any pattern to his travel. Calabrese lived in the Roxborough section of Philadelphia, but he did most of his business downtown and in South Jersey. He was on the road a lot. One day he'd be in the neighborhood. The next day he might be in the Northeast. Then a day later he'd be in Atlantic City. He usually ended up at his own bar in New Jersey, but no one wanted to make a move on him there. He always had three or four of his henchmen around. What's more, there was always a chance that some members of the Pagans, a notorious motorcycle gang with whom Calabrese dealt drugs, might be on the scene.

Scarfo made it clear he wanted nothing to do with the bikers. For the Philadelphia mob boss, they were the ones who defined the word "ruthless." So DelGiorno was told to take his time and to get it right. He started doing business with Calabrese, occasionally borrowing money. Once he bought some stolen jewelry from him. Calabrese was cautious, but willing to deal. He made and canceled appointments and failed to show up for meetings. He was never where he was supposed to be. By the end of the summer, DelGiorno and Iannarella decided they'd always be ready. So they packed a bag with two guns, two masks and two pairs of gloves and threw it in the back seat of a car that belonged to Pasquale "Pat the Cat" Spirito who, like DelGiorno and Iannarella, was hoping for the chance to do some work.

The opportunity presented itself unexpectedly on the night of October 6 when Calabrese showed up at Cous' Little Italy.

"He comes in and sits down," DelGiorno said. "Faffy was at the bar. We're sittin' talkin', talkin', talkin' and I had to give him some money or something. Three thousand dollars. I had to give him more than that, but three thousand would do. So anyway in the meantime Chickie [Joe Ciancaglini] went into the bar and told Faffy he might as well do it now, get ready. Okay. So Faffy came back to me and he signaled me. So to make Johnny comfortable, I walk him over to the bar and I said, 'Johnny, here's that money.' Meaning, if I'm gonna hand a guy three thousand he's not gonna get killed right there, right?

"So Johnny says, 'No. Wait till you get it all together.' I can't remember what the money was for . . . It might have been for some kind of jewelry. . . . But anyway, he didn't take the three thousand. So now I says, 'We're going over the Melrose [a popular South Philadelphia diner] to eat. Me, Faffy and Pat. You wanna come?' We figured we get him in the car and we whack him. But he says no, he's leaving. So we all go out together.

"Pat Spirito pulls his car up. Me and Faffy jumped in the car. So I rolled down the window and I said, 'You sure you don't wanna come with us?' He says, 'No . . . Chick wants to talk with me.' "

Spirito drove his car down Christian Street and turned right on Tenth. As he drove, Tommy Del and Faffy pulled their ski masks, gloves and guns out of the bag. But someone had screwed up. The ski masks didn't fit. They were children's sizes and neither Tommy Del nor Faffy could get them over their heads.

"Fuck it," Tommy Del said as he threw the mask down in disgust. He and Faffy would shoot from the shadows.

As part of a prearranged plan between Ciancaglini and Iannarella, Ciancaglini was walking Calabrese down Christian Street toward Tenth. They talked as they walked, passing the Christian Street Baptist Church, which was next door to Cous', then meandering past nine brick row houses. They paused at the intersection of Christian and Adler, a street barely bigger than an alley that crossed Christian between Eleventh and Tenth. There was a bakery shop across the street, but it was closed. As Ciancaglini talked, he maneuvered Calabrese so that his back was to the narrow alleyway.

Spirito had stopped his car on Tenth at Salter, another narrow alleyway that led back to Adler. DelGiorno and Iannarella, without their masks, sprinted down Salter, then walked in the shadows along Adler, covering the fifty yards to Christian Street in a matter of seconds. They saw Calabrese standing with his back to them.

"Chickie was talkin' to him," DelGiorno said in an account of the murder he gave to the New Jersey State Police. "And then we came out of the alley. Faffy came out first. He shot him. Must have either hit him in the neck or the head . . . and he shot him again. I think that might have got him in the head. And then I moved him [Iannarella] out of the way and his [Calabrese's] back was to me and I shot him . . . in the back."

When the shooting started, Ciancaglini casually walked away from the scene. After firing off their rounds, DelGiorno and Iannarella ran back to Spirito's car. DelGiorno dropped his gun in the street. Iannarella threw his over the roof of one of the row houses that lined the alleyway. Spirito gunned the car down Tenth Street as Tommy Del and Faffy peeled off their gloves. They drove to Spirito's house several blocks away where they changed clothes. Pat the Cat took the clothes they were wearing and dropped them in a dumpster along with the ski masks and gloves.

"The next day we went about our business," DelGiorno said.

Scarfo loved it.

He sent word through Ciancaglini that he was more than pleased.

"Jesus Christ, that was great," the mob boss said. "These guys are fuckin' great."

Calabrese was left to die in the gutter, just the way Scarfo wanted it. Like the Bouras murder, it was a public execution. Newspaper headlines and television newscasts screamed about yet another organized crime hit in South Philadelphia. But police responding to the scene could find no one in the neighborhood who had seen anything. Nor was there anyone in Cous' Little Italy who could remember if Johnny Calabrese had been there that night. A few weeks later DelGiorno asked Frank Monte, who had been elevated from capo to consiglière after Scarfo became boss, why Calabrese had been killed.

"Monte said that he had a lot of strength with motorcycle guys and that Nicky was afraid of him," DelGiorno told investigators. "In my heart I believe it's because [Calabrese] . . . wouldn't give [Scarfo] any money. They knew [Calabrese] was in the drug business and making big, big money. That's my belief on why he was killed."

In fact, to DelGiorno it didn't really matter. He would later tell his son Bobby that the real mark of a man was to be able to kill when given the order. Tommy Del had done that. He had crossed over the threshold. He had done "some work." And in the sick and twisted logic that permeated the Philadelphia underworld, he was now a man worthy of respect. It had taken him more than fifteen years, but Tommy Del had finally arrived. The two-bit numbers writer and bookmaker who used to take bets while driving a United Parcel Service truck was now a man of wealth and power in the underworld. He would be asked to kill a dozen more times over the next five years. And only after Scarfo had turned his guns on him would Tommy DelGiorno question the morality of it all.

———

Three weeks after Johnny Calabrese was killed, Tommy Del's old friend and mentor, Frankie Flowers D'Alfonso, was brutally beaten. D'Alfonso was found lying unconscious in the nine-hundred block of South Tenth Street only a block from the scene of the Calabrese murder. He had a fractured skull and a broken jaw. The bones under both his eye sockets had been shattered along with his left kneecap. Two bones in his lower left leg were broken. There was a gaping wound in his head that took sixty-four stitches to close. His assailants, one armed with a baseball bat and the other with a steel rod, left seventeen hundred dollars in D'Alfonso's pocket.

When he regained consciousness at the hospital and was asked by police what had happened, D'Alfonso said, "I got hit by a truck." He refused to say any more.

The beating, in fact, was a message from Scarfo. It was delivered by Salvatore Testa and Gino Milano. Salvie Testa was an up-and-comer in the mob. He had been elevated to the rank of capo shortly after his father was blown up. The younger Testa, handsome and charismatic, commanded a crew of young mobsters like Milano, a former standout South Philadelphia High School athlete. Testa was bold, fearless and extremely violent. His father's brutal assassination had left him in a rage that Scarfo was ready to exploit. Over the next three years, Salvie Testa would lead the Scarfo forces in a senseless mob war that would leave another dozen men dead and solidify Little Nicky's hold on the organization.

The attack on Frankie Flowers was just a warm-up.

Like Calabrese, D'Alfonso was refusing to share his profits with Scarfo. Angelo Bruno's longtime friend had no time and even less respect for the new mob boss. But Scarfo thought he still had a shot at getting his hooks into D'Alfonso's lucrative financial and business network. Testa and Milano were sent to open negotiations.

The news of the murders and the beating of Frankie Flowers drew mixed reactions from the house on Gladstone Street.

While Maryann had little time for D'Alfonso and his gangster ways, she recoiled at the thought of a man she knew being nearly beaten to death. It was one thing for her to dump a plate of crab shells in D'Alfonso's lap, something else again to take a baseball bat to his skull. What's more, Maryann genuinely liked D'Alfonso's wife, Micheline, and empathized with her fear and pain. As for the murders and the newspaper headlines linking her former husband to the mob and depicting Cous'

Little Italy as a hangout for gangsters, Maryann felt a combination of rage and disgust.

"I couldn't believe what I was reading and hearing," she said. She silently said a prayer of thanksgiving that she had gotten her family away from Tommy Del. And in her heart she also thanked Cous Pilla for getting her boys fired from their jobs washing dishes at the restaurant.

Bobby, on the other hand, thought he was watching the film *The Godfather* playing on the streets of South Philadelphia. He pictured his dad in the Al Pacino role, a reluctant but coolly calculating gangster called upon to do what he had to do to ensure the future of the family. It was, of course, fantasy. But what teenager doesn't fantasize?

In January of 1982, Tommy DelGiorno, Faffy Iannarella and Pat the Cat Spirito were formally initiated into the Mafia. At a secret ceremony held in a home in Vineland, New Jersey, Tommy Del swore to "live by the gun and die by the gun" and promised to "burn like the saints in hell" if he betrayed the mob's time-honored code of silence.

In law enforcement circles, DelGiorno was now considered a cold-blooded killer. But in the mob, and more importantly in the eyes of his son, Bobby, he was a man of honor.

Chapter Nine

Tommy DelGiorno had no problem embracing Nicky Scarfo's blood-and-money philosophy. He never questioned an order to kill and he always grabbed for the cash with both fists. As a result, his first years as a made member of the mob were busy ones.

Between January of 1982 and December of 1983, a dozen mob figures were murdered as Scarfo moved to settle old scores and solidify his hold on the organization. One of the first to go was Frank Narducci, who was gunned down in front of his South Philadelphia home by Salvatore Testa. Testa avenged his father's death by pumping a half dozen bullets into Narducci's head and neck at point-blank range. Then he left him bleeding in the gutter.

Another victim was Pat the Cat Spirito, DelGiorno's getaway driver in the Calabrese killing. Spirito had a reputation for being "greedy and vicious, but with no balls," Tommy Del later told investigators. After being formally initiated into the mob, Spirito proved to be a major disappointment to Scarfo. He was a reluctant and less than ruthless hit man, blowing several murder contracts ordered by the diminutive boss. So Scarfo ordered him killed. Spirito's two closest associates in the mob, Nicholas "Nicky Crow" Caramandi and Charles "Charlie White" Iannece got the contract. In April of 1983 they lured him to a trap and fired two bullets into the back of his head.

DelGiorno knew the hit was coming. A few months earlier he had been at a social gathering with several other members of the mob. Faffy Iannarella, who was engaged to be married, started discussing plans for his wedding reception.

"It's me, Chuckie [Salvatore Merlino], Philip [Leonetti], Larry [Merlino] and Faffy sittin' at a table," DelGiorno said. "We're talkin', bullshittin'. Faffy's saying about the invitations for his wedding and who's gonna sit where. He says, 'Pat can sit with Crow and Charlie.'

"And Chuckie turns around and says, 'Don't waste that invitation.' All right? Now I realized they had decided to hit him. . . . It's a shame it had come to that [but] too many guys hated him. Philip hated him. Salvie [Testa] hated him."

And so Pat Spirito was murdered.

Tommy Del didn't give it another thought. It was just the way things were done. Besides, he had other, more important, problems. The money was now rolling in. And if people had to die in order for him to maintain his position, so be it. By his own estimate, Tommy Del was earning about one hundred thousand dollars a year from his various bookmaking and numbers operations. This was clear profit. No taxes. No FICA deductions. Just wads of cash each week. He also took fifty thousand dollars in annual salary from Cous', income that he made sure to report to the IRS. And at different points in time he had about fifty thousand "on the street" as loan-shark money or to back a drug deal.

Methamphetamine, commonly known as speed, was the big drug in Philadelphia. And controlling the sale of phenyl-two-propanone (P-2-P), a chemical used in the illicit manufacture of meth, was how the mob made tens of thousands of dollars. From time to time DelGiorno and other members of the organization would loan a drug dealer money to finance the importation of fifty to a hundred gallons of P-2-P. Since this was a loan-sharking deal it technically skirted the mob prohibition on dealing drugs. Later, as the Scarfo family got even more ruthless, DelGiorno, Caramandi and several others would routinely demand a two-thousand-dollar-a-gallon "street tax" on each gallon of "oil" a meth dealer smuggled into the country. The few dealers who balked at paying were beaten or shot. Since a gallon of P-2-P cost about five hundred dollars in Europe and could be sold for about twenty thousand dollars in the United States, most were willing to write off the street tax as an operating cost and pass the charge along to their customers.

Strictly business.

Tommy Del grabbed another pile of cash late in 1982 when he sold Cous' Little Italy to family members of Raymond "Long John" Martorano. DelGiorno came away with $150,000 from the deal, plus a small bar on West Passyunk Avenue that became his new headquarters.

"I made a lot of money in Cous', but what happened, it became like a bother to me in the sense that I actually had to do some work there," he later explained. "That's not what I was expecting. It was a nice thing to happen, but I wasn't expecting that. . . . I opened that primarily as an office."

His new establishment, the J&M Bar at the corner of Crosskeys and Passyunk Avenue, was more suitable. It was a small neighborhood tavern catering to a shot-and-beer crowd. Tommy Del could sit in a back booth and take care of his business while a bartender ran the joint. There were no hassles about ordering food. No problems with waiters or waitresses who failed to show up for work. No bookkeeping headaches. In short, none of the responsibilities that came with running a legitimate business.

The fact that a dozen more mobsters had been killed meant nothing to Maryann. Nor did she care that her ex-husband was now rolling in cash and had become the underworld big shot he had always wanted to be. What concerned her was that her son

Bobby was enthralled by it all. That scared her to death. Trying to raise two teenage boys in South Philadelphia was hard enough. She and Joe were struggling to earn a living and to pay the bills. But it was almost impossible to compete with a mob father whose lifestyle was the stuff of newspaper headlines and Hollywood movies and whose solution to any problem was to simply throw cash at it.

"The boys were growing up fast," Maryann said, "and I could see they were impressed by the easy money. I knew Tommy, my oldest, would wake up and see how wrong all this was. But my Bobby was a different story. He was thoroughly impressed by everything his father said or did. He swallowed every story, word for word. Then he'd come home and repeat them to his friends. . . . I was scared. I didn't know what to do. Joe and I tried to reason with him, but we got nowhere. Bobby kept his thoughts to himself.

"One time I confronted [my ex-husband] Tom, but he just laughed at me. He said, 'Bobby knows where the money and the power is.' If I had had a gun, I think I would have blown his brains out right then. He was a pompous ass. When all the Mafia murders started taking place and the stories appeared in the newspapers, Bobby thrived on every bit of information.

"When we were married, Tom didn't drink very much. Now, the boys told me, he drank often. And when he was drunk he used to brag to them about what was going on. He sometimes would tell Bobby, in detail, how it was done. How could anyone, especially a father, do that? But then, he wasn't much of a father to begin with."

Bobby did not share his mother's view. And shortly after his fifteenth birthday, he said he wanted to move in with his father. Tommy Del said, "Fine, whatever you want." Maryann died a little inside.

"I was losing my baby. Only a mother knows how that feels. Bobby said there was no reason except he wanted to be near his father. He said it had nothing to do with me or his stepfather, he just wanted to be closer to his father. The day he moved, we packed everything in my car. . . . I was crying. When we arrived at his father's, I blamed everything on him. I screamed in his face, 'You son of a bitch. You've brainwashed him with your money.' I think I called him every curse word I could think of. . . . Before I left I told Bobby he had broken my heart and he would have to beg on his knees if he ever wanted to come back."

Then Maryann drove home to her row house on Gladstone Street and cried some more.

Bobby moved in with his father, his stepmother Roseanne ("Roe") and his two half brothers, Danny and Michael, who were then six and seven years old. The house was more than twice the size of his mother's. It was located on South Broad Street, near Veteran's Stadium and the Spectrum, one of the more exclusive sections of South Philadelphia, decidedly upscale from Bobby's Two Street roots. Everything about the house was new and smelled of money. The furniture was top of the line. The kitchen and bathrooms had been redesigned. An addition had been added onto the back of the house to make it even bigger.

Bobby's stepmother was a fanatic about keeping things clean, neat and in their proper place. And, like Bobby's mother Maryann, her sons came before anything and anyone else. One of the biggest differences between the two women, however, was that Roseanne DelGiorno had enough money to make sure her boys got everything they needed.

Shortly after moving in, Bobby noticed that his father kept a stash of cash in a drawer of the dining room hutch. Bobby guessed there was about thirty thousand dollars, folded in wads and wrapped in rubber bands. Whenever Roseanne wanted anything, Tommy Del would tell her to get the money out of the drawer. This, Bobby learned, was "the house money."

Bobby was amazed.

When Roe took Danny and Michael shopping for new sneakers, she returned with two or three pairs for each of them. Designer sneakers. Top of the line. Sneakers that carried a price tag of sixty or seventy dollars a pair. But it didn't matter. There was always plenty of cash on hand.

Bobby knew that his mother and stepfather struggled all year to save enough for a summer vacation at a campground on the way to the Jersey shore. Tommy Del, on the other hand, forked out nine thousand dollars each summer to rent a two-bedroom, luxury beachfront condominium in Ocean City. On Gladstone Street, whenever anything in the house needed to be repaired, Joe Fisher would grab his tools and take care it. On Broad Street, when a faucet on one of the sinks was dripping, Tommy Del would say, "Call the plumber. Tell him to send me the bill."

Although they were never especially close, Bobby got along with his stepmother. And after a while, he began to feel sorry for her. Despite all the money, he saw how she was left alone most of the time; that his father, her husband, wasn't much of a companion. His mother and Joe Fisher seemed to do everything together. That clearly was not the case with his father and Roe.

Tommy Del had little time for family matters. He was always out taking care of business. When he was home, he was either sleeping or could be found sitting at the kitchen table drinking coffee and brooding. Bobby spent nearly five months living in the house on Broad Street before he realized it was not bringing him any closer to his father. The time, however, did solidify his relationship with his half brothers, Danny and Michael. They all shared the same absentee father. Danny and Michael were too young to understand or express it, but Bobby often wondered if they, too, were looking for love and attention from a man who would not, or could not, give it to them.

––––––––––

"My father was in his own world," Bobby said. "He never bothered with nobody in the house. He used to sit at the kitchen table talking to himself, drinking coffee. Then he'd go out for hours."

Bobby began to spend more and more time back in his old neighborhood. He'd ride there on his bike after school and on weekends. Sometimes he'd sleep in his old room on Gladstone Street. He hung out in the schoolyard at Second and Ritner with Anthony Forline and several other close friends—Johnny GQ, Mark Pop and Jimmy Wolf. These were neighborhood guys he had grown up with and had been around for as long as he was old enough to play outside. That was one of the things he loved about South Philadelphia. You grew up on a corner, no matter what the neighborhood. And the people there grew up with you. You were family.

Bobby continued to tell fantastic stories about his father, about all the money he had and about his connections to the mob. And he continued to insist that when he grew up he wanted to be just like him. But even Bobby realized it wasn't yet time.

Maryann watched and waited, leaving the door open despite her earlier, bitter warning to her wayward son that he would have to crawl back on his knees. She could see things were changing. Occasionally, Roe would call to complain about something or other Bobby had done.

"I reminded her that she and her husband wanted Bobby to live with them and that he came with his good points and his bad points," Maryann said. "She didn't know how to answer me. I reminded her that this was one of Tom's sons and therefore his responsibility. I knew I was getting her goat and she didn't like it.

"The next time she called to complain, I just told her to tell her husband and I hung up the phone. I wanted Bobby home more than anything, but I wasn't about to bend.

"Finally, Bobby realized his father wouldn't stay home for him. I could have told him that, but it wouldn't have mattered. He had to learn for himself. Tom wouldn't stay home for his wife and other two sons. Who was Bob? One night Bobby came over the house and said he wanted to talk to me. I just knew what he was going to say. I wanted to make him hurt, like he hurt me."

Instead, Maryann's eyes filled up with tears, and her heart began to race.

Bobby looked at her and said, "Mom, I wanna come home."

She threw her arms around him, squeezed him close, and said, "Come back where you belong."

It was a small victory for Maryann in a battle that was just beginning. Over the next four years her heart would be broken again and again as she watched her youngest son flirt with the mob, blinded by the power of a father who never had any time for his children, seduced by the wealth of a man who didn't know how to love his sons. Maryann had Bobby back in her house, but it would be a long time before he was again a part of her home.

When she had filed for divorce and first broken away from Tommy Del, Maryann feared for her life. At that point *she* had been what he wanted. His macho pride and gangster image had been tarnished when she walked out. When he warned her that she might end up at the bottom of the Delaware River, she took his threat seriously. But the years had changed all that. The passion and anger were still deep-seated and bitter, but Maryann knew that she was not in physical danger from her ex-husband and his mobster friends. She no longer feared for her life. What she feared for now was her youngest son's soul.

For his sixteenth birthday, Bobby got a brand-new white Trans Am. It was a present from his father. The only stipulation was that he'd have to maintain the car himself—pay for gas, insurance, upkeep. So Bobby took a job after school and on weekends at a grocery store where several of his father's associates worked. It was a learning experience, South Philly-style.

"The guy who owned the place, Tony, was a bookmaker for

A smiling bride and groom, Maryann Welch DelGiorno and Tommy DelGiorno pose with their wedding party in 1964.

Maryann and Tommy Del in their early years as struggling newlyweds.

Tommy Del holds his first newborn son, Tommy, Jr., May, 1966.

A one-year-old Tommy, Jr. flanked by his parents in 1967.

A young Bobby gets his first exposure to sand and sun on the South Jersey shore during the summer of 1968 with Tommy Del, Maryann, and her father, George Welch.

Maryann and Tommy Del in the kitchen of their two-bedroom rented row house in South Philadelphia with Tommy, Jr. and baby Bobby.

Bobby (*left*) and Tommy, Jr. decked out for a portrait at ages two and three respectively in 1969.

Maryann and her two young sons shortly after separating from Tommy Del in 1974.

Tommy, Jr. and Bobby in their Sunday best.

Bobby as a fifth grader at Our Lady of Mount Carmel School.

Tommy, Jr. in cap and gown for his high school graduation.

Gladstone Street in South Philadelphia. Maryann's home has a stone facade and sits among brick-fronted row homes just off the corner of Third Street.

Tommy Del (*right*) treats Bobby (*left*) and Tommy, Jr. (*far left*), to dinner at the Golden Nugget Casino prior to an Atlantic City boxing match in 1982.

Frank "Frankie Flowers" D'Alfonso, the South Philadelphia gambling kingpin who opened the door to the mob for Tommy Del.

Caught by an FBI surveillance cameraman, Tommy Del stands in the doorway of his South Philadelphia restaurant, Cous' Little Italy.

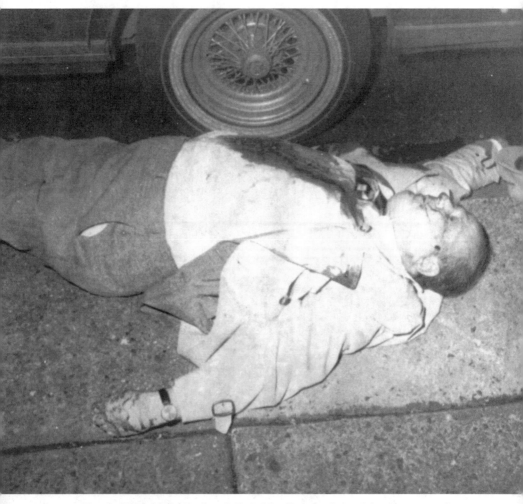

Frank "Chickie" Narducci, left bleeding and dead in the gutter in a January 1982 mob hit.

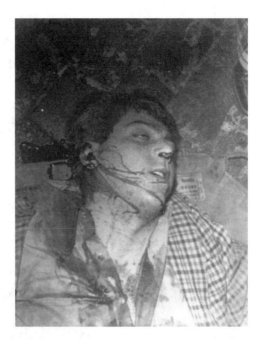

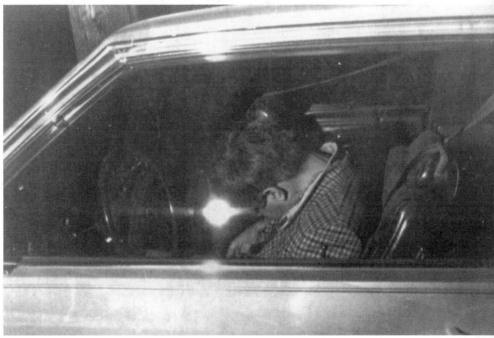

Pasquale "Pat the Cat" Spirito, a mob soldier gunned down in
April 1983 by two close friends.

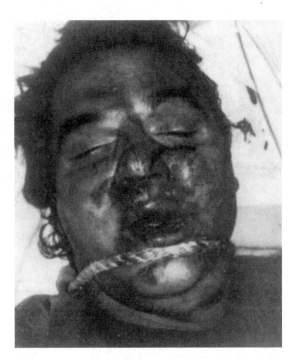

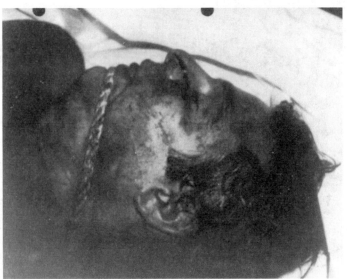

Salvatore Testa in bloody repose. The young, charismatic
gangster was killed in 1984 in an ambush set up by his
best friend.

At ease in a casino hotel suite overlooking the Boardwalk in Atlantic City, Tommy Del (*right*) and Nicky "Whip" Milano enjoy the good life.

Mobsters Tommy DelGiorno (*second row, right*), Charles "Charlie White" Iannece, Nicholas "Nicky Crow" Caramandi, and Franky "Faffy" Iannarella take in the action at an Atlantic City prize fight.

Mob boss Nicodemo "Little Nicky" Scarfo (*in suit and tie*) flanked by mob soldiers Philip Leonetti (*far left*) and three young associates in a 1986 surveillance shot at Philadelphia International Airport.

Tommy Del (*second from left*) shares a light moment with some friends, including Charlie Iannece (*in sunglasses*) and defense attorney Robert Simone (*right front*).

Mob boss Nicky Scarfo (*second from left*) in the Florida sunshine with Tommy Del (*left*) and two associates.

Firing up the grill for a barbecue in Virginia Beach, Tommy Del appears relaxed and at ease while living in the protective custody of the FBI in this 1987 photo.

Tommy DelGiorno, wearing a hood and under heavy guard, testifies before the New Jersey State Commission of Investigation during February 1992 hearings on mob infiltration of the bar and restaurant business. *Photo: © 1992 Donald Slabicki*

Bobby and Tommy, Jr. back home on Gladstone Street after leaving protective custody and returning to their South Philadelphia neighborhood.

my father," Bobby said. "He took most of his bets right in the store. On Friday nights he would hand me a whole bag of money and say, 'Give this to your father.' One time, he said, 'Tell him there's ten thousand there, and I'll have the rest during the week.' I felt important just carrying that money from the store to my father's house, like I was really involved in some kind of crime."

Tony's cousin John, who was the store's butcher, was a degenerate gambler. He taught Bobby about parlays, reverses and betting lines while showing him how to trim the fat off a T-bone and how to slice and chop chicken wings, breasts and thighs. John said he had once been a partner in the store. But he blew all his earnings betting football and baseball. Now he was just an employee.

"If you're thinking about gambling, don't," he told Bobby. "Use your money to put your own gambling book together. That way you have a better shot of winning. Always play with the odds. I learned that the hard way."

Bobby watched and listened. And what he picked up in six months was worth, in his mind at least, more than he had learned in school over the past six years. Two women who worked as cashiers also took numbers for his father. While Tony booked sports, his partner Frank took bets on horses. And Turk, who was about sixty years old and did all kinds of odd jobs around the place, had a line of "hot stuff." On any given day he might be selling watches, bracelets, shirts or television sets out the back door.

It was a typical South Philadelphia underground operation. Selling meats, cold cuts, and vegetables was almost secondary to the real action. Bobby loved it. For years he had watched his father move around in this world. Now he got his first chance to be a part of it. No one cared about the law. No one ever raised a question about right or wrong. The way they looked at it, they weren't hurting anyone. They were just out to make a few extra bucks. Nobody got his arm twisted to place a bet. Nobody was forced to buy any of Turk's merchandise. If he offered a good deal and a customer agreed to pay the price, what was the difference? Sure, out on the street there were guys getting shot, but Bobby decided that wasn't part of what was going on in the store. This was just a little harmless gambling, a little loan-sharking, some off-the-books marketing of products that had "fallen off the back of a truck."

Bobby and Tommy junior, who also worked at the store, decided to take what they were learning home to Gladstone Street. Without telling their father—or their mother and step-father, for that matter—they started their own book. As he had done with the football pools a few years earlier, Bobby took bets at the schoolyard each Sunday before the 1:00 P.M. and 4:00 P.M. football games. Tommy, who had an older group of friends, took action over a phone line he had secretly installed in his bedroom. Twice each Sunday, they'd call Tony at the store to get the point spreads and betting lines. They'd call again on Monday evening, prior to the Monday night game. It was easy, just a little paper work. Players who bet the one o'clock games always came back to bet the four o'clock games, either because they wanted to parlay their winnings or make up their losses. And, invariably, anyone who had taken a bath Sunday would try to win it all back Monday night.

Tommy junior and Bobby kept meticulous records. They'd collect from the losers on Thursday and pay the winners on Friday. Anyone who didn't pay up, couldn't bet the next week's games. But the boys never had any trouble collecting. In the neighborhood it was just assumed they were working for their father. And given the bloody current history of the mob in South Philadelphia, no one wanted to cross Tommy Del.

For Tommy junior, the bookmaking operation was a chance to make a little extra money.

For Bobby, it was much more.

"I wanted to be just like my father and his friends so bad, I couldn't wait," he said. "I wanted to walk down the street and have people say, 'That's Bob Del' just like everybody did when my father walked by. . . . I guess everybody knew what he did for a living. His name was always in the paper. If me and my father went somewhere to eat, someone would always pick up the check out of 'respect.' People were always trying to get on his good side. He was only five foot seven, but people were afraid of him."

The boys were clearing about three hundred dollars a week from their book, although one week they took a big hit, losing nearly fifteen hundred.

"We got greedy," Bobby said. "There was too much money riding on one team and instead of laying it off (to a bigger bookie) like we usually did, Tommy said, 'Let's keep it all.' But that's how you learn."

They kept the winnings in a shoe box that Bobby hid under a floorboard in his bedroom. Even with the big loss, they ended the season with $2000. They put $500 away for the next football season and split the rest. Tommy went out and bought a brand-new television set for his room. Bobby put his share, seven hundred and fifty dollars, in the bank. He had learned from his father that it was important to put money aside. Even though Tommy Del flashed a lot of cash, he always had a stash here and a stash there for an emergency. Bobby never spent all the money he was given. He'd always put some of it away. The seven hundred and fifty he put in the bank brought his account up to nearly four thousand dollars.

Not bad, he thought, for a sixteen year old.

At the store, Tony had always told him that "money makes money." Bobby understood the concept. That's why he put his cash in the bank. It earned interest while it sat there. But that wasn't exactly what Tony had in mind. This was not the Wharton School of Economics, after all. This was South Philadelphia. Tony was talking about serious money.

Like most bookies, Tony loved to gamble, especially at the casinos in Atlantic City. Most of the money he made bookmaking for Tommy Del ended up on the craps table there. A few weeks after the football season ended, he asked Bobby how his book had done. When Bobby told him it had turned a profit, Tony asked what Bobby did with his share.

"I put it in the bank to make interest," Bobby said.

"Lend me a thousand and I'll give you your money back plus twenty percent interest by next Friday," Tony said.

Bobby jumped at the chance. He was sure Tony would deliver as promised. He wasn't the kind of guy to welsh on a debt. Besides, Bobby knew that he'd never try to rip him off because of his father.

That afternoon, Bobby went to the bank and withdrew one thousand dollars. A week later he deposited twelve hundred. He had made two hundred dollars by doing absolutely nothing.

"Whenever you need anything," he told Tony, "just ask."

On two other occasions Tony borrowed a thousand. Each time he paid back twelve hundred. Then, several weeks later, looking pale and desperate, he called Bobby aside at the store.

"Can you loan me four thousand," he said. "I'm short this week on your father's money. He'll kill me."

Bobby didn't ask what had happened to the cash. He figured Tony had gambled away what wasn't his. And while he didn't really think his father would kill the man over a few grand, he recognized that Tony was dead serious about coming up with the money.

Bobby took four thousand out of his bank and gave it to Tony.

"Please, Bobby, don't tell your father," Tony said.

Bobby, who liked being treated like a man and who relished the little conspiracy, said, "Don't worry about it. I know you're good for it."

The next week, Tony handed Bobby a brown bag. Inside there was forty-eight hundred dollars. This was serious money. Like his father, Bobby had become a bookmaker. Now he was a loan shark. Soon, he hoped, he would be a gangster.

"The only thing that was holding me back was school," he said. "I had so much on my mind, a lot of things going for me. Collecting the betting money, a little loan-sharking. Once in a while we'd run a card game at the house. This was when my mother and Joe would go away for a weekend to the campground where they had a place. Then I had my job at the store. I was working there five nights a week."

At that point, Bobby's income was three hundred dollars a week. He was paid two hundred at the store and his father was giving both him and Tommy junior a hundred a week in allowance. Both boys lived at home. Neither was asked to pay anything for rent or toward household expenses. It was a comfortable existence.

On top of that, Bobby had money from his gambling and loan-sharking ventures. He'd salted away most of his shark money, building up a nest egg that would eventually reach fifteen thousand dollars.

Still, he said, "The more you get, the more you want."

One afternoon he and two friends were standing in the schoolyard around the corner from his house when a kid from the neighborhood walked by carrying a box filled with containers of copying machine ink.

"Where'd you get that?" Bobby asked.

"From the paper warehouse," the kid said. "Don't tell nobody."

The warehouse was about three blocks from the schoolyard under a ramp leading to the Walt Whitman Bridge. It was usually locked up tight. But on this day, someone had left the garage door leading into the building slightly ajar. There was a space, less than a foot wide, between the bottom of the door and the concrete floor. That's how the kid had gotten in to grab the ink. Bobby saw an opportunity to, yet again, expand on what he was learning at the store.

"What are we gonna do with ink?" one of the guys he was with asked.

"Not ink," he said. "Copy machines, computers, whatever we could get out of there. I know a guy who could sell it for us."

In the annals of South Philadelphia heists, this was not a major-league effort. Bobby and his two friends were spotted slipping under the garage door of the warehouse. Minutes after they had entered the building, two squad cars pulled up outside. A cop with a flashlight—pissed off because he had ripped his uniform shirt going under the door—cornered the boys on the third floor. He brought them out in handcuffs, cursing them all the way.

"You fucking assholes," he said. "Look what I did to my shirt."

The three boys were placed in a holding cell at a police district headquarters while breaking and entering charges were being drawn up. The owner of the warehouse was notified and so were the parents of the three would-be burglars. Two hours later a cop walked in and asked for Bobby.

"Come with me," he said. "Your mother wants to talk to you."

The cop brought Bobby to a small room. There was a chair and an opening, like a window, onto another larger room. Bobby saw his mother Maryann standing on the other side of the window. She was, he knew, extremely angry.

"The cop took me to this window where my mother was standing. . . . As soon as I put my face in front of the window, a fist came flying through. My mother punched me right in the mouth. My lip swelled right up. It was bleeding and fat. I turned to the cop and said, 'Take me back to the cell.' He laughed and said, 'But your mother still wants to talk.' So I said, 'Then you talk with her. If I talk anymore I won't have a mouth left.' "

Bobby and his friends spent five hours in the holding cell. Then they were released. His stepfather, Joe Fisher, was waiting to take him home. The owner of the warehouse, after learning that nothing had been taken or damaged, decided not to press charges. The cops, apparently impressed with Maryann's swift, no-nonsense Two Street form of justice, were satisfied to send the boys packing.

When Bobby got home, the house was in turmoil. Tommy Del had heard about the arrest. He telephoned and said he was coming over to "straighten" Bobby out. Maryann had taken the call. Her ex-husband was livid and, she believed, drunk. She told Bobby she would intercede, but Bobby told her not to.

Maryann was angry and disappointed in her son. Breaking into the warehouse was stupid. What's more, it was wrong. But she didn't want him exposed to his father, a drunk and irrational gangster who made his living taking from others. What could he possibly say to Bobby? How could he preach morality?

Tommy Del's white Cadillac pulled up in front of the row house a few minutes later. Bobby climbed into the back seat. His father was sitting up front on the passenger side. Another man whom Bobby didn't recognize was driving.

"What the fuck did you do, Bob?" his father asked. Then, without waiting for an answer, he turned to the man driving the car and said, "Look at this kid. I give him money every week. He gets work money every week. And he still ain't satisfied. He goes and tries to rob a warehouse."

They drove around South Philadelphia for several minutes without saying a word.

Then Tommy Del turned and screamed, "What is it, money?" And he reached in his pocket, pulled out a wad of hundred-dollar bills and threw them at his son.

Bobby picked up the money and threw it back at his father.

"Sometimes, I think that's all you think I want," he said, fighting back tears of anger and despair. "You think money can solve everything. I'm not one of your Mafia friends, I'm your son. I don't want your money. I want a father."

––––––––

The next morning when Bobby came down for breakfast, Joe Fisher was sitting at the kitchen table drinking a cup of coffee.

"I'm sorry for all the problems I caused," Bobby said.

Joe Fisher, the burly longshoreman who had always been there for the camping trips and the hockey games and the graduations and confirmations—and who the night before had been ready to bail him out of jail—just smiled.

"What's life without problems," he said. "But listen, try to stay out of trouble . . . because your mother's gonna kill you if you don't."

Bobby laughed out loud. His swollen lip cracked and started to bleed. Joe smiled again and offered him a cup of coffee.

"Thanks, Dad," Bobby said.

Chapter Ten

The incident at the warehouse and the blowup with his father had brought Bobby briefly to his senses. For a time he listened when his mother and stepfather warned him about the dangers of Tommy Del's lifestyle. They kept saying it was a dead-end street. That the only things worth having were the things you earned honestly. That it was better to scrimp and save and do without than to rob, steal, lie and cheat. Bobby had heard it all before, but this time it seemed to make sense—for awhile.

Soon, however, he began to rationalize the situation. During their argument in the car, his father had told him that he loved him, but that he was always busy with "his work." He had said he wanted to be around more, but he just couldn't get away. So mentally, Bobby made an accommodation. He would have his family—his mother; his stepfather, Joe; his brother Tommy; his grandparents. They would be the people he would depend on.

But he would accept his father, Tommy Del, on his terms and in his world. When you're sixteen years old anything seems possible.

"I just wanted to be near my father," Bobby said. "It was nothing against my mother or Joe. I loved that life he was living. The people he was around. How could you not like guys who handed you hundred-dollar bills?"

———

The turmoil in Bobby's house was matched by a battle going on within the Scarfo organized crime family at the same time. For almost two years, beginning with the May 13, 1982, ambush of Scarfo family consiglière Frank Monte, there had been war on the streets of South Philadelphia.

Scarfo was trying to wipe out a faction of the organization controlled by Harry "The Hunchback" Riccobene, an old Bruno ally who controlled a group of loan sharks, bookmakers and drug dealers. The Riccobenes fired first, however, taking Monte out with a hunting rifle as he stood in front of a garage where his car was being serviced. The war raged on with young Salvie Testa leading the charge on the side of Scarfo. Testa was nearly killed by a shotgun blast from two Riccobene gunmen, but survived the gunfire—which almost cost him his left arm— to terrorize the city.

Ironically, Scarfo sat out most of the action in a federal prison in Texas on a gun possession charge. But he used Testa and his own nephew, Phil Leonetti, as proxies, waging a brutal battle that forever changed the face of the Philadelphia mob. The Riccobenes sued for peace—in fact, they surrendered— after a fateful week in December 1983 when both Harry Riccobene's brother and his nephew died of gunshot wounds to the head. When Scarfo returned to the Philadelphia area from prison in January of 1984, he was the undisputed king of the Philadelphia underworld.

His mob controlled the biggest union in Atlantic City, Bartenders Local 54. Several informants later said that Scarfo was taking twenty thousand dollars a month out of the union's coffers. His henchmen were collecting a street tax in South Philadelphia not only from drug dealers but from any unaffiliated bookmakers, numbers writers and loan sharks they could find. Anyone who was not "with" a member of the Scarfo mob had to pay. Thousands of dollars were rolling in each week. Scarfo used the money to buy—through fronts—a luxurious home in Fort Lauderdale, Florida, and a forty-one-foot cabin cruiser. He called the house "Casablanca South," a reference to the classic Humphrey Bogart film that he loved. The boat he christened "Casablanca Usual Suspects," borrowing from one of the many memorable lines in the movie.

Scarfo, who had spent years struggling to make it, now had so much money that he commissioned a carpenter friend to build a hidden safe behind some paneling in the bedroom of his Atlantic City apartment. There he hid a stash that in time amounted to more than one million dollars and, according to some informants, may have climbed as high as three million. He was now on top of his world. He flew first class. Dined at the best restaurants. Wore expensive, hand-tailored suits. Drove a Rolls-Royce. It would be two years before John Gotti would splash onto the scene in New York and take center stage as America's celebrity gangster. By that point the act was already playing to capacity crowds in Philadelphia with Nicodemo "Little Nicky" Scarfo in the title role.

Yet Scarfo could not relax. Years of turmoil and of treachery had left him paranoid. Most of his underworld enemies were either dead or in jail. He was only fifty-five years old. He should have been positioned for a long and prosperous run atop the Philadelphia mob. Instead, he set a murder in motion that would undermine his credibility and destroy whatever sense of honor and loyalty remained in the Philadelphia branch of La Cosa Nostra.

Shortly after returning from prison, Scarfo decided that Salvatore Testa would have to die. The reasons, even today, are tangled in uncertainty. Testa had broken off his engagement to the daughter of Salvatore "Chuckie" Merlino, one of Scarfo's oldest friends. Merlino was then the crime family underboss and was enraged at the affront to his honor. Others whispered that Testa was more popular than Scarfo with the younger members of the organization. They predicted that, in time, Testa would challenge Scarfo for leadership. Still others said that Testa was secretly making millions dealing in drugs with a group of black gangsters in North and West Philadelphia.

At different times and to different people Scarfo would use all of those reasons to justify the murder of perhaps the most charismatic figure in the Philadelphia underworld. None of it mattered. Nobody was going to challenge Scarfo on it. The bottom line, Tommy Del later testified, was that Testa "got killed for no sensible reason." But then, Tommy Del added, "so did a lot of guys that I know."

———————

DelGiorno was in a better position than most to discuss the Testa murder. He and Faffy Iannarella had been assigned by Scarfo to supervise the hit. Nick Caramandi and Charlie Iannece were supposed to be the shooters. But Testa was even more cautious than Johnny Calabrese and setting him up proved to be more difficult than anyone had anticipated. Eventually, two members of Testa's own crew, Sal Grande and Joey Pungitore, were brought in to the conspiracy.

The order to kill Testa came down in April of 1984. DelGiorno and the others stalked him for most of that summer without success. The longer it took, the angrier Scarfo became and the more the pressure built on Tommy Del.

One Sunday afternoon early in September, Bobby drove down the shore to visit his father at the condominium in Ocean City, New Jersey. When Bobby arrived his father was sitting in front of the television set watching a baseball game and drinking a beer. He had several more before the game ended and then asked Bobby to drive him over to Atlantic City.

"I have to meet somebody and I don't want to get stopped for drinking and driving," he said.

Bobby, who was already angling to quit school and go to work full-time for his dad, jumped at the opportunity. He had often thought that he'd like to be his father's driver. It would give him the chance to learn "the business." It was a logical first step on the career track he had chosen. Just as Tommy Del had tied his fortunes first to Joey McGreal, then to Frankie Flowers and later to Frank Sindone, Bobby knew he'd need a padrone. Who better than his own father?

They left Ocean City around four o'clock in the afternoon. Tommy Del flipped the keys of his white Cadillac to Bobby, who happily slid behind the wheel. A half hour later they were sitting at a bar in the Tropicana Casino-Hotel on the Boardwalk. Tommy Del ordered a beer. Bobby got a soda. After about ten minutes, a man wearing dark, wraparound sunglasses and an open-collared shirt walked in and sat down on the stool next to his father.

Tommy Del introduced the man as Nick Caramandi, "Nicky Crow." Bobby had heard the name a few times, but had never met the man before. Caramandi was short, about his father's height. He had dark hair and a thick, South Philadelphia accent. Despite the fact that the bar was dimly lit, he never took off his sunglasses.

Bobby tried not to listen, but couldn't help overhearing the conversation that followed. His father, lips loosened after a half dozen beers, didn't seem to care who heard him.

"It was supposed to be done a month ago!" he nearly shouted. "What's the problem?"

Caramandi responded in a muffled tone. Bobby couldn't make out what he said. But then his father came through again, loud and clear.

"The little guy's gettin' mad. He wants it done right away. Why can't you just kill him on his boat?"

Feeling uncomfortable and not wanting to appear as if he were eavesdropping, Bobby moved down the bar to another stool. With that, his father turned and ordered him back. Bobby could see now that Tommy Del was drunk. His eyes were glazed and his words were slurred.

"What's the matter. Sit back over here. You're a part of this family, one of us."

Nicky Crow smiled. He seemed embarrassed and uncomfortable. He knew this was not the kind of conversation that should be taking place in public.

Bobby moved back to the stool next to his father. Tommy Del put his arm around his son and, in a half-drunken stupor, told Caramandi, "I'll get my son to do it. He'll kill the fucker, right Bob?"

Bobby looked down, not knowing what to say, as Caramandi stood up.

"I gotta go," he said. "Tell the guy it'll be done right away."

"It better be," Tommy Del said.

Caramandi reached out and shook Bobby's hand.

"It was a pleasure meeting you," he said.

"Likewise," Bobby replied, finally able to think of something to say.

Bobby and Tommy Del stayed at the bar for another half hour. Tommy drank and Bobby tried to make sense of the conversation. A murder contract. And the intended victim had a boat. He knew of only one of his father's friends who had a boat: Salvie Testa.

After two more beers, Tommy Del looked at Bobby and said, "Some day you'll be a gangster, just like me." Then, he said, "Do you know what separates the men from the boys?"

"No," Bobby said.

With that his father held up his right hand, made a fist, then extended his forefinger and cocked his thumb into the shape of a gun.

"Bang, bang," he said.

Bobby nodded.

Tommy Del smiled. "Come on," he said. "Let's go shoot some craps."

"You had to be twenty-one to gamble and I didn't have any fake identification with me," Bobby said. "But my father said if they carded me, we'd leave. We walked past the security guard into the casino and nobody said anything to me. We went up to one of the craps tables and my father pulled two rolls of cash out of his pocket, each wrapped in a rubber band. He threw the money on the table. There was five thousand dollars in one-hundred-dollar bills. He asked for chips. Each one was worth five hundred dollars. That's what he was gambling with.

"I just stood and watched him play. Boy, was he good at craps. He knew the game like the back of his hand. When it was his turn with the dice, he put bets all over the table. It was like he couldn't lose. Every number he needed to make, he made. Chips were piling up in front of him. And he just kept rolling the dice, yelling 'No seven, no seven' after he made his number.

"Then, all of a sudden this security guard walks over to me and asks to see some ID. My father turned and said, 'He's with me,' but the guard said if I didn't have any identification, I'd have to leave the casino. So my father turns around and says, 'Let's get the fuck out of here while I'm winning' and he sends me to get one of those cardboard buckets they have over by the slot machines. He filled it with the chips and we took it over to the cashier's window. She counted them up. 'That's eleven thousand dollars,' she said. 'How would you like that, sir, check or cash?' My father says, 'Cash and make it all one-hundred-dollar bills because it's easier to carry that way.' I couldn't believe it. All those hundred-dollar bills stacked in eleven piles, a thousand dollars in each pile. My father made all that money in a half hour."

Tommy Del took five of the piles, folded them into a wad, wrapped a rubber band around it and stuffed it into his pocket. Then he reached for the rest of the cash, made one big stack and told Bobby to hold out his hand.

First he counted out five hundred dollars, placing each one-hundred-dollar bill in Bobby's palm.

"That's your cut of the winnings," he said. "Put it in your pocket."

Then he told him to hold out his hand again. This time he counted out four hundred dollars.

"This money is for you and your brother, two hundred apiece, okay?" he said.

The warnings from his mother and stepfather disappeared in that stack of cash. This was what Bobby wanted. This was who he wanted to be. Joe Fisher might be able to hand him a cup of coffee after a tough night, but his father was handing him a way of life.

"Thanks Dad," Bobby said.

"Don't thank me," Tommy Del said. "Thank the casino."

———

Less than a week later, Salvatore Testa was dead.

Lured to a meeting at a candy store on Passyunk Avenue by one of his best friends, Joey Pungiture, Testa was shot twice in the back of the head by Sal Grande, who was waiting there. Later that night Caramandi and Iannece took the body and dumped it along the side of a dirt road in Gloucester Township, New Jersey, where it was discovered the next day.

Salvie Testa was twenty-nine years old. He had been featured in a front page *Wall Street Journal* article earlier that year in which he was described as a rising star in the Philadelphia mob. At the time the article appeared, Scarfo was already planning to have him killed. In the Philadelphia underworld, things never were what they seemed.

Tommy Del joked about the Testa murder a few days after it happened. He stopped at the store where Bobby was working to pick up some money from Tony.

"Ain't it a shame what happened to Salvatore?" he laughed.

"I got that money for ya, right here," Tony said.

"Good," Tommy Del said with a smile. "We wouldn't want nothin' like that to happen to you, would we?"

Several years later, from the witness stand, DelGiorno found less to laugh and smile about. He described the plot to kill Testa in meticulous detail and pointed the finger of blame at Scarfo who, he said, was consumed with fear and paranoia.

More tragic still was DelGiorno's account of how Joey Pungitore was forced to set up Testa, his lifelong friend. This, DelGiorno said, came directly from Scarfo during a meeting in Atlantic City a few weeks before the fateful session with Caramandi in the casino bar.

DelGiorno said he had told Scarfo that they were having a lot of trouble setting a trap for Testa, that he was extremely cautious and circumspect. He said he suggested that Joey Pungitore might be able to help if he could be convinced to go along with the plot. Scarfo told him that there was no need to convince Pungitore.

"He said, 'Tell Joey that he has to help us,' " DelGiorno said. " 'Tell him it is not a request, it is an order. And tell him that if Salvie in any way finds out, we're going to kill Joey, his father and his two brothers.' "

DelGiorno said he delivered the message, as ordered.

"I went and saw Joey Pung. I told him we were going to kill Salvie. He really was upset about it. He was in a state of shock, really. He says, 'I thought everything was all right.' I says, 'Well, Joey, obviously everything isn't all right.' I gave him the message that Scarfo gave . . . that if he didn't help us or did anything to get in the way of helping us that we would kill him, his father and his two brothers. I told him Scarfo said, 'I don't want no slaughter on my hands.' So he said, 'Okay.'

"What other answer did the kid have. So he said. 'The only thing is, ask Nicky if it would be all right if I brought him but I didn't have to do the shooting.'

"I said I don't see where that will be a problem, but I'll ask. . . . I ran into Nicky in Philly. . . . I told him that Joey asked not to have to do the shooting. Scarfo said, 'What's the difference if he brings him or shoots him? I don't care who shoots him as long as he's dead.' "

Sal Grande, on the other hand, jumped at the opportunity to take Testa out. It was the kind of move that he knew would please Scarfo and would enhance his position in the organization. What's more, as an aggressive rather than a reluctant hit man, he would move ahead of Joey Pungitore in the mob pecking order.

Reflecting the kind of personal animosity and bitterness that had taken over the organization, Grande made a point of publicly mocking Pungitore for months after the shooting of his best friend. Whenever he could, Grande would stop in a sandwich shop that Pungitore owned and punch out the same song on the jukebox. It was a tune originally recorded by Rod Stewart but made popular by Dionne Warwick. It was called "That's What Friends Are For."

The murder of Salvatore Testa created career opportunities all around. Caramandi, Iannece and Joe Grande, who had helped his brother Sal with the murder, were formally initiated as soldiers in the Scarfo crime family a few weeks later. At that same ceremony, Tommy Del and Faffy Iannarella were promoted to the ranks of acting capos, assuming most of the responsibilities that Testa had had in South Philadelphia. Testa's other holdings—bookmaking, gambling and loansharking operations—were spread among other family members. Scarfo took a one-third interest in a major bookmaking business that Tommy Del, Salvie and Joey Pung had been running.

The moves brought Tommy Del closer to the top of the mob, gave him greater stature within the organization and, because of the bookmaking, made him a direct partner with Scarfo in a highly lucrative business venture. Scarfo, who was spending most of his time in Atlantic City and Fort Lauderdale, left the day-to-day operations of his organization in the hands of his capos. Tommy Del was on his way to becoming the most important mobster in South Philadelphia.

Bobby was along for the ride.

He had finally convinced his parents—despite Maryann's misgivings—that he should be allowed to drop out of school.

He went to work full-time at the grocery store and worked part-time for his father, a situation that made Maryann shudder.

"I'm making good money, Mom," Bobby said. "And I won't get in any trouble. I promise."

Tommy junior had graduated from St. John Neumann and had gotten a job working construction for a friend of their father's. Good with his hands, Tommy had hopes of starting his own construction company, renovating houses in South Philadelphia. He had a girlfriend and soon would be engaged to be married.

Both boys, Maryann realized, were looking for their independence. Tommy junior, she was certain, would make it on his own. But Bobby made her nervous. He liked the easy money. While neither Tommy Del nor Maryann were aware of it, the boys had also expanded their bookmaking operation. With the coming of the football season, they now had three of Bobby's friends working for them and had arranged to take some edge-off work from two young New Jersey bookmakers they had met over the summer. The New Jersey gamblers assumed that Bobby and Tommy junior were working for Tommy Del. The boys never said otherwise. Their book was still limited to the pro football games. But they now measured their weekly action in thousands rather than hundreds of dollars.

Everything seemed to be going well for both Tommy Del and his sons. That Christmas he invited them to celebrate at a party Nicky Scarfo had planned in a restaurant on South Street. It was a gala event. Scarfo, back from prison nearly a year, finally out from under the Salvie Testa mess and making more money than even he had hoped for, was in a mood to offer tidings of good cheer all around.

Tommy Del, as he had so many years earlier with Maryann, wanted to show off his own family. But this time it would be Bobby and Tommy junior who would be asked to "dress the part."

"My father took us to this expensive men's store in Center City," Bobby said. "There were just these three-piece suits and overcoats, that's all they had. He told us we had to look sharp for the party, cause the boss was gonna be there.

"I picked up this black suit with a white pinstripe. It cost four hundred dollars. Then I got a black overcoat. It was two hundred and fifty dollars. Tommy got the same suit, only in gray. And he got a black overcoat. We each bought a hat. When we finished picking the stuff out and trying it on, my father handed me two thousand dollars and told me to pay for it. He went next door to get a cup of coffee in a restaurant.

"The bill came to thirteen hundred and fifty dollars. I counted out all the money from the roll of hundred-dollar bills my father had given me. Me and Tommy just looked at each other. That was a lot of money to pay for two suits and two coats for one party. But it felt great to be able to pay cash. It was like we were rich.

"The party was at La Cucina, a restaurant on South Street. My father told us to be there five o'clock sharp. I thought we looked like two gangsters when we walked in, but then everybody there was a gangster. Outside all kinds of limousines and Caddies were parked in the street. A lady at the door took our coats and then my father came up and said, 'Come on, I want to introduce you to somebody.' "

It was like a wedding reception. Nicky Scarfo, king of the Philadelphia underworld, was standing at the end of a receiving line greeting his guests. Tommy Del, because of his stature in the organization, moved quickly to the front of the line with Bobby and Tommy junior.

"These are my two sons, Bobby and Tommy," he said to Scarfo.

Scarfo shook hands with both of the boys and appeared genuinely pleased to meet them. He told Tommy Del, "You gotta bring your sons to my house in Florida some time."

Bobby and Tommy junior smiled. They had heard a lot about the notorious gangster, but they were surprised by how small and soft Little Nicky appeared. Seeing him in person for the first time, it was hard to believe the newspaper stories and television reports. It just didn't seem possible that this impeccably dressed little man—even Tommy Del was taller than Scarfo—had ordered the murders of more than a dozen people over the past two years. Or that the hulking gangsters who were milling around the room waiting for a chance to shake his hand were terrified of him.

Bobby and Tommy junior spent the rest of the night eating and drinking. There were tables stuffed with lobster, roast beef, turkey and all kinds of Italian food. There was an open bar, with mixed drinks, wine and beer flowing all night. A five-piece band, positioned in a balcony overlooking the room, provided the music. At any one time there were from two- to three-hundred members and associates of the Scarfo crime family, along with invited guests from several other organizations in New York and New Jersey. But no wives. And no girlfriends. In fact, the only women were the waitresses who would occasionally pass through with trays of drinks or hors d'oeuvres.

This was a private party for one of the most exclusive men's clubs in the world. Members and associates only. Outside the FBI had set up some surveillance cameras and were busy snapping pictures of the guests and writing down the license tag numbers of all the cars and limos. Inside, the most violent mob boss in America wished his family *"Buon Natale"* as crime soldiers and Mafia sycophants raised their glasses and shouted, *"Cent Anni."*

Bobby loved every minute of it.

Chapter Eleven

In 1985 the New Jersey State Commission of Investigation (SCI) held hearings into organized crime's infiltration of the boxing industry in Atlantic City. Tommy DelGiorno was one of those subpoenaed to testify. He appeared before the commission and tap-danced, denying any interest in the fight game other than as a fan and frequent ringside patron when the casinos staged bouts.

Bobby knew otherwise.

"My father had five or six fighters," he said. "He had a trainer. And whenever they fought, we all would go down to see them. That was a big deal to him. He liked that, everybody following him. He would get all his friends tickets and we'd stay in this two-room suite in whatever casino-hotel they were fighting.

"One time, at the Tropicana or the Playboy, we had a two-floor suite with a Jacuzzi in the bathroom and a big wet bar in the living room. After the fight, me and my brother and the son of one of my dad's friends went back to the suite and ordered five hundred dollars worth of food. We had lobster, shrimp cocktail, clams casino, New York strip steak. Anything we could think of, we asked for. Champagne. We used to order Dom Perignon all the time. It was, like, $175 a bottle. Real expensive. And the best part was we didn't have to pay.

"My father got comped because he was such a big gambler. He didn't have to pay for his room or his food. All we had to do was sign his name."

Tommy Del loved to gamble at the casinos and he loved to sit ringside and watch his fighters. But Bobby said he had another reason for traveling to Atlantic City.

"My father used to have all kinds of girlfriends down there. He usually used the fights or 'business' as an excuse to go down. He took me and my brother a lot of times. He'd say, 'Meet us down there.'

"One time, I remember, we were in the bar and my father had these two girls with him. We were just standing there, drinking. This one girl musta been twenty-one, twenty-two years old. The prettiest thing I ever saw. Really hot-looking. My father was drunk. He had his arm around her, treating her to drinks. Treating everybody to drinks. So my father called me over. He said, 'I want you to meet somebody.' He had his arm around this girl and he says, 'I want you to meet your new mother. This is going to be your new mother. Give your new mother a kiss.'

"I was kind of embarrassed, but she just started laughing. That's just the way he was. He always had girlfriends. He liked the young girls.

"I remember another time, it was near Christmas. We went down to this jewelry store on Sansom Street. He knew the guy who owned it. We go there. My brother, my father. He's gonna buy us Christmas presents.

"The jeweler was a big gambler. He owed my father a lot of money. So we go in there and my father tells us to pick out something we liked. I was looking at this diamond pin shaped in the letter 'D' for DelGiorno. . . . Then my father says he needs some other stuff. He says, 'I got three girlfriends and I got to get them some things.' The jeweler's showing him pearls, diamond necklaces, gold chains. My father picks out three different things, one for each girlfriend. He's got the stuff in a bag and he turns around and he's looking and he's looking and he says, 'Damn, I know I'm forgettin' something.' So I says, 'Dad, did you get Roe anything?' And he just grins and says, 'Damn, that's who I forgot. I forgot my wife.' And then he says to the jeweler, 'Just throw anything in there.' "

While the SCI hearings did little to rid the fight game of the mob—the fact that boxers and gangsters were doing business was hardly an earth-shattering revelation—they did shine a spotlight for the first time on Tommy DelGiorno. Until that point, he had always taken second or third billing when it came to publicity. He was the "associate" arrested along with Frankie Flowers. He was the "hidden owner" of the restaurant where Angelo Bruno had had his last meal. He was the "reputed mob soldier" spotted with other key members of the organization in mob clubhouses and at the casinos. It was the SCI, however, that identified Tommy Del as a significant member of the Scarfo crime family. By that point DelGiorno was already a capo, but in those days—long before a slew of informants began dissecting the organization for investigators—information from the underworld filtered up slowly to law enforcement.

At the same time, the New Jersey State Police Organized Crime Intelligence Bureau targeted Tommy Del in a major gambling investigation. It would turn out to be much more. The state police mob squad had been tracking the Philadelphia crime family for years, and veterans there were both amazed and shocked that a psychopath like Nicky Scarfo had risen to the top. Nailing Scarfo, however, was proving difficult. He was suspected of murdering an Atlantic City lawyer and part-time municipal court judge in 1978, but there was not enough evidence to bring him to trial. He was tried for the 1979 murder of an Atlantic City cement contractor, but was acquitted—along with Phil Leonetti and Larry Merlino—because prosecutors were unable to come up with anything to corroborate the account of one cooperating eyewitness.

Attempts to wiretap Scarfo's phone or place an electronic listening device in his apartment or office yielded little new information. Like the late Carlo Gambino, Scarfo seldom spoke on the telephone. He preferred face-to-face meetings, usually during a stroll on the Boardwalk where electronic listening devices were useless amid the crowds and squawking seagulls.

Tommy Del was a much easier target. In the summer of 1985, state police detectives broke into the mobster's condominium on the Boardwalk in Ocean City and planted a bug in the kitchen area of the complex. Their only fear was that Roe DelGiorno, described by investigators as a "compulsive cleaner," would stumble on the device. At the same time the state police got a court authorization for a wiretap on DelGiorno's Ocean City phone. Throughout the summer of 1985 and again during the summer of 1986, the tapes rolled while Tommy discussed everything from his gambling and loansharking operations to his growing disdain for Scarfo. Mixed in were some typical domestic disputes, including an angry shouting match in which Tommy threatened to kill his wife's aunt.

"That motherfucker, she should get killed," Tommy Del said in a rage.

"Why don't you get your machine gun and just kill everybody," Roe shouted back, sounding as frustrated and annoyed with her husband's macho posturing as Maryann had years before.

After becoming a cooperating witness, Tommy Del would downplay the incident, claiming he never intended to murder the woman but made the threat to get under his wife's skin. "I used to tell her that all the time to aggravate her," he said.

He was giving her agita, Mafia-style.

The state police played a waiting game with their tapes, building a case that, while often overlooked because of the federal and city prosecutions that followed, actually set in motion the destruction of the Scarfo organized crime family. While no one could predict it at the time, Tommy Del's tenure at the top of the Philadelphia mob would be a short one.

Death, meanwhile, came closer to Gladstone Street.

On February 9, 1985, Frank "J. R." Forline, the uncle of Bobby's neighbor and best friend, Anthony Forline, was found shot to death. Frank Forline, who owned a concrete supply company in Sharon Hill just outside of Philadelphia, was described by police as a loan shark and gambler who operated on the fringe of the South Philadelphia mob. He was found lying in the cab of his pickup truck in the parking lot of a K mart in Marple Township. He had been shot five times in the head, neck and body. Investigators described the shooting as a mob hit. The murder has never been solved.

Three months later, on May 18, Broadway Eddie Colcher died.

Maryann, Bobby and Tommy junior heard about it several days after their old friend had been buried. Broadway Eddie was forty-seven. He died of kidney failure, apparently brought on by diabetes, which had plagued him for years. He died on a Saturday and was buried the next day.

"My father didn't even go to the funeral," Bobby said. "He never even mentioned it. Eddie got sick and my father and his friends just dropped him, didn't bother with him no more. They took his book away and ignored him."

Frank D'Alfonso, however, the mob couldn't—or wouldn't—ignore.

After his brutal beating in 1981, Frankie Flowers maintained a low profile. He was mentally and physically scarred by the attack and seldom traveled far from the Ninth Street area. "He walked with a limp, looked like he had a stroke . . . and was afraid for his life," said D'Alfonso's son, Frank junior, in describing his father to a Philadelphia jury years later.

D'Alfonso had remained neutral during the mob war that raged in 1982 and 1983. And while he continued to operate as a bookmaker and loan shark, he tried to stay out of the limelight, avoiding the attention of both law enforcement and Scarfo, the despotic mob boss whom he detested. His name surfaced again, however, when the SCI began looking into the boxing business. State investigators tied him to Plinky Palermo, an aging South Philadelphia mob figure with lots of connections in the fight world. They also began to probe D'Alfonso's interest in a lucrative closed-circuit television operation that was broadcasting some of the big Atlantic City bouts.

Scarfo, still angry and frustrated over his inability to get a piece of D'Alfonso's action, followed the SCI investigation with interest. He considered it a personal affront that Flowers made no offer to share his profits with the organization as he had done during the Bruno era. He also viewed D'Alfonso's stubborn independence, even after the beating, as a public sign of disrespect.

It the spring of 1985, Scarfo decided that it was time to send Frankie Flowers another message. But this time it would not be delivered with a baseball bat and a steel rod. This time it would come through the barrel of a gun.

Periodically, Scarfo would convene meetings of the upper echeleon of his organization to discuss family business. These sessions usually took place in a restaurant or bar with enough privacy to ensure that the conversation wouldn't be overheard, but also with a high enough public profile to thwart any attempt by law enforcement to set up surveillance. So it was that one afternoon in May, Scarfo and his top associates sat down for lunch at The Wok, a trendy Chinese restaurant on Walnut Street in the middle of Philadelphia's Center City commercial and business district. The restaurant attracted a well-heeled clientele of lawyers, bankers, office workers and shoppers. No one paid much attention to the group of casually dressed middle-aged men sitting at two tables in a far corner. There Scarfo, DelGiorno, Salvatore and Lawrence Merlino, Faffy Iannarella and Philip Leonetti—the brain trust of the organization—spent three hours discussing the business agenda of the Philadelphia mob. Murders, past and present, were a major topic of discussion.

At the meeting Scarfo bragged about how he had planned the 1979 slaying of Michael "Coco" Cifelli, a drug-dealing mob associate shot to death as he talked on a pay phone at the entrance to a South Philadelphia restaurant. And Salvatore Merlino continued to gripe about how the late Salvatore Testa had jilted his daughter.

"He was always complaining about Salvie," Tommy Del said. "I think he wanted to dig him up and shoot him again."

But the main purpose of the meeting, DelGiorno said, was to plan the execution of Frankie Flowers. Scarfo, without going into details about his reasons, said he wanted D'Alfonso killed. He ordered DelGiorno to supervise the contract.

"He told me that he decided to hit Flowers," DelGiorno later testified. "He said to use the two Milanos—Gino and Nicky—and Frank and Philip Narducci [as the shooters]."

For weeks after that meeting, mobsters positioned themselves in a room over a produce store in the Ninth Street Italian Market and watched D'Alfonso's movements. While cautious, Frankie Flowers apparently felt safe in the neighborhood where he had spent most of his life.

On the evening of July 23, he left his house and walked around the corner to buy a pack of cigarettes at a grocery store. It was 8:20 P.M. on a warm South Philadelphia night. D'Alfonso was sitting on a crate in the middle of the block near Catharine and Percy Streets enjoying a smoke when two men ran up behind him and fired five shots into his back and head. The gunmen dropped their weapons and kept running to a waiting car. In seconds they were gone and Frank D'Alfonso was dead.

Reaction to the mob hit in law enforcement circles demonstrated how little investigators really knew about the Scarfo organization. "He was a businessman more than a gangster and a friend to most of these guys," one police source told reporters in the wake of the D'Alfonso murder. "The killing surprises me because if the word came down from Scarfo, it seems that DelGiorno could have gone to bat for him."

What investigators did not yet realize was that Tommy Del went to bat for nobody but himself. He had used D'Alfonso and Colcher to gain entry to the mob but had dismissed them as inconsequential once he had moved further up the ladder. Broadway Eddie became a nobody whose passing went unremarked. Frankie Flowers was just another piece of business. DelGiorno was overwhelmed by the power and the money that came with being a capo in the Scarfo organization. And he did whatever he had to do to hold onto and expand that position. There was no way he would balk at the order to hit D'Alfonso. He never even considered it.

"I killed on orders of Scarfo," he said matter-of-factly.

Four days after the shooting, Frank D'Alfonso was buried following a funeral mass at St. Paul's Roman Catholic Church. Across the street was the church hall where he used to run the bingo games. About two hundred people attended the funeral. Afterward, they filed quietly out of the church and passed the black hearse waiting to take D'Alfonso's remains to the cemetery. Behind the hearse were limousines for the grief-stricken family members. And behind the limos were five trucks. Each was filled with flowers.

The D'Alfonso murder would be the last during the bloody reign of Little Nicky Scarfo. There would be several other shootings and an equal number of brutal beatings as the organization expanded its extortion of drug dealers, numbers writers, bookmakers and loan sharks. But no one else would be killed in the year that followed. DelGiorno, Iannarella, Caramandi and a dozen other mobsters who roamed the streets of South Philadelphia were sending thousands of dollars a week down to the shore to Scarfo. Little Nicky was finally beginning to realize the tremendous wealth that came with being a mob boss. But Scarfo wanted even more. His greed was insatiable, and was matched only by his wanton use of violence.

Tommy Del used his wealth and influence not only to solidify his position in the mob, but also to enhance his standing with his two oldest sons. Maryann was dumbfounded when her ex-husband presented Tommy junior with "an early wedding gift" in the summer of 1986. Engaged to be married in another year, young Tommy had begun looking for a house. He had spotted one in his mother's neighborhood that was for sale for twenty-five thousand dollars. He had five thousand socked away for a down payment. Tommy Del handed him a brown paper bag filled with the other twenty. He also guaranteed Tommy junior a spot in the plumber's union despite a waiting list of hopeful apprentices. Tommy Del had a connection with a business agent that, he said, would assure his son a position.

When he asked Bobby if he'd like to take up that trade, his younger son balked.

"Dad, I could never pass the test," Bobby said.

"What test?" Tommy Del answered. "Tommy's in and if you want, you got a job there, too. I know the guy who runs the union and he owes me a big favor."

Bobby, however, had grander ambitions. And Tommy Del was ready to help him realize them. Several weeks after he gave Tommy junior the "wedding gift," he took Bobby over to a New Jersey car dealership and told him that in honor of his nineteenth birthday he could pick out any car on the lot.

Bobby was then driving a 1981 Grand Prix. It was his fourth vehicle in less than three years. He had crashed his Trans Am into a telephone pole only a few months after his sixteenth birthday. Then he got a van, but some guys from another corner, who had been battling with Bobby and his friends, trashed it. After that Tommy Del gave Bobby the used Cadillac that he was driving. But one night, while Bobby was driving around with a girl he had picked up from another neighborhood, the girl's irate boyfriend threw a cinder block at the windshield. Bobby swerved. The cinder block crashed through the back side window, filling the back seat with glass. And the Caddy slammed into a parked car. Bobby fled the scene, but the car was never the same again. After getting it repaired, he gave it to his grandmother and bought the Grand Prix.

"I don't know what it was," Bobby said. "But I just never had no luck with cars."

But now his luck was changing.

Standing in the middle of the car lot in South Jersey, Bobby's eyes narrowed in on a white Chrysler Fifth Avenue with a blue ragtop roof. It was top of the line. List price: twenty-three thousand dollars. Once again, Tommy Del explained, the guy who owned the dealership owed him a favor. Bobby was speechless. Less than an hour later he was riding around South Philadelphia in an automobile worth as much as his brother's new house. It was, he knew, his dad's way of balancing the books. Tommy Del doled out his affection in dollar bills. In 1986, he loved each son twenty-thousand-dollars worth.

After handing Bobby the keys to the new car, Tommy Del reached into his pocket and peeled off five one-hundred-dollar bills. He handed them to Bobby and said, "Buy some new clothes. If you're gonna start working for me, you got to look respectable."

————

"I couldn't believe it," Bobby said. "All in one day. My dreams coming true. A brand-new Fifth Avenue and a new job. I thought I had it made.

"The following week I went over to my father's house to report for work. He said I was gonna be a collector for his street numbers business. I had to make four stops a week. But he said I was on call twenty-four hours a day. He said 'That means, if I call you, no matter where you're at or what you're doing, you come.' He said Tory Scafidi, who was a soldier in the mob, would show me the stops. Then he warned me about the business. He told me to trust nobody. He used to say, 'Keep your friends close, but your enemies closer.' He told me to never let anyone know what I was thinking and he said one little mistake and I could end up in the trunk of a car. It wasn't like he was trying to scare me. He was just letting me know this wasn't all fun and games.

" 'This ain't like what you see in the movies,' he said. 'This is real. Once you're in, there's no second chances, no pulling out.' Then he said if I felt I couldn't handle it, to just say so. But I said, 'Dad, this is what I always wanted.' "

Maryann felt sick and helpless.

How, she wondered, could she and Joe compete with a man who walked around with five thousand dollars in his pocket, who stuffed twenty thousand into a brown paper bag and handed it to one son while giving the other a brand-new car that every other kid in the neighborhood was drooling over? How do you turn a kid's head away from the flash and glitter when it's sitting right there in front of him? How do you convince him that it's wrong, when his own father is telling him to go ahead and grab for it?

Chapter Twelve

Nicky Scarfo was a mob boss for the 1980s: bold, brash and full of avarice. In the short term, this made him a very rich man. In the long term, it brought down his organization. While Angelo Bruno at least had paid lip service to the time-honored concepts of respect and loyalty, Scarfo ruled through fear and intimidation. There were no sitdowns with the mob boss to iron out disputes or clear up misunderstandings. Greedy and treacherous, Scarfo wanted it all. And he wanted it now. His was a slash-and-burn philosophy, not unlike the approach of the pin-striped outlaws who were ransacking Wall Street at this same time. It was more Attila the Hun than Machiavelli.

"When you get involved with him, you know . . . you take the good and take the bad," Tommy Del would say. "The good is you can run around a lot and have everybody in your circle afraid of you because you got him behind you. The bad is, once in a while you got to do him a favor."

Usually the favor involved whacking somebody. But on a few occasions Scarfo went for the money instead of the blood.

This was the case when he heard that a group of drug-dealing loan sharks from Northeast Philadelphia were using his name as leverage to collect debts from their customers. Since Scarfo had nothing to do with their operation, he figured he was entitled to a fee—a commission, so to speak—for being a part of their merchandising campaign.

He sent a local bookie named Sparky to collect.

The scam was ingenious in its simplicity. Sparky asked to borrow $250,000, telling the loan sharks it was for a drug deal he was putting together. The guys from the Northeast, as Scarfo knew they would, called down to South Philadelphia to see if anyone in the organization would vouch for the bookie. Several members did. Sparky got his cash and began to make his weekly payments. The interest alone was several thousand dollars a week. But after three or four weeks, on Scarfo's orders, Sparky stopped paying. The guys from the Northeast, as Scarfo knew they would, called downtown again to ask those who had vouched for Sparky to straighten out the problem.

"They were told to forget about their money," an informant said later. "Scarfo had it and that was it. They were told to just be thankful they weren't dead. What were they gonna do?"

On another occasion, Ralph Staino, a member of DelGiorno's crew, stole one hundred gallons of P-2-P from a drug dealer who was paying the mob's street tax. Staino had found out that the dealer had the chemical contraband—a key ingredient in the manufacture of methamphetamine—stashed in an apartment in Germany, and he sent someone over to grab it. If the laws of the underworld were being strictly applied, Staino should have been ordered to return the P-2-P. And if he had refused, he should have been killed. Protection from rip-offs was what the street tax was supposed to be buying, particularly protection from members of the organization collecting the tax.

But Tommy Del, knowing Scarfo's lust for money, decided to look the other way. Instead of solving the drug dealer's problem, he manuevered his way into the scam, threatening to kill Staino unless he turned the P-2-P over to him. He then told

Scarfo he had come up with a deal that would earn them two million dollars. Scarfo didn't want to know the details. He just asked when he'd see the money. Staino had already gotten fifty gallons of the stolen P-2-P into the country. At the going rate of twenty thousand dollars a gallon, that netted the organization a million dollars. Tommy's cut was two hundred thousand. Scarfo got five hundred thousand. The rest of the money went to several other mobsters involved in the transaction. The chance for another million was lost, however, when customs agents confiscated the second fifty-gallon shipment as a Staino associate tried to smuggle it into the United States.

Scarfo reacted in typical fashion. Instead of being satisfied with his first cut, he berated DelGiorno for losing his second half-million dollars.

Greed and arrogance had turned the diminutive mobster into an underworld despot who enjoyed belittling and mocking anyone he considered weak or ineffective. It was another way to flex his muscle, to show he was boss. Little Nicky had waited a long time for the power and wealth. And he wanted everyone to know that he had arrived. His house in Fort Lauderdale became a meeting place during the winter and spring for members and associates of the mob and also for New York Mafia figures who were in the Florida area. Early in January he would hold a New Year's celebration there, a catered affair not unlike the Christmas parties that were now annual events at La Cucina. And while Bobby and Tommy junior never made it to Fort Lauderdale, their father was a frequent visitor.

Ownership of the home was another one of Scarfo's scams. For tax purposes he had to show how he could afford to live in the six-hundred-thousand-dollar waterfront hacienda. So he had his lawyer set up a corporation, Casablanca South Leasing, Inc., and, for three thousand dollars each, several of his associates bought in to a time-sharing plan that, on paper at least, entitled them to spend several weeks living in the home each year.

One of those buying into the plan, DelGiorno told investigators, was a popular Philadelphia disc jockey, Jerry Blavat. Blavat had been a longtime friend of Philadelphia mob figures, dating back to his days as a sometime driver for Angelo Bruno. Known as the "Geater with the Heater," he also owned a nightclub in Margate, New Jersey, near Atlantic City, where Scarfo and the others often stopped for drinks or a meal. Blavat ran legitimate businesses and, his lawyer maintained, was never anything more than a friend to Scarfo and the others. There is no evidence to the contrary. Whether he took full advantage of his time-sharing, however, is something Tommy Del thought unlikely.

"One weekend we went down there," Tommy Del told New Jersey investigators. "It was on a Sunday and we were all in the house and Spiker [mob associate Anthony Gregorio] or one of them was making spaghetti and meatballs and [Scarfo] said that Blavat was coming. . . . Blavat came into the place around ten o'clock or something, 10:30 that morning. . . . He came in, said hello to everybody. He went over. He went and sat down with Scarfo for a little bit talking to him. He went and he ate a meatball sandwich, came back to the table and said goodbye. And so when he was leaving, I said to Nicky, 'Where's he goin'?' He said, 'Back to Philly.' So I said, 'Wait a minute. You mean to tell me this guy flew to Florida to eat a meatball sandwich?'

"[Scarfo] said, 'No, no, no. He comes here because he's one of the guys that leases the house and he thinks that because he shows up that the surveillance will pick him up and if they ever ask him if he's really leasing he could say yeah.' "

Scarfo's role as lord of his Fort Lauderdale manor and gracious host of mob meetings and "confabs" there belied a current of unrest within the organization. In rapid succession, and for reasons that appeared based more in his own paranoia than in reality, the mob boss turned first on his old friend Salvatore Merlino and then on DelGiorno.

Merlino and his brother Lawrence, then a capo in the organization, were "taken down" at a meeting in March of 1986.

Both men were reduced to the rank of soldier and lost all their authority within the organization. Salvatore Merlino, Scarfo said, had become a drunk and an embarrassment. In fact, one month earlier he had begun serving a four-year prison sentence after being convicted of trying to bribe a police officer who stopped him for drunken driving. Lawrence Merlino, more a contractor than a gangster, fell out of favor simply because he was Salvatore's brother. At a raucous mob meeting at a private room in a Sea Isle City, New Jersey, restaurant, Scarfo denounced both Merlino brothers, threatening to kill them and their families unless they shaped up. He then promoted his nephew, Phil Leonetti, to underboss, and elevated Tommy Del and Faffy Iannarella from acting capos to capos. With Salvatore Merlino away in jail and with Scarfo and Leonetti operating primarily in Atlantic City, DelGiorno and Iannarella became the top mob figures in South Philadelphia.

Whether it was pressure from the added responsibility or simply the constant fear brought on by the double-dealing and treachery that had become the trademarks of the organization, Tommy Del began to spend more and more time looking at life through the bottom of a bottle of booze. And when he drank, he often became nasty and belligerent.

———

"My brother and my father never really got along," Bobby said. "They were always arguing. My brother never really liked what he did. He used to tell me I was crazy for wanting that kind of life. My brother, he just wanted a job and to be left alone. . . . One night me and my brother were out drinking with a couple of his friends and we ended up at my father's bar, the J&M. My father and a few of his friends came in, all drunked up. My father tends to talk too much when he gets drunk, you know. He aggravates and gets on your nerves. It was Nicky Whip [mob solider Nicholas Milano], little Joey Merlino, my father and Faffy. They had been out drinking. My father calls my brother over and then he turns and puts his arm around

Nicky Whip. Then he said to Tommy, 'This is a real son. This is what you call a real son.' My brother really felt bad. He just gave my father a dirty look and walked away. I thought he was ready to cry. I think he wanted to kill my father, that's how mad he was.

"My father really took his friends first. . . . He treated them first. Nicky Whip was young, in his twenties. He was a gangster. A killer. He's treatin' him better than he is his own son.

"The next day, my brother wouldn't go over my father's. But my father, he acted like nothing had happened. That's the way he was. If something happened, the next day he just forgot about it. He thought money or things would make it up. . . . He always took the side of his business partners over his family. One time I got in a fight and he took the other kid's side before he even heard my story because the kid's father worked for him. . . . I didn't go over his house for, like, three weeks. When I finally did go over there, I sit down in the kitchen. My brother was there too, watching a ball game or something. My father was sittin' on the other side of the table and before I even got to say anything, my father reached in his pocket, grabbed a hundred-dollar bill, crumbled it up and threw it at me. He says, 'This is what you came for, ain't it?' I wanted to kill him. He made me feel so small. Like I was just after money. I had come to apologize, to make up. But he just had that way about him, like everybody was after his money, like he was somebody because he had all this money.

"So I got up and I said, "I don't want your fuckin' money.' And I threw the hundred-dollar bill back in his face. I said, 'Stick your money up your God damn ass.' And I ran out the door. He sent my brother to run after me, saying he was only kidding around. I didn't think that was very funny at all.

"That's cold, you know. When it gets down to all you could think about is money. And I was gettin' that way, too, toward the end. He had me so brainwashed, I was startin' to think like him. . . . I just wanted to do everything he did and be just like him. . . . His money and his friends always came first. And he always would make an excuse. He'd say, 'I gotta make a livin', don't I?' "

Tommy Del's world began to unravel in the summer of 1986, even as his wealth continued to grow. The stolen P-2-P deal was causing problems for the organization. A partner of the drug dealer who was ripped off was threatening to go to war with the mob over the two million dollars he lost. Scarfo didn't like that kind of aggravation.

And another scam, involving a corrupt Philadelphia city councilman and an attempt to extort one million dollars from a developer, blew up when the developer ran to the FBI. This was a deal involving a Delaware River waterfront project called Penns Landing, which the city had been trying, for years, to get off the drawing board. Finally, in 1986, a company had been selected to begin the first, seventy-million-dollar phase of the project. Using their ties to the corrupt city councilman as leverage, the Scarfo organization tried to shake a million dollars out of the deal by threatening to tie up two key pieces of legislation needed before the project could move forward.

But Nicky Crow Caramandi, the point man in the extortion plot, got picked up trying to extort an FBI undercover agent posing as the developer's project manager. The city councilman, his legislative aide and Caramandi were all indicted. Scarfo, who had approved the scam, began to worry. DelGiorno, who was supposed to be supervising Caramandi, worried even more.

That summer, the New Jersey State Police tapes coming from the wiretap and electronic bug in the Ocean City condo contained more and more outrageous, drunken monologues from Tommy Del, who would rant and rave about the organization and the people who ran it. On one tape, which later made its way into newspaper reports, DelGiorno belittled Scarfo and Leonetti and the rest of the mob leadership. "They're all pussies," he said. "Four Irish guys from Northeast Philly could run the mob better."

Several mob soldiers in DelGiorno's crew began to complain about him to Scarfo and Leonetti, claiming he was often drunk and irrational and that he berated them for no reason. "He would get drunk and make a list up," Leonetti said later. "[Telling his soldiers] that I'm going to kill you. I'm going to kill you. He'd say, 'Remind me tomorrow, I'm going to kill all you guys.' Real sloppy."

Tommy DelGiorno had become a problem. Nicky Scarfo decided to deal with him in typical fashion. In July, in the midst of the investigation into the extortion plot and with the drug dealer still issuing threats, Scarfo sent word to DelGiorno that he was "taken down," reduced to the rank of soldier. He would now report to Iannarella. Even more ominous from Tommy Del's perspective was Scarfo's decision not to divvy up earnings from the bookmaking operation that he, DelGiorno and Joey Pungitore shared. Usually they split the profits every three or four months. In August, they had more than three hundred thousand dollars sitting in their kitty. But when asked, Scarfo said to let the cash sit for a while.

DelGiorno saw that as an obvious indication that he might not be around much longer.

"That was much too much money to keep up," Tommy Del subsequently told a jury. "So I had suggested that we split some of it. And Scarfo said, 'Nah, let's hold it up.' Knowing him, he would never leave that kind of money up when it wasn't necessary. That gave me a hint.

"See, he figured wait a couple more months and I would be dead, then he'd only have to split it two ways," Tommy explained. "I know the way this guy thinks, how he operates. . . . I had seen guys who he had killed and I knew the way it was done."

It was Scarfo's greed that tipped Tommy off. On the surface, the tyrannical little mob boss was telling Tommy to straighten out, to cut out the drinking and carousing and to reestablish himself within the organization. But in reality, DelGiorno knew Scarfo had already decided to kill him. It was just a matter of time. His demotion was permanent and, if Scarfo had his way, it would be terminal.

Tommy Del also began to notice that guys he bet with were holding back. "Everybody stopped paying, you know. You don't do that unless you are a guy who is going to get killed." DelGiorno had been on the other end of the gun often enough to read the signs. Clearly he had a problem. Late that summer the situation intensified when two detectives from the New Jersey State Police paid a visit to his South Philadelphia home. Their message was short and to the point. They said they couldn't tell him how they knew, but it was their obligation to warn him that there was a murder contract out on his life. The contract, they said, came from his boss, Nicky Scarfo.

Tommy Del played dumb to the detectives, but the visit shook him up. He thought about running away, just taking as much of his cash as he could get his hands on and leaving the city. But he hesitated. Then he toyed with the idea of firing first, of taking out Scarfo. Through what remained of that summer and into the early fall—even while he showered money, presents and jobs on his two sons—Tommy Del lived on the edge. Now, like Johnny Calabrese and Salvie Testa before him, he was the one looking over his shoulder. He was the guy who ducked meetings and never followed the same routine. He was the hunted.

Bobby picked up on the problem shortly after he started working full-time for his father. One night early in the fall of 1986 he was out drinking in a club on South Street with some friends. South Street was a trendy strip of funky boutiques, restaurants, bars and after-hours clubs where people partied every night. Most of the younger members and associates of the Scarfo crime family frequented the area. While standing at the bar, Bobby spotted the son of another mob figure and offered to buy him a drink. The kid brushed him off, first ignoring him and then telling him, "I already got a drink."

"The guy treated me like trash," Bobby said. "So the next day I go over to my father's house and tell him what happened.

My father tells me he's having some problems with his business partners, that he got 'taken down' by his boss. And he told me to stay away from his friends' sons, not to trust any of them."

Tommy Del said nothing about a murder contract, but Bobby knew he was worried.

Sunday morning, November 2, 1986, as a steady rain fell on Broad Street, two men in trench coats knocked on Tommy Del's door. It was 9:30 A.M. DelGiorno recognized the two as the New Jersey State Police detectives who had visited him in August. Sergeant Ed Johnson, who was spearheading an organized crime investigation into the Scarfo family, told him they were there to talk again about the plot to kill him. This time Tommy said he wanted some proof. Johnson pulled two cassette tapes out of the pocket of his coat.

"I'm here to play these tapes," he said.

Tommy Del was stunned. For a few seconds he didn't say anything. Then, recovering, he asked two questions. Where were the tapes from and whose voices were on them.

Johnson was short and to the point. The tapes were made in Ocean City, New Jersey, he said. One was Tommy Del's own voice. The other was an interesting conversation between Faffy Iannarella and Sal Grande, the ruthless young hit man who two years earlier had killed Salvie Testa.

Tommy Del invited the two detectives in. He was clearly agitated. Nervous. He told them to hurry up. He wanted to hear the tapes, but he said he was expecting some people over the house in a little while. Johnson, taking charge of the situation, said it wasn't a good time or place. He said they'd need at least an hour. He then suggested that they meet later in the day in a hotel out by Philadelphia International Airport. Tommy Del agreed. Johnson said he would call when everything was set up.

From Broad Street, Johnson and Detective Charlie Crescenz, another member of the Organized Crime Intelligence Bureau, drove out to the airport and booked Room 308 at the Marriott Hotel. The room was nothing fancy. There was a bed, a television and a sitting area—two chairs and a small couch around a coffee table. Johnson set a cassette player on the table, telephoned DelGiorno and then started a pot of coffee. Tommy Del arrived about fifteen minutes later. He had regained his composure and was once again the South Philly tough guy.

"I'm not interested in cooperating," he said.

Johnson said that wasn't the purpose of their visit.

"We just want to inform you of the grave situation you're in with your boss," the detective said.

DelGiorno took a seat on the couch and Crescenz handed him a cup of coffee. Johnson picked out the first tape, a short conversation made on August 16 in a condo rented by Sal Grande in the same complex in Ocean City. The state police had a bug in Grande's place all summer long.

Tommy Del listened intently, leaning forward so as not to miss a word. Grande and Iannarella were discussing the fact that DelGiorno had been "taken down" by Scarfo. Iannarella wondered about Tommy's fate. Then DelGiorno heard Grande's response. The phrase seemed to hang in the air of the hotel room. Tommy could almost see the smirk on the young hit man's face.

"Ain't nothin' gonna happen to him . . . yet," Grande said.

Johnson just looked at DelGiorno. Then he removed the tape and put the second one in the cassette player. Now DelGiorno heard himself talking about Scarfo, Leonetti and the rest of the mob. His words were somewhat slurred. He was obviously drunk. Tommy listened for ten minutes, then told Johnson to turn off the tape.

"You don't have to play anymore," he said. "I remember it vividly . . . I remember the day."

But Johnson was taking no chances. He reminded Tommy Del what else he had said on that tape.

"Do you remember the remainder of the day you were drinking and you started to get very loose-lipped," Johnson said. "You identified yourself as a superior in this organization, and then you went on to identify a number of other people."

"Yeah, I remember," Tommy Del said as he reached under the sweater he was wearing and began to massage his chest with his right hand.

"Now your predicament," Johnson continued, "is that tomorrow New Jersey is going to indict you, Scarfo, and the others. And eventually, this tape is going to be turned over to the defense attorneys in the case and their clients, the guys you were belittling, will hear it all."

The meeting at the Marriott lasted for two hours. The state police had built a major gambling and loan-sharking case against DelGiorno, Scarfo, and fifteen other members of the organization based largely on some eight-hundred hours of conversations recorded over two summers in Ocean City. Already in trouble for the drug heist and the Penns Landing waterfront extortion, DelGiorno knew that the New Jersey indictment would seal his fate.

The next day, DelGiorno, Scarfo and the others were arrested. Word of the secret state police tapes surfaced, and Del-Giorno moved to the top of Scarfo's hit list.

"Everybody got rounded up," Bobby said. "Nicky Scarfo and Philip Leonetti were arrested in Jersey and the others, my father, Faffy, all of them, were picked up in Philly. So I had to go bail my father out. The bail was set at $250,000, so we had to come up with $25,000 in cash—10 percent—to bail him out. My father had money hidden in the ceiling of his house. I go over and Roe goes downstairs and in the ceiling is all this money. She takes it out and counts out what she needs.

"So I drive my stepmother over to bail my father out. We waited, we musta waited about two hours because all these people, whoever was bailing Faffy, Grande, Joey Pung out, they all brought cash and the cops had to count it all out three or four times. It was all in twenties and tens and fifties. It took a long time. But they all got bailed out.

"That night, after my father is home, I drive back to Gladstone Street in my father's car. I used to take it for him, clean it, get it washed. It's one of the things he had me doing when I started working for him. The next day I was gonna take it to the car wash, shine it all up and bring it back to him.

"So the next day, it musta been ten o'clock, ten-thirty in the morning. I'm taking the car back. I pull around the corner at Broad Street and I look over to my left and there's this car with three guys in it, just waiting there. I couldn't see who they were. They all had hats on. They were just sittin' there. It was a Lincoln Towncar. So I'm driving down Broad Street and here this car starts following me.

"As I pull in front of my father's house, I jumped out and I looked and there was Tory Scafidi [mob soldier Salvatore Scafidi] in the passenger side. He tried to turn his head, but I seen him. So, he like, waved to me as the car went past. The other two guys had hats on and the one in the back slouched down and I really couldn't tell who it was. It mighta been The Whip [Nicky Milano]. I'm not sure. . . . So I was wondering why they didn't stop."

Bobby went into the house and told his father what had happened. Tommy Del, sitting at the kitchen table drinking a cup of coffee, went cold with rage.

"Those motherfuckers," he said. "They want to fuck with me."

"What's the matter?" Bobby asked.

"You were driving my car?" Tommy Del said, ignoring Bobby's question and telling him to again recount, in detail, what had happened.

"Yeah," Bobby said. "Remember. I took it home last night."

Tommy Del sat quietly for a few minutes, staring at his coffee cup. Then, in a voice laced with both fear and anger, he told Bobby, "I think they were gonna kill me. But then they seen that it was you, so they just drove by."

"Then he started talking," Bobby said. "For the first time, I heard him talkin' serious. It was him talkin'. It wasn't this mob guy that he was, or that he thought he was. It was him as a person. He don't have his army no more. He's all by himself. He's got nobody to turn to. . . . He said, 'They're gonna kill me. It's all bullshit. The boss thinks I drink too much. The only reason is, he [Scarfo] wants to make more money by cuttin' me out.'

"Now he's talking to me," said Bobby "asking me for advice. He never, ever, asked me for advice. I'm sittin' there confused. He says, 'I have two options. I can go and try and kill Nicky [Scarfo], but that would be crazy . . . or I could turn informant.' But he says that that's just something he's thinking about and he tells me not to tell anybody.

"Then he tells me he's got a couple hundred thousand put away and he says we could start over. And he asks me whether me and Tommy would go into the witness program if he became an informant. I said, 'Dad, I don't know.' And he says, 'But Bob, they're gonna kill me.'

"I felt bad. I was confused. I shoulda said no right from the beginning. . . . Here's a guy, all my life, he thought he was a king. He was on top of the world. He thought it would never end. . . . I never seen him nervous like that. Scared. Very scared."

———————

Two days later, Detective Ed Johnson again called DelGiorno and set up another meeting. This one would take place in the parking lot of the airport hotel the following Sunday, November 9.

Once again it was raining. Johnson was waiting in his car when DelGiorno pulled up. The detective walked over and sat in the passenger side of Tommy's Cadillac. He suggested they rent a room and have another discussion. Tommy, who had already been figuring the angles, said he wanted to talk, but he wanted the feds there as well. Johnson was agreeable. He said he'd set the meeting up for the following night but that

Tommy had to give him something to bring back to his superiors.

"What can I tell them they can expect from you?" he asked.

"Everything," Tommy Del replied.

Chapter Thirteen

Maryann lost her two sons on November 11, 1986. Even now, it is a date circled in black on the calendar in her mind. The night before, in a room in another hotel near the airport, Tommy DelGiorno finalized a deal with the government. In exchange for protection for himself and his family and a plea bargain to all the crimes which he had committed, DelGiorno agreed to testify against the organization. He was the first made member of the Philadelphia mob ever to strike such a bargain.

Bobby and Tommy junior, after discussing the matter for hours, had reluctantly agreed to go into hiding with their father, stepmother and two half brothers. Both boys thought they'd be gone for six months to a year. Then they hoped—and Tommy Del let them believe—they'd be able to return to South Philadelphia.

All that remained, on the night when they were to leave, was one last visit to the house on Gladstone Street.

Maryann was in the kitchen cooking when Bobby and Tommy junior walked in.

"Sit down, have some dinner," she said.

"No, mom, we can't," Bobby said. "We gotta talk to ya. Come on in the parlor and sit down."

Maryann sat on the couch in the tiny living room with her husband. She could tell from her boys' expressions that something was wrong. Just how wrong, she couldn't have imagined. They quickly told her that their father was going to be a witness for the government and that there was a contract out on his life. Then they said there was a chance they might be killed and that they would have to go into protective custody with their father.

At first, Maryann didn't understand what they were saying.

"Why?" she said. "You two live with me. That's not possible."

"Mom," Tommy junior said softly. "We have to leave."

Maryann began to shake and then to gag. She could not catch her breath. Tears welled in her eyes.

"I knew it, I knew it," she screamed. "It's all blowing up in his face. I knew it would come to this. That's why I divorced him."

For Maryann, it was a nightmare. She had fought to keep her sons away from their mobster father and now he, with the help of the government no less, was taking them away from her. Joe Fisher reached over and tried to comfort his wife, but Maryann could neither hear what he was saying nor take any solace from his presence.

"Where is he?" she screamed, her tears turning to a bitter rage. "I'm gonna kill him. I'm gonna kill him."

Bobby and Tommy junior tried to calm her down. Both insisted that this was just a temporary move, that after their father had finished testifying they'd be able to return home.

"When are you going?" Maryann said between sobs.

"Tonight. In a little while."

"Where are you gonna stay?"

"We can't tell you."

"How can you go and not tell me where you are? What am I supposed to do? I'm your mother. . . . That son of a bitch."

For more than an hour, the boys and Joe Fisher tried to console Maryann. Then it was time to leave. She sat sobbing quietly on the couch as they walked out the door. Memories flooded back of her babies, of her struggle to bring them up with little or no help from their father, of the sad and happy times on Gladstone Street. Of Broadway Eddie. Of the Christmas presents. Of Halloweens and graduations and birthday parties. She was always there, while Tommy Del was nowhere to be seen. God, oh God, how could this be? The only things of value she had ever taken from her first marriage were the boys. They were all that mattered to her. Their big shot father with his money and his guns had proven to be the coward that she always knew he was. All his talk about the mob and all his gangster bullshit meant nothing. He could shoot people in the back. But when it was time to defend himself, he turned and ran. The hell with him, Maryann thought. But God, oh God, how can he take my babies?

That night, shortly before midnight, a Winnebago camper pulled out from behind a home in the twenty-nine-hundred block of Broad Street in South Philadelphia. There was an unmarked New Jersey State Police car in front of the camper, and another behind it. Inside, with his wife and his four sons, was the man who would bring down Nicodemo "Little Nicky" Scarfo.

The DelGiornos had packed hurriedly, throwing clothes and other necessities into green trash bags and a few suitcases. The state police promised that the rest of their belongings would be sent once they were permanently situated. Tommy Del clutched a blue gym bag that contained cash and jewelry. Bobby guessed that his father had close to $200,000 on hand, although later police would say DelGiorno took about $137,000 with him into hiding. Tommy Del had also slipped Tommy junior a handgun, telling him to hide it. They might need the gun in the future, he said, if he decided "to go back to the old ways."

Teary-eyed members of the family hugged and kissed Roe,

Danny and Michael as detectives looked on. Bobby and Tommy junior, still reeling from their emotional goodbyes on Gladstone Street, looked on in stunned silence as their paternal grandparents and Roe's family tried to cope with the forced departure of their loved ones. Tommy junior's fiancée, Chrissy, begged to go along, but the state police refused to take her with them.

No one quite knew what to expect as the caravan pulled out of South Philadelphia. Danny and Michael, then just ten and eight years old, were excited. To them it was the start of a great and mysterious adventure. But the rest of the DelGiornos wore more somber expressions. Tommy Del had crossed over a line that meant living the rest of his life with a Mafia murder contract on his head. Roe, as any young mother would be, was concerned about her family, especially her two young boys. Bobby and Tommy junior, sitting in the camper as it headed north, were literally and figuratively in the dark.

In the days leading up to their secret departure they had been repeatedly told that protective custody wouldn't be that bad, that it would be like a vacation, that in six months or so they could return to South Philadelphia. They hoped that was true. But within a week, they came to believe that, in Bobby's words, "it was all bullshit."

Casually at first, but on a consistent basis, the troopers who were guarding the family began to make it clear to the two older boys that they would be better off breaking all ties with the past.

"There's nothing back there for you but trouble," they would say, emphasizing that to return to South Philadelphia was to return to the lair of the mob.

Their father was the biggest mob informant in the history of the Philadelphia Mafia. There was already a contract out on his life. And Scarfo had made it clear that he wasn't above holding family members responsible for the sins of their fathers, sons or brothers.

Joseph Salerno, Jr., an Atlantic City plumber who had testified against Scarfo in the 1980 murder trial of cement contractor Vincent Falcone, was a prime example. This was the case in which Scarfo, Leonetti and Lawrence Merlino were acquitted. But the jury verdict wasn't enough for Scarfo. He thought he had to make an example of the plumber. The problem was that Salerno was in hiding under the Federal Witness Protection Program. Salerno's father, Joe senior, however, was living in South Philadelphia and traveling to Wildwood Crest, New Jersey, every summer, where he owned and operated a small motel.

On the night of August 10, 1982, a man wearing a designer sweatsuit and ski goggles knocked on the motel office door. When Salerno answered, the man pulled out a pistol and pumped a bullet into his neck. The elder Salerno survived the attack but a long-held Mafia tradition was shattered.

"Based on the past, Joseph Salerno senior had little reason to be frightened," the Pennsylvania Crime Commission noted. "[Because] tradition held that the mob did not harm an innocent relative or member of an enemy's family—a brother, a sister, a father. It just wasn't done."

Nicky Scarfo changed those rules, and thumbed his nose at the authorities while doing it. A day after the Salerno shooting, Scarfo and several of his henchmen were spotted walking around Atlantic City wearing the same type of designer sweatsuit as the gunman who shot Joe Salerno senior.

Now Tommy Del was the guy Scarfo wanted looking down the barrel of a Mafia gun. But anyone in DelGiorno's family would be an acceptable substitute. This was the bind that Bobby and Tommy junior found themselves in. They were paying a price—a steep and unreasonable price, they would eventually decide—for their father's life of crime. Both the FBI and the state police were insisting that they would be targeted by Scarfo's hit men because of their father's decision to become a government informant. Bobby, who had gloried in his father's role as a macho mobster, wanted to help his father. But he was being asked to give up his life—his family, his home, his friends, his very identity—to do it.

On the one hand the detectives were telling him if he went back to South Philadelphia he would be killed. On the other, South Philadelphia, the place and the people, meant everything to him. He couldn't imagine living anywhere else. He couldn't imagine never seeing his family and friends again. Sometimes he thought he'd be better off dead, that maybe he should just go back home and take his chances. At other times he and his brother would rail against their father for the spot he had put them in.

"Why doesn't he stand up like a man?" Tommy junior would ask. "All his life he told us never to be a rat. Now what is he?"

"Yo, Tom," Bobby would say, trying to calm down his brother and at the same time avoid the undeniable truth in what he was saying. "This is Daddy we're talking about. They were gonna kill him. What could he do?"

But for the first time, somewhere deep in his subconscious, Bobby began to question his father's way of life. For the first time he began to ask himself if the money, the cars, the clothes, the "easy living" of a mobster were really worth it.

Bobby, even more than his older brother, chafed at the confinement and restrictions that the state police imposed upon him. He was used to coming and going as he pleased. Now he had to ask permission to go outside. And a trip to the store or the movies required security clearance and an escort.

Their father took thousands of dollars into hiding. He had his wife and his two young sons with him. Bobby and Tommy junior liked their half brothers, but their relationship with their stepmother had deteriorated to little more than mutual tolerance. Their friends and family were back in South Philadelphia. And as each day went by, South Philly seemed farther and farther away.

Less than a week after their clandestine departure, the Del-Giornos were set up in a state police "safe house" in northern New Jersey. The house, in a small town in the north-central part of the state, was on a large, fenced-in estate. There was a swimming pool in the back yard and beyond the fence was a wooded area. The closest neighbor was a half mile down the road. Danny and Michael adapted immediately. For a time they didn't even have to go to school. They were with their mother and father, enjoying an extended vacation. There was a large yard to run around in and, once the weather warmed, there would be a pool to swim in. Their house on South Broad Street in Philadelphia was nice, but nothing like this.

Adding to the younger boys' excitement was the constant presence of detectives with guns and walkie-talkies and cars equipped with two-way radios and shotguns. Danny and Michael were too young and too naive to realize what Bobby and Tommy grasped almost instantly. They were prisoners. There were no bars, but this was a jail. Their every move was monitored. Any time they left the house, a detective would have to go with them. They needed permission—and an escort—to go anywhere.

Tommy junior would grow more hostile as the weeks went by with no indication of when— or if—the confinement would end. Bobby, who clung to the belief that he was engaged in an effort to save his father's life, fought off a foreboding sense of homesickness, denying at first what Tommy said was the reality of their situation: that they'd never be able to go back to South Philadelphia.

For Bobby, that was incomprehensible.

Even before they made it to the safe house, he was dreaming about home. On the very first night, after collapsing in nervous exhaustion on a bed in a motel somewhere in New Jersey, Bobby thought about home. The tension and pressure had drained him, left him numb. All he wanted to do was close his eyes and sleep and hope. Maybe, he thought, this wasn't really happening.

"There was a state trooper driving the Winnebago and there were troopers in cars in front of us and behind us. We drove for about four hours that night. We finally pulled into this motel. There were three more undercover police cars there waiting for us.

"We all got out of the camper and walked up to the second floor. I asked one of the troopers what room was mine. He says, 'Well, Bob, we got the whole second floor, so pick two if you want.' I was so tired I walked into the first room, fell on the bed and passed out.

"I still remember what I dreamed that night. I dreamed that I was home, waking up in my own bed, running down the stairs; and my mother's in the kitchen cooking breakfast. I run up to her, give her a big hug and say, 'I'm never gonna leave you, Mom. I had this terrible dream that I left.' And my mother says, 'I'll never let you leave.' "

Then Bobby woke up.

And he started to cry.

In the months that followed, as he and his brother grew bored and tired and angry while living in the safe house, that dream would come back to haunt Bobby's nights. He couldn't shake it. He would go for three or four nights without it, then a piece would return. He'd see himself in his room, or in the kitchen. He'd smell the eggs cooking and see his mother at the stove. He'd hear her voice. And then he'd wake with a start and there'd be that empty feeling in his stomach.

He was nineteen, and he was away from home for the first time in his life. Really away. This wasn't a vacation at the shore or a trip to Florida. He missed his mother, his grandmother and grandfather. He missed his friends. He missed the schoolyard where he used to hang out and the neighborhood he grew up in. He missed being able to walk out of his house on Gladstone Street and see, sitting on a stoop two doors away, Anthony Forline, the guy who was as close to him as his brother. He missed the Saturday night beef-and-beer parties that would bring together everybody from the neighborhood. He missed being able to walk two blocks to his grandmother's house. He missed climbing out his bedroom window at night and sitting on the roof of his mother's tiny row house and looking up at the stars and dreaming about the future.

There weren't any dreams in Jersey—only nightmares.

The DelGiornos spent their first two days in hiding at that motel. Security was so tight that when the boys wanted to go out and play football in the parking lot, they had to get clearance. It took an hour to get the okay.

"This is the kind of trouble we had to go through just to play a game of football," Bobby recalled. "First we had to wait for the okay from the supervisor who was in charge of the guard detail. Then we had to wait for him to assign two of his troopers to stand outside with us. When we finally got to play outside I felt like a little kid. There was a cop at each end of the parking lot, like they were babysitting us.

"There was nothing for us to do but play football and eat. We stayed at that motel for two days, until my father started to complain. Then they moved us to another hotel at a ski resort. It had an indoor swimming pool, weight room and a game room for my younger brothers. But we only stayed there one night because the state police said a lot of Mafia people from New York came to that resort. That's when Roe threw a fit. She started yelling, 'I'm not living this way, going from one hotel to another. Tell 'em I wanna be put in a house or else I'm going back to South Philly.'

"Roe was right. We were being yanked around like yo-yos, moving around like gypsies."

Five hours after Roseanne DelGiorno's outburst, the state police told Tommy Del they had found a "safe house" where they'd be able to stay on a permanent basis. They all piled back into the Winnebago. The two state police escort cars, one in front and one in back, fell in line, and they headed out.

The house had six bedrooms, five bathrooms, maid's quarters, a den, a playroom with a ping-pong table, a weight room for exercising and a swimming pool and cabana out back. There was a two-car attached garage and a two-car detached garage. There were security cameras set up all over the estate, along the winding driveway that led from the road to the house and along the back and side yards. The den on the first floor served as the state police office, where a bank of television cameras allowed a trooper to scan the grounds.

Somebody rich owned the place, although Bobby never found out who. Nor did he learn how the state police got access to it.

The DelGiornos settled in as best they could.

Tommy Del would be away from the home for days at a time, attending debriefing sessions or court hearings where his testimony was being used to substantiate the charges that had been lodged against Scarfo and the others and to build several other cases that state and federal authorities hoped would bring down the mob.

For the law enforcement agencies that had been battling the Scarfo organization—with little success for more than five years—Tommy Del was a valuable and lethal weapon. Not so, his family. For the New Jersey State Police and, later, the FBI, the DelGiornos were a source of constant aggravation. And no one was more aggravating than Bobby.

A week after moving into the safe house, Bobby took off. He had been planning the move for two or three days and was amazed at how easy it was just to walk away. The night before, he took fifteen thousand dollars in cash out of the blue gym bag where his father had hidden all the family funds. The money was from Bobby's loan-sharking and bookmaking operations, all the cash he had saved up over the past three years. He had given the money to his father to hold onto the night they left Philadelphia. Tommy Del had put it in the bag with the cash and jewelry he took into hiding.

The money and the clothes he was wearing were all Bobby took with him when he left.

It was a Friday around 11:00 A.M. After breakfast he started for the back door when his younger brother, Danny, ran up to him.

"Where you going, Bob?"

"Out back in the woods to look for deer," Bobby said.

"Can I come?"

The two headed out the door, past one of the detectives who asked where they were going.

"Out to look for deer," Danny replied.

Once in the back yard, Bobby told his younger brother to climb up into the tree house and keep watch.

"If I'm not back right away, that just means I've gone deeper into the woods," Bobby told him. "You stay up in the tree."

Bobby climbed through the fence that separated the grounds of the estate from a clump of woods and then headed out, moving in the direction of what he thought was a roadway. Ten minutes later he was out of the woods and moving toward a gas station. He asked a young girl there if she could call him a cab.

"A cab out here, are you crazy?"

It was then that Bobby realized how out of touch he was with reality. He didn't even know where he was. All he knew was that this was North Jersey, not far from New York City. And now he also knew he was somewhere without taxi service; somewhere a long way away from South Philadelphia.

"Is there a bus or a train around here that I can get to Philadelphia?" he asked.

"There's a train," she said, "but it goes to New York."

Bobby had to control his emotions, to think clearly. He had been gone less than ten minutes, probably not long enough for anyone back at the house to get suspicious. But he was running out of time. He had to get to the train station, get to New York and then connect with a train to Philadelphia. He thanked the girl and, breaking into a trot, headed off in the direction she had indicated.

The train station was nothing more than a commuter stop, an outdoor platform that filled up each morning with office workers on their way into the city. But shortly before noon, the platform was practically deserted, adding to Bobby's feeling of isolation and contributing to his growing anxiety. For thirty minutes he sat on a bench clutching a train ticket, expecting that any moment the gravel parking lot behind him would be filled with state police cars, sirens screaming, red lights flashing. He fingered the ticket like a rosary bead and prayed to God that the train would be on time.

Five hours later, he was getting off another train at Thirtieth Street Station in Philadelphia. There he had no trouble hailing a taxi. A broad smile lit up his face as he jumped into the back seat and told the driver, "Take me to Second and Ritner."

Bobby had the cab driver drop him off about a block from the neighborhood schoolyard where he and his friends always hung out. It was nearly 6:00 P.M. when he stepped out of the taxi. The sun had gone down. What had been a bright fall afternoon was turning cold. But Bobby felt a warmth that was beyond description as he began to walk the sidewalk in his neighborhood. He was home.

He turned a corner and looked across the street toward the schoolyard. It was like he had never left. There, under the lights, stood John GQ, Jimmy, Mark Pop, all his friends from the neighborhood. Bobby moved toward them, but stayed in the shadows. He scanned the streets around the schoolyard, looking for a car that might seem out of place, a car with someone sitting in it, watching. Satisfied that wasn't the case, he moved in closer. If this was a typical Friday night, the guys would be drinking beer in the schoolyard and planning what to do for the rest of the evening.

"They each had a quart of beer in their hands and they were leaning against the wall of the school," Bobby said. "I hollered over to them, 'Hey, you faggots, you got a quart of beer for me?' Everyone looked up, but they couldn't see me because it was dark and they were standing under the schoolyard lights.

As I walked closer, Mark Pop yells, 'It's Bobby. It's fucking Bobby.' Then he runs up and lifts me in the air and he's hugging me and the other guys come running over, hugging me and asking me all kinds of questions.

" 'I thought we'd never see you again,' John GQ says. 'All the newspapers are saying you, your father and your whole family's been put under protective custody.'

"While this is going on, Anthony Forline comes strolling around the corner. He sees me, runs up and jumps on me. Then he says, 'Bob, I gotta talk to you. The FBI's been to my house. They think me and you planned your escape and I was going to drive somewhere and pick you up with the fifty thousand dollars. They say you stole fifty thousand dollars. Your mother's going crazy. She don't believe 'em, but she's real upset.' "

Forline, in his excitement, had gotten his story somewhat twisted. It was the New Jersey State Police, not the FBI, that had questioned him.

"State Police, FBI, what the fucks the difference," he said when Bobby asked him to repeat the story. Also, it was fifteen thousand, not fifty thousand, and the money wasn't stolen, it was Bobby's to begin with. This was, to Bobby's way of thinking, just another example of how the authorities take a piece of information and distort it to suit their purposes. Bobby had begun to see them do that with his father—detectives would offer subtle suggestions to Tommy Del, suggestions that Bobby and his brother later suspected were designed to ensure that their father's testimony would conform with evidence and other testimony the prosecution planned to present.

It was all a game.

Now Bobby decided he was going to play.

He sent Jimmy around the corner to check out his street. Sure enough, Jimmy spotted two plainclothes detectives sitting in an unmarked car on the corner. Nobody, however, was watching the alleyway that ran behind his mother's house.

Now Bobby sent Anthony Forline back to knock on his mother's door.

"All the attention will be on you," Bobby said to his best friend. "Once you get in the house, make sure you keep my mother occupied. Make sure you keep her downstairs."

Anthony headed off for Gladstone Street. Like a quarterback in a pickup football game, Bobby started handing out assignments to the others. His plan was to sneak in the back window to his bedroom. Under a floorboard in the closet was a .357 magnum, a gun he had bought two years earlier from a local drug dealer. If Bobby was going to be walking around South Philadelphia with both the state police and the Mafia after him, he wanted to be armed.

"If anybody's gonna come up behind me and try to put some bullets in my head," he told Anthony and the others, "I want to be holding something besides my dick in my hand."

They gave Anthony a two-minute head start so that he could distract the detectives who were watching the street. Then Bobby, Mark Pop and Knave, another one of the guys, headed out. Knave was supposed to stand at the entranceway to the alley. If anyone came around, he would whistle. That would be a warning for Bobby and Mark Pop.

John GQ stood in the schoolyard with a puzzled look on his face.

"What about me?" he asked.

"You?" Bobby said. "You got the hardest job of all. Here's twenty bucks. Go to the bar and bring back two cases of beer. Make sure it's Bud."

"And make sure it's cold," said Mark Pop.

———————

"Me and Mark Pop started down the alley. We got to my house and both of us climb over the fence. Mark gives me a boost onto the roof that was near my bedroom. I look down and tell him, 'If you hear any yelling, just go back around the schoolyard.' As I'm walking across the roof I'm praying the window isn't locked. I pulled on it and it opened, so I climbed in. I could hear Anthony talking to my mother, but at this point I'm most interested in gettin' the gun. I open the closet door, lift up the rug and move the floorboard and there it is. I just look at it for a few seconds, feeling so powerful. I grabbed it and, at that point, I wasn't afraid of anything or anybody. No Mafia. No nobody. I just sat there holding that gun.

"Before I go back out the window, I creep over to the top of the stairs to see what my mother was saying. I could tell she was crying. I hear her tell Anthony that she hopes I'm all right. Anthony's telling her, 'Maryann, I know your son. Bobby can take care of himself.'

"At that point I'm thinking how, here I am, right dead in the middle of everybody's life except my own. I felt like running down the stairs and just hugging my mother. But I knew if I did that, she would turn me over to the police for my own safety. The last thing I wanted was to go back to that safe house where there wasn't anything but trees and grass."

Bobby was living his nightmare. This was his house. This was his bedroom. The sounds, the smells, the feel of the place were all familiar, comforting, solid. His mother was right downstairs, sitting at the kitchen table talking to Anthony. It was a common, ordinary scene. A piece of his past. Bobby headed for the window. He knew if he stayed any longer, he'd start to cry. All he wanted was to come home.

Five minutes later he was back in the schoolyard with Mark Pop, Anthony and the others. They each had a beer in their hands and were planning their next move when a girl from the neighborhood walked up.

"Bobby, what are you doing here?" she said.

"I live here, remember?" he said.

"But I heard there's a bounty on your head."

"And I heard there's a bounty on your ass," Mark Pop yelled, chasing her away.

"What was that all about?" Bobby asked.

No one answered.

"What's she talking about, Ant?" Bobby said.

"The word on the street is one hundred thousand dollars," Anthony Forline said. "That's how much for whoever kills your father or you or your brother."

The reaction of the New Jersey State Police during the twenty-four hours that Bobby was "free" indicated just how valuable law enforcement considered Tommy DelGiorno.

State police detectives swarmed all over Bobby's South Philadelphia neighborhood, correctly surmising that a nineteen-year-old who was born and bred on the concrete sidewalks around Second Street would head for home. Cops staked out the neighborhood. They sat in unmarked cars on a half dozen corners. They had surveillance posted outside his grandmother's home and, of course, they were inside and outside his mother's.

In the end it was a tearful and despondent Maryann Fisher who found Bobby and talked him into returning with the state police. But that would not occur until the morning after Bobby got his gun.

He and his friends, full of bravado after polishing off both of the cases of Bud that John GQ had brought back to the schoolyard, headed for a beef-and-beer party at the Irish Club on Second and Mifflin that night. With detectives staked out all over the neighborhood, Bobby and his buddies partied past midnight with about two hundred people. Then Bobby, drunk but still alert enough to realize he was being looked for, crashed at his friend Jimmy's house.

"They'll be looking for me at Anthony's or Mark Pop's," he told Jimmy through the drunken haze that had enveloped them all.

"You could stay with me as long as you want," Jimmy said.

A state police detective was at Jimmy's door the next morning. Word had filtered back about the party and the police were questioning every one of Bobby's friends. Jimmy tried to hold

---

the detective off, basically playing dumb while Bobby listened from a back room.

"Listen, you punk, this isn't some street-corner fight, this is a life and death situation," the detective said.

"Who's life you talking about?" Jimmy shouted back. "Bobby's? Are you kidding? You could give a fuck. All you care about is that if Bobby doesn't go back, his father won't testify."

Then Bobby heard the slam of another car door and his mother was inside the house, pleading with Jimmy.

"Please tell me where Bobby is," she said, her voice full of fear, anger and sadness.

Bobby walked out. He and his mother embraced. Tears filled his eyes. They streamed out of hers. Bobby was in a daze. He couldn't quite focus. In the background he heard the state police detective suggest that they all go somewhere for a cup of coffee. Somewhere where they could talk. Bobby went willingly.

The somewhere was the New Jersey State Police office in Bellmawr, New Jersey, just across the Walt Whitman Bridge from South Philadelphia. It was the only place they could be sure they were safe, the detective explained.

Bobby, his mother and two detectives sat in a small office discussing the situation.

"Look, Bobby, we know it's rough," one of the detectives said, "but try to go along with us on this. We'll give you whatever we can. We'll find you a job. I understand you've got family out in Oregon. We can relocate you there. We'll pay for everything. Set you up real nice."

The only Oregon Bobby was interested in was Oregon Avenue in South Philadelphia.

"You're so busy playing cops and robbers, you're missing the whole point," Bobby said. "Don't you understand? Where I want to be is home, with my mother, with my family, with my friends."

Bobby fought to hold back the tears welling up again; this time they were tears of anger and frustration.

"How would you like it if you had to leave your family and friends and was told you'd never see them again? Tell me what you would do."

Like the night before at the schoolyard when he first asked about the murder contract, no one answered. Then one of the detectives asked the other to take Bobby's mother to another room for a few minutes. When she had left, the detective sat down behind his desk and stared directly into Bobby's eyes.

"Do you know how serious this situation is? Do you know your father has already admitted to committing fourteen murders? Do you know what they're going to do to him if he doesn't testify?"

The implication was clear. If Tommy Del reneged on his agreement to cooperate so that his family could return to South Philadelphia, then the state would prosecute him for the murders he had admitted committing. And while the detective might have been exaggerating slightly—Tommy Del would eventually admit to his own involvement in five gangland murders—that did not change the fact that Bobby's father could face life in prison or the electric chair.

The irony was that if Tommy Del did testify, then he and his family would have to remain in hiding because they were already under a death sentence from the Scarfo organization.

It was a no-win situation for Bobby.

And for Maryann.

All she had been thinking about for the past twenty-four hours, from the moment the state police called and told her that Bobby had fled, was her baby turning up dead in the gutter, tortured horribly and shot in the back of the head by some Mafia goon. Now she had found him, but she couldn't protect him. For his own safety, she had to send him back to his father and the state police. She had to be content with an occasional call or letter from God knew where. She had to live her life without knowing where her boys were or what they were doing.

As she sat pondering the situation in the state police office, the phone rang. It was Tommy Del. He wanted to talk with Bobby.

"He'll talk to me first," Maryann said, grabbing the receiver from one of the detectives.

Bobby, from the other room, could hear his mother screaming and knew immediately that it was his father on the other end of the line.

"This is all your fault, you son of a bitch," Maryann said. "Now I have to convince him to come back. If I do, I don't want you to lay a hand on him. Do you hear me? I don't even want you to raise your voice to him. You caused all this. If I knew where you were, I would get a gun and blow your fucking brains out. You're nothing but a coward. Why aren't you dead?"

Quickly, one of the detectives grabbed the phone out of her hand.

"Maryann," he said, "we can't let you issue death threats. I understand how you feel, but this is a state police office here. You threaten to kill somebody, you're breaking the law. Please, try to calm down."

Bobby was handed the phone in the other room and listened while his father begged him to come back.

"Bob, they're gonna kill you if you stay in South Philadelphia," Tommy Del said. "Come back and I'll make sure you can have visitors, whoever you want, whenever you want. Who knows. In a couple of years, when this is all over, you could probably go back home."

"I'll come back," Bobby told his father. "But when this is over, I'm coming home for good."

After he hung up the phone, the state police detective told Bobby he had done the right thing. Bobby just stared at him.

"Your family's gonna come out on top of this," he said.

"The only people who are going to come out on top are you guys and the FBI," Bobby shouted. "I don't know who's worse, the mob or the police."

Bobby spent another thirty minutes alone with his mother. They hugged, and she squeezed him tight. He told her he would be back as soon as his father had finished testifying at all the trials. He said the state police would arrange for her to visit with him. He said to tell grandmom and grandpop that he would see them soon. Then he was gone, whisked away in an unmarked state police car for a trip up the New Jersey Turnpike to Newark.

There another detective in an unmarked car was waiting to take him back to the safe house. The detective was about six foot two and weighed nearly 250 pounds. He wore jeans, a sweater and a black leather jacket. His hair hung down around his collar. He had an earring. He was unlike any of the other members of the state police Bobby had met.

"My name's Jim," he said, reaching out to shake Bobby's hand.

"Bob DelGiorno," Bobby replied with what must have been a quizzical look in his eye.

"I work undercover, narcotics. That's why I look like this."

For the next three months, however, Jim was going to work the detail guarding the DelGiornos. Bobby liked him immediately. Even more so when they were alone in the car driving from Newark.

"Listen," Jim said, "I grew up in Jersey City so I know what it's like to be away from the city. Most of the guys on this detail don't know the difference.

"So, if you wanna get laid or just go out drinking or whatever else, just name it and we'll try to figure out a way to do it. Just do me one favor."

"What?" Bobby asked.

"Don't run away on my shift," the detective said.

Bobby smiled. Finally, he thought, an honest cop.

Chapter Fourteen

Maryann's nightmare began when the boys left with their father. And it intensified after Bobby went back with the New Jersey State Police. She would close her eyes and try to sleep, but all she could hear were the voices of her two sons. In the nightmare they were little boys again, and they were lost. Maryann could hear them calling.

"Mommy, Mommy, help us," they would say. "Please, Mommy, find us."

Suddenly, she would see them.

Maryann would reach out. Their hands would almost touch. But they would slip away, disappear, and she'd hear them crying again.

"Mommy, Mommy, help us."

There was no way to make the voices stop. Even when she was awake, Maryann would hear them. Joe Fisher, concerned about his wife's state of mind, had insisted that she visit her family doctor. He prescribed Valium for her nerves and a mild sleeping pill to help her get some rest. Still, she tossed and turned all night. Paced and fretted all day.

On a Tuesday morning late in November, two days after she had convinced Bobby to return to the safe house with the state police, Maryann sat alone on the couch in the living room of her home on Gladstone Street. Joe had left for work. The house was empty. Maryann took a Valium and a sleeping pill. Then she took another. She picked up a photograph of Tommy and Bobby—a picture taken when they were just six and seven years old—and she began speaking to it. She got up, went into the kitchen, poured herself a cup of coffee and took two more pills.

"Believe me," Maryann said several years later, "I didn't start out to kill myself. But you have to understand the situation, you have to put yourself in my place. My two children were taken away. I had no idea where they were and whether, if they walked out of the house, they would be killed."

Sitting at her kitchen table, holding the same picture, drinking a cup of coffee, tears filled her eyes as Maryann talked about the day she nearly took her own life.

"I was just sitting here. And I had their picture. And I kept looking at their picture. And I started to shake, and I took another pill. And then another one. And it just got easier as I took another and another. I just thought I was worse off than any person in the whole world.

"I was talking to the picture and I just said, I don't want to live anymore. I figured life wasn't worth living.

"I was holding the picture and I began talking to them, thinking about when they were little and all the good times we had. . . . All that happiness was gone now. I was crying again. I took two more sleeping pills. I wanted to sleep the world away. Nothing was working. I couldn't calm myself and I couldn't sleep. I know it was wrong, but I hurt so bad. I just wanted to shut the world out forever.

"I took all the pills. I was crying and talking to the boys out loud. 'Please forgive me. I'm not strong enough to go on with my life without you. You'll never be safe. . . . You'll never come home to me.'

"The next thing I remember is waking up in intensive care

in Mount Sinai Hospital. . . . And my doctor, Peter Gross, was there holding my hand. And I said to him, 'Why did you bring me back. I was content where I was.' He talked to me. He told me that I had to be here for when they came back. He said I had to be here for their phone calls. He said I had to be strong."

Later that day, Maryann's parish priest came to the hospital to hear her confession. She explained her despair. She knew that trying to kill herself was a mortal sin and she asked for God's forgiveness. She wanted to be there for the boys. But Maryann also told the priest that she hated her ex-husband and wanted him dead.

"Maryann," he said softly, "I understand how you feel, but you're not a judge. You're not a jury. Let it go."

"Father, forgive me, I can't," she said. "Some day I'll see him dead."

The priest talked with Maryann for more than an hour that day and for hours more in the weeks and months that followed. Each time he blessed her, but he said he could not give her absolution as long as her heart was filled with hate for her ex-husband.

She has not been to confession since.

———

Maryann spent three days in intensive care while her condition stabilized and four weeks in a psychiatric ward. Joe Fisher, who had unexpectedly come home for lunch on the day she overdosed, had rushed his wife to the hospital, saving her life. Now he was at her side, holding her hand and urging her not to give up. Bobby and Tommy junior were not told what had happened. There was just a vague reference to their mother's "nervous condition" and the fact that she checked into the hospital for some help. They were able to call her there occasionally and, at one point in the middle of her treatment, the state police arranged a brief visit in New Jersey.

"I don't even know where it was," Maryann said. "The state police came to the hospital and took me and Joe somewhere over in Jersey. That's where I saw my sons for the first time since Bobby ran away. We talked. It was nice. I know I was kinda dopey because of the medication. We were in a restaurant."

The visit ended on a sour note, however, with Bobby and Maryann arguing over Tommy Del.

"He had them brainwashed," she said. "He had them thinking he was the good guy now and he was doing this for them. It took them a long time to realize that wasn't how it was."

For Bobby the first six weeks in protective custody had been an emotional roller coaster. He still clung to the belief that what he was doing was necessary in order to help save his father's life. He wanted to believe that, to feel that finally his father needed him. Wanted him. On the other hand, there was his mother, Joe, his grandparents and South Philadelphia. How could he give all that up? And for what? The state police would pump him up, insisting that what his father was doing was important, that no one had ever done it before, that he was putting his life on the line.

So Bobby would swing between the two extremes. The day he and Tommy junior met with Maryann, Bobby was touting the state police line. The next day he called his mother and apologized.

"It was hard," he said, "to know what to do and who to believe. Eventually, I saw my father for what he was, but in the beginning, even after I had run away and came back, there were still times when I thought he was doing this for us. He wasn't, though. Everything he did, he did for himself."

While Maryann fought to overcome her depression, Bobby and Tommy junior, unaware of how severe their mother's condition was, opened a battle of their own against the stifling boredom of life in rural New Jersey.

They were isolated and cut off from everything and everyone they knew. Bobby considered taking off again, but he thought about his mother's anguish and the promise he had made, so he sat tight.

Danny and Michael, at least, had some semblance of a normal life. They were living with their mother and father. Their grandparents and cousins, Roe's family, came up to visit. The state police would pick up the tab for big family dinners at restaurants in New York City, tabs that would run to three or four hundred dollars. For the younger boys it was a vacation, an adventure. For Bobby and Tommy junior it was a jail sentence.

For the taxpayers of New Jersey it was expensive.

Before it was all over, the New Jersey State Police would spend more than $140,000 protecting Tommy Del and his family. This would include housing, living expenses, security costs and incidentals, such as weekend trips, hotel bills, meals, food, clothing and anything else Bobby could finagle.

"When I first came back after I ran away, I didn't have many clothes." he said. "My mother was supposed to be sending them to me, but it was taking forever to get them. I needed a jacket and I went in and asked the supervisor of the squad if someone could take me to the mall. He says sure and then he says, 'Don't forget to bring enough money.'

"I blew up. I was still mad about being away and I told him, 'Look, I didn't ask to be here. You take me away from my home, make me lose my job. Where would you like me to get the money? You call whoever you gotta call and you tell them I'm on the next train out of here back to Philly if you don't get me a jacket.' "

That afternoon, one of the troopers took Bobby to a nearby mall. He returned with a $150 leather jacket, compliments of the taxpayers of New Jersey. Bobby liked the jacket. But more than that, he knew it would get a rise out of the state police. He wanted to bother them; to return some of the misery they had brought into his life. He smiled at the thought of the supervisor trying to explain to his boss down in Trenton about an expense voucher for a stylish bomber jacket.

Bobby also learned something else.

"I knew I could get anything I wanted by throwing a fit. The only reason I did that is because, I knew, after my father was done testifying, they weren't going to give two fucks about any of us, me, my brother *or* my father."

Certain members of the guard detail, however, were more tolerant than others about what Bobby and Tommy junior could and couldn't do. One squad, in fact, arranged for Tommy junior's fiancée to come up to a ski resort in northern New Jersey for the weekend. The outing cost the state $2,700. It started with a visit to a ski shop where Bobby, Tommy and Tommy's fiancée, Chrissy, picked out the latest in ski apparel.

"I knew they were paying, so I was grabbing everything in sight," Bobby recalled.

Then they checked into a hotel. Tommy and Chrissy got one room. Bobby, who was hoping to "get lucky," got a separate accommodation. And the two troopers assigned to guard them shared a third room.

"We ate filet mignon and lobster tail," said Bobby. "We drank wine with dinner and then went clubbing at night. It was great. Usually, it was me and the two troopers. Tommy spent most of the weekend with his girlfriend. They'd have dinner with us, but then they'd go off by themselves. Me and the troopers went skiing during the day and after dinner we'd go drinking.

"The first night, everyone was tired after dinner and we all said we'd go back to our rooms to get some sleep. But one of the troopers made the mistake of giving me his credit card in case I woke up first for breakfast. He told me to just charge it and sign his name. Two hours later, after I was sure they were asleep, I headed for the bar at the hotel. I musta spent two hundred dollars. Every girl that walked in there, I bought her a drink.

"Then, the next night. They took me clubbing. I had a fake ID that said I was twenty-two, but the doorman wanted to see a driver's license with a photo, which I didn't have. One of the troopers tried to slip him ten dollars and the doorman says, 'I can't take that. It would be a bribe. I'm waiting to get into the state police academy, and I don't want to do anything to hurt my chances.' So the trooper pulls him aside, takes out his badge and says, 'We gotta look out for each other.' He let me right in, no problem.

"I liked these guys. They were just regular guys trying to do their job, and I didn't hold any of this stuff that was happening to me and Tommy against them. We were drinking at the bar and one of the troopers starts flirting with a girl sitting across from us. And the girl's boyfriend was getting real upset cause she seemed to be liking the attention she was getting.

"So the trooper calls the bartender over and he tells him he wants to buy drinks for the guy and his girlfriend. He orders the girl a piña colada and he tells the bartender to give the guy a glass of milk.

"We met another girl that night, and they told her I was the son of some rich movie producer from Hollywood and they were my bodyguards. She believed them and was real impressed. We drove her home and we got stopped for speeding. One of the troopers got out and walked back to the police car and pulled out his wallet, showed him who he was. We didn't get a ticket and the girl was even more impressed. 'Who are you guys?' she said.

"We had a great time. It was a great weekend. But on the ride back to the safe house, the troopers got worried about the bill. One of them kept saying, 'I can't believe we spent twenty-seven-hundred dollars. My God, twenty-seven-hundred dollars for a weekend.' "

The getaway at the ski resort was a temporary break in the tedium that had become routine for Bobby. There was only so much television he could watch, only so many video movies he could rent, only so many times he could occupy himself playing cards at the kitchen table.

When the boredom became unbearable, he would usually do something that got him in trouble. On one occasion, he and Tommy turned the house into an armed camp, creating the only serious security alarm the state police had to deal with during their five-month stay at the safe house.

Tommy had brought some large firecrackers with him when they went into hiding. One night when their father was away testifying in Philadelphia, and Roe, Danny and Michael were asleep upstairs, Bobby and Tommy decided to have a little fun.

"We wanted to liven things up. Two of the troopers were watching television and the third was in the office watching the security cameras. So me and Tommy went upstairs to the maid's quarters, which was right above the office. We put a long wick on the firecrackers so we'd have enough time to get back downstairs. Then we lit the wick and dropped them out the window. They fell right in front of the office door.

"We ran down the back stairway and sat down at the kitchen table in the other end of the house, pretending we were playing cards. All of a sudden, we hear this *boom*. Tommy hollers to the troopers, 'What's that noise?' They start scrambling all over the place.

" 'Get out of the kitchen,' they're saying. 'Get in the living room. Keep your heads down.' I wanted to laugh out loud. There was tears in my eyes I was trying so hard to keep a straight face. The trooper in the office came running out with an M-16. The others had pulled out machine guns. They each took a living room window and started talking in real low voices. 'You think it was some kind of bomb?' one of them says. 'It probably wasn't hooked up right,' another says, 'or we wouldn't be here right now.' The trooper who was in the office says, 'It scared the shit out of me. I thought it was all over for us.'

"Me and Tommy are on the floor trying not to laugh. We look at each other and we realize these guys are gonna kill us when they find out it was all a joke. Then one of them says, 'Call down to headquarters and get us some support up here.' Before anybody moves, Tommy jumps up and starts laughing and pointing at me and yelling, 'It was his idea. It was his idea. Bobby threw a firecracker out the maid's window.' Then we were both rolling on the floor laughing. One of the troopers, the guy who was in the office, said, 'I don't think it's very fucking funny.' But the other two couldn't help themselves. They started cracking up, too.

"Later, me and Tommy got in trouble because the supervisor told our father. But most of the other troopers in the squad thought it was hilarious."

Neither their father nor the squad supervisor ever heard about another one of their adventures, a trip through the netherworld of Jersey City go-go bars and of New York's notorious Forty-second Street, compliments, once again, of the state of New Jersey.

It started on a Friday night at the Meadowlands Racetrack where, despite the fact that they were underaged, Bobby and Tommy junior spent an evening betting the horses and drinking beer with the two troopers assigned to guard and entertain them.

"We had been complaining for a while about there not being anything to do. Also, I hadn't been with a girl for a long time and one of the troopers knew this was bothering me.

"So they said they would take us to the racetrack for the night. At first there was a big argument that we shouldn't go near New York. That the mob might spot us. But finally, my father spoke up for us, said we'd be all right, that nobody knew us. So two troopers took us. We went to the racetrack, ate dinner there, had a window seat as we bet the races. The tab was close to three hundred dollars, and I bet a hundred of it was beer money. The state paid for everything. I was really loaded and so was one of the troopers. But I had won close to a hundred and fifty dollars betting on the races.

"So instead of going right home, we asked, 'Could we go out?' I wanted to go to New York, Forty-second Street. You know. The one trooper was saying no, but the other was so drunk, he said, 'Come on. Let's go.' First we went to this bar in Jersey City. It was a go-go joint.

"All four of us are in there, giving the girls money. They

were dancing naked on the bar. And I'm begging this one trooper to take us over to Forty-second Street. He was a little nervous about it, afraid he might get caught. But I said, 'Come on. Look at me. I'm nineteen. I'm locked up all day with nothing to do. This is the only chance I got.'

"So he gives in, and we go to Forty-second Street. I told them I would pay for everybody's blow job once we got there. The one trooper says, 'No, no.' And my brother, he was drunk, too, but he says, 'Nah.' But the other trooper and me were so drunk, we both wanted to. He was up for it.

"We pull up to this corner and there's about eight hookers standing there. We pull the car a little into this alley and two of the hookers come over. My brother and the other trooper get out of the car. I'm in the back seat. The drunken trooper's in the front seat. He gives my brother Tommy his badge and his gun. One hooker gets in the back and the other gets in the front.

"I see my brother stick the gun in his pants and the badge in his back pocket. Him and the other trooper are gonna stand guard at the alleyway while we're with these hookers in the car. Ten minutes later, we get out and there's my brother Tommy, waving the gun and the badge at all the other hookers who were standing there. He's saying, 'All of youse, up against the wall. Youse are all under arrest.' Then he drops the gun on the ground.

"The other trooper goes running over. 'Yo, Tommy. Come on. You're gonna get us all in trouble.' Tommy didn't know what he was doing and these hookers, they didn't know what to think. Here's this drunk waving a badge and a gun at them. What a night.

"We finally got Tommy back in the car and we headed back home, back to the safe house. We got in about five o'clock in the morning. The other troopers wanted to know where we were all that time. We told 'em we went out for a few drinks after the races, and then stopped for breakfast."

———

The encounter on Forty-second Street was the first of two occasions when state police detectives would permit one of the DelGiornos to have sex with a prostitute. The other occurred in a hotel near Paterson, New Jersey.

Tommy Del and three state police detectives were returning to the safe house and had stopped for dinner in a restaurant lounge on the first floor of the hotel. It was February 10, 1987. That morning Tommy DelGiorno had made his debut as a government witness, testifying against Scarfo at a bail hearing in U.S. District Court in Philadelphia. The judge in the case denied Scarfo's request for bail after Tommy Del fingered him as the boss of the Philadelphia branch of La Cosa Nostra and as a gangster who had orchestrated—and bragged about— more than a dozen mob murders.

DelGiorno and his state police guardians were in a euphoric mood. Scarfo, who had literally gotten away with murder for almost twenty years, was now on the defensive. Finally, it looked like the good guys were going to win.

Over dinner, Tommy caught the eye of a woman drinking alone at the bar. She seemed to like him. He clearly liked her. For one-hundred dollars she told him she'd show him how much she cared.

The state police looked the other way. But defense attorneys eventually learned of the liaison and tried to use it to discredit both the state police and Tommy Del whenever he took the witness stand in the criminal trials that followed.

"At first I said no," Tommy Del testified, "but then I gave in to my weakness."

"So the state police provided you with a prostitute, is that correct?" one lawyer would ask incredulously.

"How much did you have to pay for this momentary devotion?" another would say, his voice dripping with sarcasm and disdain.

Then Robert Madden, a former Assistant U.S. Attorney who represented several of the mobsters DelGiorno helped convict, would move in for the verbal kill. Madden would get

DelGiorno to explain in detail the circumstances surrounding the encounter. Then he would get him to acknowledge that all the time he lived in protective custody—including the time he was in bed with the prostitute—would be applied against any jail sentence he eventually received. At that point, Madden would look at the jury and ask Tommy Del, "Is this what you would call doing hard time?"

Prosecutors could do nothing but weather the legal storm. The three troopers who were guarding Tommy Del that night were each suspended for a year after the incident was uncovered. But the encounter with the hooker surfaced every time DelGiorno testified in court. Eventually, Tommy Del learned how to blunt the thrusts of the defense attorneys and turn the affair to his advantage.

"You think a hooker would be enough to get me to testify?" DelGiorno once asked a defense attorney who had implied that it was one of the reasons he was cooperating with authorities.

"I don't know, would it?" the lawyer replied.

"It woulda hadda been *some* hooker," shot back Tommy Del as the courtroom burst into laughter.

———

Landing Tommy DelGiorno as a witness had been an investigative coup for the State Police Organized Crime Intelligence Unit. It was, in retrospect, the seminal event in the destruction of the Scarfo organized crime family. But the bumbling that marked the five months the DelGiornos lived in state police custody quickly overshadowed the investigative work that brought Tommy Del into the fold.

State police authorities were publicly embarrassed by the disclosure that three of the troopers who had been assigned to guard Tommy Del had also pimped for him. And they were humiliated a few weeks later when DelGiorno reported that seventy-four thousand dollars in cash had disappeared from the blue gym bag he kept hidden in his closet in the safe house.

At first, Bobby and Tommy junior were the prime suspects.

Over their loud and vociferous objections, they were forced to take lie-detector tests. Once they were cleared, suspicion shifted to a member of the guard detail. That's when Bobby learned that even a guy with a badge could be a crook.

One of the troopers who worked the security detail was eventually arrested and charged with stealing the money. A fifteen-year police veteran, he was convicted and sentenced to five years in prison, ironically, the same jail term that Tommy Del would eventually receive for his years of murder and mayhem.

"I am shocked and saddened at this turn of events," Clinton Pagano, then superintendent of the state police, said the day the arrest was announced. "The action of this trooper is a disappointment."

But for Bobby and Tommy junior disappointment didn't begin to describe it. For the two boys, it was becoming more and more difficult to tell the good guys from the bad guys. There were some troopers they genuinely liked. Others they respected. But their experience with law enforcement as an institution led them to the belief that the whole system was twisted. The end justified the means. The investigators and the prosecutors handling their father weren't interested in honor or justice. What they wanted were convictions. Tommy Del, a liar and a cheat all his life, a guy who was once a target of these same law enforcement officials, was now their star witness. He had once been a hit man for the mob on the streets of South Philadelphia. Now he was shooting for the government from the witness stand. All that mattered, in either case, was that he get the job done.

In April of 1987, the DelGiornos were transferred from state to federal custody. At that point, they began living under the protection of the Federal Bureau of Investigation. There would be no more prostitutes. No more ski trips.

But there was plenty of golf.

And lots of booze.

"The FBI turned our tragedy into their vacation," Bobby said. "They were more worried about making par than protecting us."

Chapter Fifteen

While Tommy Del and his family lived in relative comfort in state police and then FBI custody, Little Nicky Scarfo rotted in jail. The flamboyant mob boss was arrested on January 7, 1987, at the Atlantic City Airport in Pomona, New Jersey, as he returned from a New Year's holiday stay in Fort Lauderdale. Scarfo, who had posted bail following his indictment in November in the New Jersey gambling and racketeering case, was picked up on federal charges of conspiracy to commit extortion in the Penns Landing waterfront development scheme. Additional federal, state, and city charges would follow. This time, there would be no bail.

Tommy Del had outlined it all for the feds. So had Nick Caramandi. "The Crow" began singing to the FBI a few days after Tommy Del went into hiding with the state police. Convinced that Scarfo planned to kill him for botching the Penns Landing shakedown, Caramandi called the FBI from his prison cell and was whisked away to a government safe house. Eventually, he joined DelGiorno on the witness stand. Together they would testify at a series of trials that rocked the Philadelphia underworld and resulted in the convictions and prison sentences of more than fifty mob members and associates.

Scarfo's arrest at the airport was the beginning of all that. The fifty-eight-year-old mob boss, tanned and neatly dressed as he walked off the plane, would never again visit the home that he loved in Florida, never again sail out on the cabin cruiser that he cherished, never again walk the Boardwalk in the city where he was once king. Denied bail, he would spend the next two years being ferried between his prison cell and various courtrooms where he would be tried for racketeering, conspiracy, drug dealing and twice for murder.

Each time, Tommy Del was there to point the finger at him.

DelGiorno's debut as a witness came at the February bail hearing in Philadelphia. And his first public mea culpa was in March when he appeared in New Jersey Superior Court in Mays Landing to enter a guilty plea to the racketeering charges that were pending there. The plea formalized the agreement he had reached with the New Jersey Attorney General's Office to cooperate and testify against his former mob cohorts. It also set the stage for a more detailed plea bargain his lawyer had arranged with the feds involving five murders and one attempted murder.

DelGiorno, appearing none the worse for wear after ninety days in hiding, showed up in court that Friday morning dressed like the high roller he used to be. He wore a neatly tailored, double-breasted charcoal gray blazer, light gray slacks, white shirt and dark blue tie. He occasionally glanced around the empty courtroom, but his expression was one of curiosity rather than concern.

Several burly state troopers were positioned along the walls and near the doors. There was also a contingent of Atlantic County sheriff's deputies. All were armed. Tommy was a prize and no one was taking any chances. Barry Goas, the deputy attorney general who headed up the squad that had been debriefing DelGiorno, represented the state. Gerard P. Egan, a young Philadelphia lawyer and former member of the U.S.

Attorney's Office for the Eastern District of Pennsylvania, was Tommy's defense attorney. The hearing lasted about twenty minutes, just long enough for Goas to outline the state's case against DelGiorno and describe some of the details of his cooperating agreement. Tommy Del sat quietly at the defense table, conferring once or twice with Egan. When it was time for him to enter his plea, he rose and faced Superior Court Judge Paul Porreca. The case was based on hundreds of hours of wiretapped conversations recorded in the Ocean Colony condominium. While it centered on gambling, sports betting and bookmaking, the formal charge was racketeering. The judge asked DelGiorno what his definition of that term was.

"Loan-sharking, gambling, drugs, extortion, Your Honor," Tommy replied.

"What role did you play in those events?" Porreca then asked.

"Your Honor, I did it all," he said.

At that point, March 27, 1987, Tommy Del had been doing it all for about twenty-five years.

Tommy Del had gotten his bravado back when he decided to become a cooperating witness. Now, instead of the mob, he had the FBI and the New Jersey State Police to back up his swagger. And so he reverted to form, talking tough and acting smart. But this time he was cast in a different role. Now he was a witness instead of a wiseguy. In fact, a federal prosecutor would say that at the time, DelGiorno was the most important witness in the history of law enforcement's battle against the Philadelphia mob. As a former capo in an organized crime family, he was also one of the highest-ranking mob figures in America ever to break the Mafia's time-honored code of silence.

The Scarfo organization would pay dearly for DelGiorno's decision to testify. But then, so would the federal government. While the New Jersey State Police had run up a tab of about

$140,000, the feds would spend more than twice that amount caring for DelGiorno and his family over the next two years.

"I remember when we first went with the FBI," Bobby said. "They were way different than the [state police] troopers. They were more relaxed and laid back, as if nothing was gonna happen. We moved to Virginia Beach. My father had a choice, either to rent a house or buy it and keep the rent. So that's what he did. He bought a house for $160,000. I think he paid cash for it. . . . It was in a development, real nice. Like a house in the Jersey suburbs. Four bedrooms, a kitchen, dining room, den, two-car garage. And he put a $23,000 pool in the back yard—diving board, cement all around. We hated mowing the lawn, so he cemented most of the back yard. Really nice. All together, it was over $180,000.

"So the FBI was giving him $1,500-a-month rent. That was going into my father's pocket because he owned the house. That was our safe house. The FBI had a condo about two miles away from us. They were guarding us. If anything had happened, they'd of seen it in the papers or heard about it on the news. It was like their vacation. They stayed at a condo with a pool and tennis courts. Everybody used to fight to go on our detail, cause that's where they would stay. Two people used to be on the detail for a week at a time.

"A couple of the agents loved to golf. They used to get my father and go golfing three or four times a week. This was between times when he wasn't back in Philly testifying.

"They also paid all our bills. Phone bills. Electric bills. Everything. Cars. We had three cars. Oldsmobiles. Leased. Me and my brother each had a Cierra. My father had a bigger car. The Olds 98, I think. All the insurance was paid. And my father got $600-a-week allowance on top of the rent and paying all the bills. He was doing all right, my father. I think he was actually saving money. He was really soaking the FBI.

"He'd go golfing or he'd go to the driving range. The agents would stop by a couple times a week to check up on us or to take him golfing and then sometimes they'd go out drinking at night. Sometimes he'd go with them. And once in awhile, me and my brother would go. . . . My father would get drunk and talk his shit, about what he used to do and this and that. . . . I used to love to hear those stories, but now it bothered me. Here he was a rat. All my life he taught me not to rat, and now he's ratting and he's still got the balls to talk about all these gangster stories. The killings and all the money he used to make.

"So for being a murderer and everything else he did, he was treated pretty good. . . . But me and my brother, Tommy, we were gettin' sick of it."

Shortly after being relocated to Virginia Beach, the simmering resentment that the two boys had been trying to control flashed into the open.

Tommy Del, Bobby, Tommy junior and two FBI agents had gone out for drinks at a local restaurant. As they sat around talking, the discussion, as it usually did, reverted back to South Philadelphia and the plays and players in the Scarfo organization. On this night Tommy Del was talking about the day Bobby almost got shot, recounting the tale of the three hit men who followed him up Broad Street when he was driving his father's car. Bobby knew the details intimately. But Tommy junior had never heard the whole story. As the talk continued, one of the FBI agents confirmed what Bobby and his father had suspected, "Nicky Whip" Milano was believed to be one of the gunmen who had been assigned to kill Tommy Del.

With that out on the table, Tommy junior flipped out. Bobby realized right away what was going through his brother's mind. He thought back to the incident at the J&M Bar when Tommy Del had thrown Nicky Whip in Tommy junior's face. "This is a real son" Tommy Del had said that night in the same liquor-slurred voice he was using now. Bobby could still see the nasty grin on his father's face as he put his arm around Milano. And he remembered vividly how his older brother had fought to hold back the tears as his father publicly humiliated him in front of a bar filled with wiseguys.

"My brother tended to argue with my father all the time anyway," Bobby said. "So this time, when they get on the subject of Nicky Whip, my brother just stood up and says, 'Now where's your fuckin' son? Your fuckin' son was gonna kill ya.' And then he just walked out of the restaurant and went back to the house.

"My father just, like, stooped down in his chair. He didn't know what to say. He acted like he didn't know what Tommy meant, but he knew."

———————

If Bobby and Tommy junior were a headache to the state police, they became a migraine to the FBI. The two boys hated their confinement and, as their relationship with their father deteriorated, they began to openly question what they were doing there. Tommy junior took some solace in the fact that the feds had permitted his fiancée, Chrissy, to go into hiding with him. They were now living together in the house in Virginia Beach. But Tommy still got into an argument almost every time he talked with his father, and it quickly became evident to everyone that the situation could not continue.

Bobby looked elsewhere for relief from the tension and pressure. He started to frequent clubs and bars in the area, drinking and carousing and occasionally getting into fights. He found it difficult to make new friends. "I was always worried about slipping and using my real name," he said. "We all had new identities. And I felt like I wasn't really myself. . . . What I really wanted to do was go home. I just wanted to be back with my friends in South Philadelphia."

And so he did.

He would take off on a Friday afternoon, telling his father and the FBI, if they bothered to ask, that he was staying with a friend in Virginia Beach or Norfolk and that they'd be partying all weekend. Then he'd drive for six hours and pull up in front of the home of one of his friends from the old neighborhood. Anthony Forline always knew when Bobby was coming.

He'd let him know in advance. But Bobby would have to crash somewhere else, usually at Mark Pop's house because Anthony lived on Gladstone Street and Bobby's presence there would attract too much attention.

The trips to Philadelphia helped Bobby cope with his situation, but they also intensified his longing to return home permanently. He and his friends would go out drinking Friday night into Saturday morning and for that brief period of time it was like he'd never left. But Bobby would always leave the next day. He didn't want to push his luck, nor did he want to risk drawing his friends into a confrontation with the mob. While Scarfo and more than a dozen other major mob figures were behind bars awaiting trial, there were still plenty of their associates out and about, along with a group of younger wannabe gangsters—the sons, brothers and cousins of made members of the organization who would like nothing better than to make an example of a DelGiorno, any DelGiorno.

Periodically, Bobby would also manage to see his mother, stepfather and grandparents. Sometimes he'd slip into the house on Gladstone Street or into his grandmother's home on Snyder Avenue. During the summer months, he'd drive over to the campground near the Jersey shore where Maryann and Joe had a trailer. Maryann loved those visits best. She would arrange for Bobby's friends to come down for a barbecue. Joe would fire up the grill and load it with hotdogs and hamburgers. Cans of beer would be chilling in a cooler and Maryann would sit in a lounge chair and just watch as Bobby and his friends sat for hours laughing and joking and telling stories.

Maryann knew the boys were a little wild. They had, after all, grown up on the streets of South Philly. Bobby was not a Rhodes scholar, nor were any of his friends. He wasn't cut out to be a doctor or a lawyer. She didn't kid herself about his potential. She never made the argument that his father held him down, that without Tommy Del he would have gone on to college or law school. She knew that wasn't the case. But Maryann also knew Bobby's heart. He might get into fights and raise some hell, he might drive you crazy with his antics, but he wasn't a gangster. He wasn't ruthless.

All she wanted was for her boys to have a chance. Tommy Del, and now the federal government, had taken that away. So she took what little she could out of the secret visits Bobby—and then Tommy junior—would make. And she lived on the dream and the hope that someday they would be back with her in South Philadelphia.

"One time we were all down the campground," Maryann said. "Bobby was there with a bunch of his friends. And we see this car, a big black car, driving up the street, looking at the numbers on all the trailers. There's two men in suits and they stop in front of my trailer. I go out and they say, 'We're here for the body.' My heart starts pounding. Bobby's hiding inside the trailer. Joe comes out.

"Turns out they were from a funeral parlor. There had been a death at another trailer in the campground, the address was similar to ours, and they had gotten the numbers mixed up.

"We all laughed about it later, but at the time I was a nervous wreck."

———————

While Maryann worried and agonized about her sons, her former husband became a fixture in newspaper headlines, testifying at a dozen trials that, over the next two years, would destroy the Scarfo organized crime family. But while he was hailed as a star witness by prosecutors, Bobby and Tommy junior saw him as little more than a rat who, in saving his own neck, was destroying their lives. Their argument, of course, was rather simplistic, but the two boys had a very narrow, self-centered perspective. What they saw was their father being paid to testify. The cars, the house, the golf trips, the bar tabs were all part of that payoff. Debriefing sessions in which Tommy Del would go over his testimony were, to Bobby and Tommy junior, coaching sessions where their father was told what to say and how to say it.

All of this, of course, would be disputed by the federal government. Tommy Del was a crucial and important witness, prosecutors and FBI agents would argue. But he was not told what to say. His deal with the government was to testify honestly and completely. There was no promise of a payoff. Nor were there any guarantees.

A succinct explanation for the reason the government cuts a deal with someone like Tommy DelGiorno was once given by the former federal attorney who had successfully prosecuted Panamanian dictator Manuel Noriega. The attorney had used the testimony of a number of admitted drug traffickers and international lowlifes to win the case. "Swans don't swim in sewers," he said, explaining that these kinds of people were the only ones in a position to know about the inner workings of the Noriega organization.

Joel Friedman, head of the federal government's Organized Crime Strike Force in Philadelphia, said the same thing about DelGiorno and the sewer that was the Scarfo crime family. "Indisputably, DelGiorno was engaged in grave criminal conduct, for profit, for a long time," Friedman wrote in a sentencing memorandum. "While he undoubtedly harmed society substantially by this conduct, his involvement positioned him to be able to be of great assistance to law enforcement. The reality of real world law enforcement is that without the cooperation of deeply involved individuals such as DelGiorno, it is extremely difficult to make significant progress against entrenched criminal organizations like the Mafia."

Given their different philosophies and perspectives, it is not hard to understand why the two DelGiorno boys did not get along with their federal keepers.

"They were nothing but spoiled brats and crybabies," one agent said of Bobby and his brother.

"Yeah, and *they* were assholes with badges," Bobby says in reply.

———

Six months after the move to Virginia Beach, Tommy junior's relationship with his father was worse than ever, and he broached the idea of returning to South Philadelphia. The two boys were having lunch at a local restaurant when Tommy laid his plan on the table. What if they followed their own father's example and ratted him out.

"To who?" Bobby asked.

Tommy, who had obviously been mulling the idea over for quite a while, said it was simple. He'd volunteer to testify for the defense in the big racketeering trial that was coming up. He'd tell the jury all about their father, the money he was being paid, the way he was being rehearsed and the fact that he still had a gun and had talked about "going back to the old ways" if things didn't work out.

While Bobby wanted nothing better than to get back to South Philadelphia, he didn't understand how that would help them. But Tommy said he'd only be willing to testify if they had an agreement that no one would bother them once the trial was over. He suggested that they could get that arrangement by contacting one of the mob defense lawyers.

"Our deal will be we just want to be left alone," Tommy said, "so that we won't have to worry about being killed for something our father did."

"What guarantee do we have?" Bobby asked. "How do we know they'll keep their promise? They might kill us anyway."

"If my testimony helps them win the case and get off, they'll appreciate it," Tommy said, perhaps somewhat naively. "What chance do they have now?"

In fact, with Tommy Del, Nicky Crow and a dozen other witnesses, the federal government was building what eventually would prove to be an airtight case against the Scarfo crime family under the Racketeer Influenced and Corrupt Organizations Act. Designed to incorporate the operations of a criminal organization as part of a conspiracy charge, the so-called RICO statute had become a major weapon in the war against the mob. Federal prosecutors in Philadelphia planned to use it against Scarfo and sixteen other members of his organization, including his nephew and underboss, Philip Leonetti; the brothers Salvatore and Lawrence Merlino; Faffy Iannarella; and most of the other major figures in the South Philadelphia mob.

Bobby listened while his brother laid out the details of his plan over lunch that afternoon. Bobby was hesitant, but he didn't know how to back away once Tommy junior made the proposal. It was Tommy's fiancée, Chrissy, however, who slowed things down. Back at the house, the boys brought her into a conversation about their plan. Chrissy, they realized, was the most objective of the three of them. She had chosen to follow Tommy into hiding and could look at the situation without the emotional baggage that Bobby and Tommy junior carried.

"Chrissy wondered about whether we could trust anybody," Bobby said. "She said it wasn't just the mob we ought to be concerned about. She said we'd have to worry about the federal government too, if Tommy testified for the defense. So after that, we just decided to forget about it for awhile. Actually, I was happy she talked my brother out of it. I knew if he wanted to do it, I would back him one hundred percent, but I was worried. I thought too many things could go wrong."

With that, the boys went back to their life in hiding. Each was now working at a job at the nearby Norfolk Naval Base. The feds had managed to get them attached to a civilian work crew. They answered phones, did some office work and, for a while, Bobby drove a forklift.

Tommy junior would do his job, go home and spend his time with Chrissy. He could no longer stand to be with his father and made little attempt to socialize with the rest of the family. Both he and Bobby loved their half brothers, Danny and Michael, but the strain and tension of their make-believe existence made it impossible to lead a normal life.

Bobby would live from paycheck to paycheck, hitting clubs and bars in the Norfolk–Virginia Beach area during the week and sneaking back to South Philadelphia at least once and sometimes twice a month. As he had done earlier with the state police, he decided that his only satisfaction would come from making life miserable for his father and the feds. So he ignored their warnings about trips home. They had begun to suspect what he was doing, but Bobby didn't care. He was entitled to his recreation the same way his father and the FBI agents were entitled to theirs. When they stopped going to the golf course, he said, he'd stop going to South Philadelphia.

"They really didn't care about us," Bobby said. "It was all a joke. They didn't want to be bothered. And my father, he was either away testifying or, when he was home he was drinking or playing golf.

"One time, my father was up in Philly testifying and they had one agent on the detail watching us. So he asks me if I wanna go golfing. So I said I don't golf, but I offered to go with him. I was his caddy, carrying his clubs like a real jerkoff. He's got his beeper on the golf bag I'm carrying. We get to the ninth hole and it goes off. He wasn't golfing very well and he was really aggravated. So he says, 'God damn it.' And he tells me to check and see what number it is. I look and I tell him it's our number, the house number in Virginia Beach.

"He says, 'Damn it. I'm right in the middle of a game.' And he tells me, he gives me a quarter, and he tells me to run back to the clubhouse and call and see what's the matter.

"It took ten minutes to get all the way back to the clubhouse. I get there and I call home and Roe answers. I ask what's the matter and she says they just got a crank phone call. Somebody asked, 'Is Tom there?' and then they hung up. She was a little panicky. I could understand it. She was worried somebody knew where we were living. You know, she's there all alone with Danny and Michael.

"So she asks for the agent. And I have to tell her he's still out on the golf course, that he sent me to call her. She tells me to get him on the phone. So I run all the way back out there and tell him what happened and that my stepmother wants to talk to him.

"And he goes, 'It's probably some guy with a wrong number.' He's acting really mad that somebody is interrupting his game. But he walks back to the clubhouse and calls Roe on the phone. And he's trying to calm her down. I hear him telling her it's probably just a wrong number and to relax. And I can tell from what he's saying that Roe is really mad.

"But then when he gets off the phone, instead of going back to the house, he says, 'Come on, let's finish the game.' And he goes back out and plays the other nine holes. . . . Nothing was wrong, but God forbid, if something was wrong, we woulda been out on the golf course. That's how much they cared.

"They used to live at the condo, five minutes from the house. And they'd say call us if there's any problem. Like if the mob sent some hit man, he was gonna let us make a phone call."

———————

Encouraged by a few agents who loved the sport, Tommy Del became an avid golf enthusiast during that first year in hiding. He not only went out and played nearly every day, but he and the agents talked incessantly about their games and about some of the great courses in the country. Eventually, Bobby said, they managed to mix business with pleasure at federal expense.

"My father really got into golf. And this one time we were sitting at the table in Virginia Beach and two of the agents were over for dinner. And they're talking about all these nice courses they've played on, in Dallas, Texas, in Charleston, South Carolina, and some other spots. And my father mentions that he wants to go look for a permanent place to live, this is for when he's done testifying. And where do you think he says he wants to visit? Dallas, Charleston, all the spots the agents had just been mentioning. And so they took him. He got the okay from the squad supervisor to make this trip to look for a spot to live, but really he and the agents were just going to play golf on those courses. That's what he told me afterwards. They didn't go look at houses, they went to play golf and pass some time. And the agents went right along with it. It was a vacation."

Bobby, on the other hand, continued his getaway weekends to South Philadelphia. One Friday night early in March of 1988, he and a group of friends found themselves in a nightclub in Northeast Philadelphia. Before Bobby knew it, he and his friends became embroiled in a fight over a girl. She had been coming on to Bobby's friend Mark Pop despite the attention's of another young man, the son of the club's owner.

"At first, Mark walked away from the guy," Bobby said. "But I could tell that he only did that because I was there, and he was worried about me getting in trouble. So I says, 'What's the matter, Mark? I'm away for a year and you turn into a pussy?' That's all he needed to hear, because then he knew it was all right with me. He just wanted me to give him the okay.

"So there was about six of us and this guy, the owner's son, a young guy who thought he was a gangster or something, he had about eight guys around him. Mark goes back over to the guy who's talking to this girl and he says, 'Heh, asshole, let me ask you something. You think if I hit you right now, we'd all get our asses kicked?' The guy laughs, really cocky, and says, 'You sure would.' And Mark says to him, 'Well, guess what. You ain't gonna see any of it.' And he punches the guy right in the head. Knocks him out."

With that the place erupted. Bar stools flew. Punches and bodies went flying across the room. Bobby ended up with a broken nose. Everyone else was bruised and bloodied.

"We got beat up pretty good," Bobby said later.

After about ten minutes, order was restored by some of the older guys in the bar. Bobby and his friends were asked to leave.

"But Mark was still pissed off," Bobby said. "He had lost this gold chain. Somebody ripped it off his neck during the fight. It was worth about three-hundred bucks. So right near my car is this cinder block . . ."

Bobby and his friends piled into his car and drove around to the front of the nightclub. They stopped in front of a large bay window. Mark got out of the car.

"He had the cinder block. He lifted it over his head with both hands and then he just tossed it through the window. All you heard was this big crash. . . . Then Mark stood there for a couple of seconds and gave the whole bar the finger. He just stood there holding his middle finger up in the air."

With Bobby and the others screaming at him to move, Mark finally jumped back in the car. Bobby gunned it and sped down to South Philadelphia and the safety of the neighborhood.

Less than twenty-four-hours later, Bobby was back in Virginia Beach. Word of the bar fight and cinder block, however, got there before him. When he walked into the house, his father and two FBI agents were sitting at the kitchen table. One of the agents asked where he had been. Bobby said he was at a friend's house near Norfolk.

"You're a fucking liar," Tommy Del screamed.

"We checked, Bob, you weren't there all weekend," one of the agents said in a calm but stern tone. "We know you haven't been there for the past three weekends."

Bobby heard the agent, but decided to respond to his father.

"Who are you to call anybody a fuckin' liar," he said.

"And who are you," he said to the agent, "to tell me who I can see and where I can go? I'm not the criminal here. I'm not under arrest." Then he pointed toward his father and said, "He is. But he does whatever he wants and no one says shit to him."

The argument lasted about twenty minutes with the two agents trying to calm down both Tommy Del and Bobby. The agents, clearly fed up with Bobby's escapades, nevertheless tried to explain that it was his safety they were concerned about. The Philadelphia office had gotten a call. Bobby was being spotted more and more frequently. It was only a matter of time before one of Scarfo's friends would hear about it.

But Bobby wasn't buying into the explanation.

"You think I'm stupid," he said to the agent. "You don't care what happens to me. You're just worried that you'll look bad if it happens while the FBI is supposed to be guarding me."

With that, Bobby got up and walked out of the kitchen. He headed upstairs for his brother's bedroom. Tommy junior was the only person he could talk to. But when he got there, the room was empty. All the furniture was gone. And so were Tommy and Chrissy.

This led to another shouting match in the kitchen. This time it was Bobby asking the questions and the feds refusing to answer. At first they wouldn't tell him where Tommy junior and Chrissy had gone. Then they said there had been another big fight between Tommy Del and Tommy junior. Afterward, Tommy junior had insisted on moving out. The FBI agreed to relocate him. He and Chrissy were now living somewhere else.

"Where?" Bobby said.

"We can't tell you."

"Give me the phone number so I can call him."

"We can't do that either."

"If you don't put me in touch with my brother," Bobby said in a cold, clear and strangely calm voice, "I'm calling the *Philadelphia Daily News*. And tomorrow there'll be a story in the paper about where we're living and what my father's been doing."

Chrissy and Tommy junior were living on their own in the Lancaster, Pennsylvania, area. It was Pennsylvania Dutch Country, rolling green fields and horse buggies, windmills and barns, men with beards and women in bonnets. Bobby called that night. Tommy said he couldn't take it anymore. He was tired of fighting with his father. He was tired of the lies and the deception. He and Chrissy were going to start over. He asked Bobby to move in with them.

Two days later, Bobby drove to Lancaster to check it out.

He wanted to get away from his father, but once he saw the bucolic countryside, he knew that wasn't the answer. He and Tommy junior talked it over. Bobby frankly admitted that life in Lancaster wasn't for him. He knew if he lived there, he'd be driving back to South Philadelphia all the time. He worried that he might be spotted, followed, and end up leading the mob right to his brother and Chrissy.

They talked about different places where Bobby might be more comfortable. Then they got out a map and began looking for spots near both Philadelphia and Lancaster so that Bobby could live on his own, but still be close enough to stay in contact with his friends and family.

The next day Bobby drove back to Virginia Beach. He told the FBI he wanted to be relocated like his brother. He had a list of demands. He wanted a job, a furnished apartment with the first four months rent paid and a phone installed. He said he wanted to keep the FBI-leased car he was driving. And he said he wanted to take his clothes, his money and the rest of his belongings. He said he wanted to be on his own, to start a new life the same way his brother had. But he didn't want to move to Lancaster.

He said he had found a better place, a place where he thought he would feel more at home and where it would be easier to fit in.

He said he wanted to move to Baltimore.

Chapter Sixteen

When Tommy DelGiorno and Nick Caramandi agreed to cooperate late in 1986, they became the seeds for the biggest racketeering investigation in Philadelphia history. Federal authorities called it "Operation Harvest Time."

Throughout 1987, FBI agents, Philadelphia homicide detectives and investigators with the New Jersey and Pennsylvania State Police pooled their resources and, at least temporarily, put aside interagency squabbles to build a RICO case that everyone hoped would bring down the Scarfo organization.

Prosecutors knew that a key defense strategy would be to attack the credibility of DelGiorno and Caramandi who, by the time they took the witness stand, had openly admitted their own involvement in a series of murders, extortions, drug deals, shakedowns and bribes to union officials and politicos. For that reason, every piece of hard, physical evidence that would support their story was important.

In January of 1988 a federal grand jury handed up its indictment in the Harvest Time case. The eighty-eight-page document outlined the operations of a criminal enterprise that spanned the bloodiest decade in Philadelphia underworld history. Scarfo headed a list of defendants that included the entire hierarchy of his organization. Among the others charged in the case were Scarfo's nephew and underboss, Philip Leonetti; his former underboss, Salvatore "Chuckie" Merlino; mob capos Joe Ciancaglini and Frank "Faffy" Iannarella; and nearly a dozen mob soldiers, including Sal Grande, Charlie Iannece, Gino Milano, Larry Merlino and Joey Pungitore. There were also seven unindicted coconspirators named in the case. All had been major mob figures in Philadelphia. All were now dead. They were Angelo Bruno; Antonio "Tony Bananas" Caponigro; Phil Testa; Frank Monte; Frank "Chickie" Narducci; Sal Testa; and Pasquale "Pat the Cat" Spirito.

The racketeering acts listed in the indictment tracked the life and times of Nicodemo Scarfo, perhaps the most violent Mafia boss in America. They included extortions, shakedowns, drug scams, loan-sharking, bookmaking, numbers writing, ten murders and four attempted murders. By the time the indictment was announced, most of the Scarfo mob was already behind bars. Scarfo himself had been convicted seven months earlier of conspiracy to commit extortion in the Penns Landing shakedown. A Philadelphia city councilman and his legislative aide, both charged in connection with the mob shakedown, were found guilty in a separate trial. There were also two murder cases pending, each brought by the Philadelphia District Attorney's Office. In one, Scarfo and eight associates were charged with the murder of Salvie Testa. In the other, Scarfo and eight codefendants, some of whom were also named in the Testa case, were accused of killing Frankie Flowers. In fact, less than a month after the grand jury leveled its Harvest Time charges, Scarfo and his codefendants were sitting in Common Pleas Court in Philadelphia helping their attorneys pick a jury for the Salvie Testa murder trial. By April, when Bobby moved to Baltimore, the trial was already under way and his father was about to take the witness stand.

"When I first told the FBI I wanted to move to Baltimore, they agreed," Bobby said. "But then they dragged their feet. The agent who was supposed to be arranging it said he was too busy with other things. They had this big trial going on in Philadelphia, a murder trial, and he couldn't get to it. They would tell me they were looking for a place for me and a job, but they were just buying time. They didn't want any problems while the trial was going on. They wanted everything to go smooth."

Bobby, on the other hand, wanted out. He was convinced the FBI would not act without a push, so, in typical fashion, he decided to shove. He drove to Baltimore on his own and began looking for apartments. He cruised around several different neighborhoods and finally settled on an area in the southeast corner of the city, not far from the waterfront. The newspapers would later refer to the area as Highlandtown, but several residents called it Canton. It didn't matter to Bobby. All he knew was that it reminded him of South Philadelphia.

The neighborhood was a complete package. He could walk out his front door and be surrounded by the city. The streets were lined with row houses. There were stores, bars and restaurants on the corners. A Catholic church, Saint Casimir's, was a block away. Although Bobby wasn't much for going to mass, he thought it would be nice to hear church bells on Sunday morning again. It would be like Gladstone Street and the bells from Our Lady of Mount Carmel.

"I was tired of having to get in the car and drive everywhere. When we lived in Virginia Beach, you had to get in the car to go to the store. In Baltimore, everything was right there. The houses were all on top of each other. It was what I was used to. There was a laundromat, a liquor store, a pizza parlor and two bars within a block. There was a grocery store right across the street. Everything was right outside my door. It was great. I thought I could be myself again."

Bobby negotiated the rent himself. He didn't have a job, so he faked his employment references. He covered that, however, with an offer to pay four months rent in advance. In cash. By April 1, 1988, he had the apartment, a two-story walkup in the twenty-nine-hundred block of O'Donnell Street. It included two bedrooms, a living room, kitchen and bath. The rent was $350 a month. Bobby's unit was in the middle of the block, part of a string of two-story brick row houses between South Curley Street and Linwood Avenue. The entrance to Bobby's apartment was on the side of the building, off a narrow alleyway that ran out to O'Donnell Street.

With the tacit approval of both his father and the FBI, Bobby began moving in during the second week in April. He made several trips from Virginia Beach to Baltimore, unloading boxes of his belongings, lugging them up the alleyway and into the apartment. He also called his mother and grandparents and told them the good news. They could come and visit him any time they wanted, he said. It was practically a straight line down Interstate 95 from Gladstone Street in South Philadelphia to O'Donnell Street in Baltimore. Bobby had already clocked it. Without going over the speed limit, you could make the trip in under two hours.

Finally, on Saturday, April 16, he moved in for good. Anthony Forline, his oldest and best friend, drove down to help him unpack and set up. Bobby arrived first and waited outside in case Anthony had any trouble locating the address. As he stood on the sidewalk, he looked around his new neighborhood and decided he liked what he saw. The place felt right. When Anthony arrived an hour later he said the same thing. First he grabbed Bobby in a bear hug. Then he looked around and said, "Is this Baltimore, or South Philly? If somebody had blindfolded me and taken me here, I wouldn't be able to tell the difference."

"I know, Ant, it's great," Bobby said. "Come on in. Let me show you the apartment."

Bobby gave Anthony a quick tour, then suggested they drive down to the Inner Harbor, Baltimore's swank new tourist attraction, for some lunch and to catch up on old times, before returning to the apartment to unpack the boxes and set the place up. In less than fifteen minutes, they were sitting in a restaurant overlooking the harbor eating hamburgers. Bobby told Anthony he was tired of hiding, tired of lying. While he still had an assumed name, at least here he could be himself. He talked about getting a job. The FBI, he said, had lined up a couple of interviews for him for the following week. The feds were finally coming through. They had also given him a check to cover two months rent. Anthony talked about moving down to Baltimore and sharing the apartment with Bobby. It was a casual, leisurely lunch on a soft, spring afternoon full of prom-ise. It was a time to joke about the past and dream about the future. It was the fresh start Bobby wanted. And it was great, he thought, having a friend like Anthony there to help him get it going.

"We got back to my apartment about one o'clock in the afternoon. Anthony ran over to the liquor store and bought a case of Budweiser so we could have a few while we unpacked all my stuff. It took us about five hours, but it was worth it. The place looked great. Anthony was a lot neater than I was and made sure we set everything up right. By the time we were done, we were pretty drunk. Then we sat around talking about what we were gonna do that night. The Flyers were playing the Washington Capitols, but I didn't have cable yet, so we decided to find a bar where we could watch. It was a playoff game, and we didn't want to miss it.

"So we go upstairs to shower and change. There were two more bags up there that we forgot. While I'm in the shower, Anthony starts to unpack them. Then, as I'm getting out of the shower, I hear this clicking noise. I look in the bedroom and Anthony's got my gun out. I forgot it was in the bag. He says, 'Bob, where do you want me to put this?' He had the gun in one hand and a box of bullets in the other. Then he says, real serious, 'Would you ever use this gun on anyone?' I told him if someone was trying to kill me and I had no way out, I probably would. But I said a person could *say* anything. Until it came to the moment to make that decision, you would never really know.

"Anthony said he didn't think he could ever shoot somebody, no matter what. 'Just holding it in my hand makes me nervous,' he said. I took the gun, loaded it and then put it in a leather holster. Then I gave the holster to Anthony and asked him to hide it in the bottom of a shoe rack next to my bed. I always felt safe having a gun near me. It made me feel invincible."

While Anthony showered and dressed, Bobby went to check out the bar on the corner. It was a neighborhood tavern, like dozens of others he knew back in South Philadelphia. With his expensive leather jacket, neatly pressed pants and shirt and a large gold chain with a diamond encrusted "D" around his neck, Bobby was out of place the minute he walked in the door. The look he got from the barmaid, a pretty young blonde, told him as much. He asked if they had cable. The barmaid said no.

"Why are you staring at me like that?" Bobby asked.

"It's the way you're dressed," she said. "Nobody comes in here dressed like that. Are you from out of town?"

Before Bobby could answer, the barmaid shot him another question, this one with a harder edge.

"Are you a cop?"

"If I was a cop, would I be dumb enough to say, 'Yeah, I'm a cop,' " Bobby said. "But no, I'm not a cop. I just moved in two doors down. My apartment's up the alleyway."

With that a man in a business suit who had been standing at the other end of the bar walked over and introduced himself. His name was Eddie. The bar was Eddie's Lounge. Both Eddie and the barmaid smiled at Bobby and welcomed him to Baltimore. Then they got into a discussion about where he might find a cable television set. They suggested another bar, the Irish

Pub, about a block away. Bobby thanked them and headed for the door.

"Listen, if you can't find cable, come back here," the barmaid said. "This place jams on a Saturday night."

Bobby headed back to his apartment to fill Anthony in on the details. There was no cable at Eddie's Lounge, he said, but there was a pretty blonde barmaid. If they didn't find the Flyers game in another bar, Eddie's Lounge might be a good place to spend the night.

"How pretty is she?" Anthony asked.

"All blondes are pretty. Especially after you've been drinking beer all afternoon," Bobby said.

"We walked out of the apartment and out on O'Donnell Street we hear this screaming. We look over toward Eddie's Lounge and there's three guys kicking and punching another guy who's on the ground, laying on the sidewalk, yelling, 'Leave me alone. Leave me alone.' Anthony looks at me and says, 'Well, Bob, I guess you feel right at home now.' We walk over to the Irish Pub which turns out to be a real pit. Dirty floor. Ripped bar stools. And people who looked right at home in the place. Anthony says, 'Bob, I don't care if the drinks are free, I'm not staying here.' So that's how we end up back at Eddie's Lounge.

"Eddie says 'Hi' when we walk in and after we sit down at the bar, the barmaid comes over and says the first drinks are on her boss. I introduce Anthony to the barmaid. I tell her he's from Philadelphia and I'm from Virginia Beach. Already I made a mistake, because I wasn't supposed to mention Virginia Beach to anyone. But I was pretty drunk by that point. So I hand Anthony a fifty dollar bill and tell him to buy the whole bar drinks. He calls the barmaid back over. 'The whole bar?' she says. 'The whole bar,' Anthony says again with a smile. He was already working on getting her back to the apartment after the place closed. She smiles. 'That's a lot of money,' she says. I pat Anthony on the back and tell her, 'Don't worry. He's got lots of money.' "

For Bobby and Anthony this was nothing new. The sharp clothes, the smart talk, the flirting were all part of a routine they had perfected during dozens of Friday and Saturday nights in places just like this in Philadelphia and South Jersey. Slightly drunk and more at ease, they ordered another round of beers and soaked in the atmosphere. It felt like home. The only difference was they were alone. They didn't have Mark Pop or John GQ or any of the other guys from the neighborhood to back them up. Bobby stood just five foot six and weighed, at best, 150 pounds. Anthony was about 40 pounds heavier, but not much taller. In fact, Anthony had always been the peace-maker in the group, the most sensible and the least likely to fly off the handle. Neither was a barroom brawler. But Bobby had a mouth at least a foot taller than he was. It frequently got him in trouble.

Buying a round of drinks for the bar had loosened everyone up, made them all a lot friendlier. Several people stopped by to thank the two newcomers and to welcome them to town. Bobby and Anthony spent three more hours drinking beer, flirting with the barmaid and shooting an occasional game of pool. It seemed to be a good way for Bobby to open a new chapter in his life.

Then it got ugly.

––––––––

"About eleven o'clock, eleven-thirty, these three guys walk in and sit down at our end of the bar. They look familiar to me, but I'm pretty drunk and I can't place them. This one guy calls the barmaid over and then he turns, looks at me and says, 'What's your name?' I says, 'Bob, what's yours?' He says, 'Steve.' Then he asks where I'm from and I say Virginia Beach and he says, 'You don't sound like you're from down South. You sound like you're from New York.' I couldn't think for a second. I was trying to remember my story. So I told him I was born and raised in Philadelphia, but moved to Virginia Beach when my father got a job down there. I wanted to make the story close to the truth so I wouldn't forget it the next time I came into the bar and saw the same people. I didn't want to get caught in a lie.

"At first, this guy Steve was all right. We joked around a little bit. Then he calls the barmaid over and says, 'Give this asshole from Philly a drink on me.' But he laughs and says he's only kidding and tells the barmaid, 'Give my new buddy a drink.' So I didn't get mad. . . . Down the other end of the bar they had the news on the TV, so I asked the barmaid to ask if anybody had heard the score of the Flyers game. And this guy Steve says, 'The Flyers suck. The Capitols are gonna kill 'em.' And then he starts acting like a real jerk, trying to make me look like an ass in front of the barmaid."

True to form, Bobby's mouth worked quicker than his mind. He reached into his pocket, pulled out a twenty dollar bill and slapped it on the bar. "How bad do you like the Capitols?" he said. "Put your money up here and show me."

"I could tell from the look on his face that he didn't even follow hockey. He was just trying to get on my nerves. This was my way of making him shut up. Even the barmaid seemed to be fed up with him. 'Go ahead, Steve,' she said. 'You're all talk. You think you know everything. Bet the man twenty dollars.' Steve looks at me and says, 'What are you trying to do, hustle me? You probably already know the score.' But before I can even say anything, the barmaid tells him, 'That kid hasn't left his bar stool all night. How would he know the score?' "

There have been confrontations in bars over lesser events. Bobby and Anthony had been in more than a few. But it is hard to imagine something as inconsequential as an unanswered bar bet leading to murder. Filled with beer and bravado, Bobby pulled his twenty dollar bill back off the counter.

"Never mind," he said mockingly to the barmaid. "He doesn't want to bet."

Stephen Hemerlein stared coldly at Bobby, then smiled.

"Kid," he said, "you really have balls. Maybe it's because you're new around here and you don't know who the fuck I am."

With that he told the barmaid to give Bobby another drink, got up from his own stool and walked over and put his arm on Bobby's shoulder.

"You better be glad I like you," he said in a voice barely above a whisper, "because if I didn't, you'd be dead right now." Then he smiled and walked back to his own stool.

At that point, Bobby recognized him. He was one of the guys outside Eddie's Lounge earlier in the night kicking and stomping the guy on the sidewalk. Anthony, who had been shooting pool, made the same connection. He came over to ask about the confrontation, then told Bobby, "Just don't talk to that asshole anymore."

It was good advice, which Bobby promptly ignored.

Shortly after midnight, Hemerlein and his two friends got up to leave the bar. As they were buttoning their jackets, Hemerlein looked at Bobby and said, "I'll be back, asshole."

"I hope not, asshole," Bobby replied.

With that Hemerlein, who stood about five foot ten and weighed 180 pounds, lifted Bobby off his bar stool and slammed him up against a jukebox. Normally, this would be where Mark Pop would jump in and fists would start flying. Instead, Anthony moved in to break things up, but he was grabbed by Hemerlein's two friends.

"I got lucky because the owner came running over, grabbed this Steve and said, 'No fighting in the bar.' Steve says, 'I was just talkin' to him.' So Eddie says, 'You could talk all you want outside.' That's when Steve says, 'Come on Bob, just you and me, outside.' I look at Anthony and nod, trying to tell him to keep an eye on the other two guys. And then we walk outside. We're heading down the street and this guy's got his arm on my shoulder like he wants to talk to me. But when we get to the alleyway that leads to my apartment, he grabs me by the neck and starts knocking my head against the wall. He's dragging me up the alley. It's dark. You can barely see. And he's banging my head on one side of the alley and then the other, working his way down the alley toward the yard outside my apartment.

"Later, I find out his two friends followed us out of the bar, but we had already disappeared in the alley and they walked right past and down to the next corner. Anthony came out after them and he hears noise up the alley and comes running. . . . This guy Steve has me on the ground, choking me. It's only a matter of time before his two friends find us and then me and Anthony will get stomped like the guy on the sidewalk. So Anthony runs in the apartment and gets the gun.

"I'm trying to keep this guy from choking me to death. The next thing I hear Anthony holler, 'Get off of him. Get off of him.' I could hardly breathe. This guy turns toward Anthony and says 'Fuck you' and then jumps up and rushes toward Ant. I'm watching this in a daze, still trying to breathe and trying to see in the dark. I see Anthony backed up against the wall in the alleyway and him and Steve are grabbing and pulling at something. I see their shoulders moving up and down. And then I hear this loud bang and the guy's head looked like it exploded. There was blood everywhere.

"I jumped up faster than the guy could fall to the ground. He just slumped against the other alleyway wall and slid down. Anthony was just standing there, holding the gun, not saying anything. I yell to him, 'Ant, Ant, are you all right?' He says, 'He pulled the gun. It just went off. It just went off.'

"I couldn't see the guy's face because there was so much blood. I ran over and put my hands under his shoulders, trying to make him stand up, to walk. He was so heavy. I screamed to Anthony, 'Help me.' But Anthony was just standing there, staring, like he was in shock. I was dragging the body, trying to get him to walk, to say something. Finally, Anthony snapped out of it. 'Bob,' he said, 'tell me he's not dead. Tell me he's not dead.' I put the body down. I was soaked in blood. 'He's dead, Ant,' I said. 'He's dead. We got to get out of here before his friends come.'

"But Anthony just leaned over the body saying, 'Get up. Get up. Please get up.' "

Bobby dragged Anthony down the alleyway and out onto O'Donnell Street where his car was parked. Anthony got behind the wheel and started it up. Bobby ran around the other side and was about to jump in the passenger seat when Stephen Hemerlein's two friends came back out of Eddie's Lounge. Unable to find either Bobby or their friend, they had apparently circled the block and gone back inside to wait for their return.

"Where's Steve?" they yelled.

Bobby pointed down the alleyway. "He needs help," he hollered. Then he got into the car and he and Anthony sped away. They drove around the strange city for nearly an hour, lost, confused and scared.

"What should we do?" Anthony asked.

"I don't know," Bobby said. "I don't know."

They thought of heading for Philadelphia, but realized that was a dead end. Bobby had left his jacket with his wallet back at the bar. The police were probably already looking for them.

"Give me the gun," Bobby said. "I'll say I did it. What's the difference. My life is already all fucked up."

"But it was an accident," Anthony said. "The gun just went off. We ought to just turn ourselves in and tell the truth."

Shortly after 1:00 A.M. on the morning of April 17, 1988, Bobby DelGiorno and Anthony Forline pulled into the Bethlehem Steel plant entrance in Sparrow's Point about fifteen miles southeast of the city. Bobby, soaked in blood, stepped out of the car and told the startled Pinkerton guard, "We just shot someone. I think he's dead."

Maryann got the call Sunday night from her ex-sister-in-law. She and Joe had just returned from a weekend at their campground. As they walked in the door, the phone was ringing.

"Are you sitting down?" her former in-law asked.

"What?" Maryann said. "We just walked in the door."

"Are you sitting down?" said the voice on the other end of the line again. "This time your son's really done it."

Maryann expected to hear another tale about Bobby and the FBI or Bobby and Tommy Del. She was aware of the friction that had been building and, in a way, relished the fact that her two boys had had it with their father.

"What are you talking about?" Maryann said into the phone. Then she grew quiet, turned white and listened.

Seconds later Joe heard her screams and came rushing downstairs. He found her in the middle of the kitchen banging a wooden spoke against the kitchen table, crying uncontrollably.

Joe brought her into the living room and made her sit on the couch. He took both her hands and held them tightly.

"Maryann," he said. "What is it?"

The story came out in fits and bursts, along with a rush of curses aimed at her former husband. Once again, Maryann blamed Tommy Del for what had happened. If it weren't for him, Bobby would have never left South Philadelphia, he would have never been in Baltimore, and Anthony, sweet, innocent Anthony, would have never gone to visit Bobby there.

Maryann told Joe all that she knew. Slowly gaining control of herself, she repeated what she had learned from the phone call. The details were sketchy. All that was certain was that Bobby and Anthony were being held in Baltimore on first-degree-murder charges. There had been some kind of fight, there was a gun and a twenty-four-year-old man had been shot in the face and killed. The initial accounts included police speculation about the motive behind the shooting. One source said it grew out of a fight over a pool game. Another hinted that the murder was part of a drug deal gone sour. Until she had a chance to talk with Bobby directly, Maryann refused to believe any of it.

Once again she felt helpless in the face of events over which she had no control. It was another cruel joke, another bitter twist of fate. Bobby was practically home. His move to Baltimore was the first step toward a complete split with his father. Finally, he had recognized the empty fantasy of the gangster life and decided to put it behind him. Baltimore was a fresh start, a new beginning. And if everything went right—after the trials were over and the publicity had died down and Scarfo and the others were put away for good—then her Bobby and her Tommy could come back home. Maryann was content with that. In the meantime, she and Joe had been talking about trips to both Lancaster and Baltimore to see the boys. Nothing had been planned yet, but with the spring and warmer weather, she was already looking forward to a ride through Pennsylvania Dutch Country on a Saturday afternoon or a stroll around the Inner Harbor on a bright Sunday morning.

Instead, her first visit to Baltimore was to the city jail. Visiting hours were Tuesday morning. She and Joe were there when the doors opened.

Bobby and Anthony had been in jail for two days, but it seemed like two months. It was cold and dirty and so were they. The place had the look, the feel, and most of all, the smell of an underground subway. It was dank and damp with the hint of urine in the air. Originally, the two new prisoners had been separated, each assigned to a different cell block, but Bobby's cellmate, a young black guy named Jerry, knew his way around the prison and managed to get Anthony switched to the same block. The three prisoners became fast friends. They ate together, exercised in the gym and spent whatever free time they had talking.

Jail was very much a routine, a lot like being in school. Your whole day was scheduled. There was always someone telling you what to do next. And wherever you went, you had to wait in line. Jerry, however, knew how to work the system. When Anthony and Bobby turned their noses up at the mush being served for breakfast, their new friend asked if they'd prefer cereal.

"Just take your trays and wait over there," he told them after Bobby and Anthony had been handed helpings of a thick, gray-white substance neither of them recognized.

"That's grits," Jerry said. "But since this is your first time eating here, I'll treat. I know a few people. Let me see what I can do."

Bobby watched from his table as Jerry walked over to one of the prisoners who was serving breakfast. He couldn't hear what was said, but in less than a minute, Jerry was back at their table with six small boxes of cereal and three pint containers of milk.

"Thank you," Bobby and Anthony said in both surprise and disbelief.

Jerry quickly became their guide through the netherworld of prison. He told them the chief rule inside was to mind your own business. And the corollary to that was "never rat, even if you gotta take the blame for something." Bobby could only smile, thinking of his father. No one in jail knew who he was—he was booked under the name Robert D'Antonio, the name the FBI had given him. But it was Robert DelGiorno who appreciated the irony in Jerry's advice.

"Always look out for your cellmate, because he's the one you're gonna be spending most of your time with," Jerry said. "Don't trust anyone else, but never underestimate anybody in here. Mostly everyone in here is a threat to society, that means they're a threat to you. The object is to survive."

During the day, time passed. There was always something to do or someplace that you had to be. But at night, things slowed down. And that's when Bobby had to focus on and think about his situation. He was alternately angry, afraid, and confused. He thought about the first-degree-murder charge. He and Anthony could get life in prison. Or the electric chair. They tried to tell the cops it was an accident, but, just like the feds and his father, the Baltimore police twisted words around, changed their statements to suit their purposes. Now they were saying Bobby and Anthony had lured Hemerlein to the alley, set him up. They mentioned drugs and robbery. Nobody would listen to the truth. Nobody cared.

The FBI had sent an agent to see him in jail, but the feds seemed more concerned with whether Bobby had blown his family's cover than with the charges pending against him. They wanted to know if he had told anyone who he really was and where his father was living. They wanted him to go into isolation for his own safety, but they wouldn't do anything for Anthony, so Bobby refused. Now he was on his own. There was a bail hearing coming up later in the week. Who would post the money for him and Anthony? Would the judge even set bail? Would they get out? He had always thought a gun meant power, that it made him invincible. Now, when he closed his eyes he saw Stephen Hemerlein's face explode and felt the blood, hot and sticky, seeping through his pants and shirt as he tried to move the body.

———

Bobby saw his mother for the first time Tuesday morning, April 19. Accompanied by a guard, he was lead from his cell to a small visiting room where Maryann and Joe Fisher sat waiting at a table.

"You've got fifteen minutes," the guard said.

Tears filled Bobby's eyes when he saw his mother. She looked small and sad. Maryann started to cry.

"I'm sorry," Bobby said. "I'm sorry to put you through all this shit."

"Bobby, I'm your mother. I'll do anything I can to get you and Anthony out of this."

"Just stay calm," Joe Fisher said to Bobby. "Talk slowly and tell us what happened."

The fifteen minutes flew by. Bobby explained as best he could. Joe and Maryann said they had hired a lawyer. Anthony's parents had done the same. The two lawyers were waiting to meet with the boys that morning. They hoped to arrange for bail, maybe get the charges reduced.

"Bob, just keep your head clear and tell the lawyer everything, down to the last detail," Joe said.

"We love you," Maryann said as the guard came to take Bobby away.

Chapter Seventeen

Three days and two hearings later, Bobby and Anthony—helped in part by the disclosure of Bobby's true identity to the judge handling the case—finally made bail. Keeping Bobby in prison created a security risk that neither the FBI nor officials with the Baltimore City prison system wanted. Even before the second bail hearing—and against his will—Bobby had been whisked out of his cell block and placed in an isolation wing. "There were some Chinese terrorists there and a couple guys who looked like they were crazy," Bobby said. "I felt safer with the regular prisoners."

Bobby spent one night in the isolation unit, sleeping on a mattress damp and smelling of piss, before being called down for his second bail hearing. By that point, both prosecution and defense attorneys were in agreement on bail, which the judge set at one hundred thousand dollars for each defendant. On April 22, following a brief hearing, Maryann and Joe Fisher put up two thousand dollars and the deed to the house on Gladstone Street to satisfy the ten thousand dollar [ten percent] cash requirement for Bobby's bail. [Later that day, Tommy Del came up with eight thousand dollars in cash and Maryann and Joe got the deed back.] The Forline family put up its home to bail out Anthony. The two defendants, charged with first degree murder, were ordered to appear for trial in the Circuit Court of Baltimore on October 19. Until then, both were free.

Sitting in jail, waiting for their release, Anthony had told Bobby, "The first thing I'm doing when I get home is going and getting two cheese steaks and some South Philly french fries." Bobby, who would have to return to Virginia Beach, didn't have that option.

"They brought me and Anthony out cuffed together on the day we made bail. We knew we were gonna be released, so we were saying our goodbyes, knowing that because of the mess we would have to stay away from each other until after the trial. One of the guards wished us luck, and we thanked him. Then when he took the handcuffs off, we just stood there looking at each other for a second. Anthony grabbed me in a hug and said, 'I'm gonna miss you, buddy.' I said, 'It won't be forever, Ant. Just till we get this all straightened out.' We walked through this door and there was Anthony's mother and father and his whole family. He took off running for them, tears were coming out of his eyes.

"I looked up and there was my mother, crying and running toward me. She grabbed me and then Joe came up and gave me a hug, and I started crying. Anthony looked over and waved goodbye, and he and his family walked out the door. I walked over to a bench and sat down with my mother and Joe. We had about twenty minutes before the FBI was coming for me. I didn't want to go. I wanted to stay with my mother and stepfather, but I knew that if I made any trouble it might be bad for my case. My mother said, 'We know you have to go, but the FBI told us if you play your cards right, they'll do everything they can to help you out in this case.' I just thought to myself, 'Yeah, now they really got me by the balls.'

"I felt bad about what happened, about all of this. And especially about getting Anthony in the middle of it. But I didn't want to go back with my father and the FBI. That's what I was trying to get away from."

The FBI had booked Bobby on the next flight out of Baltimore for Virginia. The agent who picked him up after the bail hearing said the flight would be leaving in about three hours so he asked if Bobby wanted to stop by the hotel where his father was staying to wash up before heading out to the airport. Tommy Del, who was scheduled to testify in the Salvatore Testa murder trial, wouldn't be going back. Instead, he'd be heading to Philadelphia and another dramatic appearance on the witness stand.

Bobby had hoped to avoid seeing his father, but the thought of a hot shower and a clean shave before getting on the plane sounded too good to pass up. The feds had rooms in Stouffer's, a fancy hotel in downtown Baltimore, right across the street from the restaurants and stores that are part of the Inner Harbor.

"My father always insisted on staying in the most expensive hotels," Bobby said. "The FBI always picked up the tab."

Bobby and the agent took the elevator up to his father's room. Tommy Del was sitting in a chair watching television. Two other agents were with him. As family reunions go, this one was decidedly lacking in pathos and empathy.

"What the fuck did you get into this time?" Tommy Del said as soon as Bobby walked into the room. "Can't you see we have enough problems already? You want to be a big shot and carry a gun? That's what happens when you have a big mouth."

Bobby sat down on the edge of the bed as the tirade continued. He was too tired to fight, too exhausted to go over it all again. It didn't matter. Nobody would believe him anyway. Why should he bother explaining anything to a Mafia gangster who used to laugh about killing people, who used to make jokes about how he would terrorize guys into paying him money and doing him favors. Bobby used to think it took guts to kill someone. Now the thought made him sick. Now he knew what death felt like, what it smelled like. All of a sudden, he felt drained. He could barely move his arms and legs. He couldn't focus. His father's words were buzzing in the background.

Forget the shower, he thought. Forget the shave.

"Take me to the airport," he said to the agent who had brought him to the hotel. "I'll get cleaned up when I get home to Virginia Beach."

"And when I get back there, I'll straighten you out good," his father yelled as Bobby turned and walked out the door.

On the ride out to the airport the agent tried to make small talk, ignoring the flare-up that had just taken place in the hotel room.

"Did any niggers bother you while you were in jail?" he asked.

"I had a cellmate who took care of me and Anthony," Bobby said. "He showed us around and made sure nobody bothered us."

"You were lucky," the agent said. "That jail was full of niggers."

"Yeah," Bobby said. "We were lucky."

An hour later, as he sat alone on the plane waiting for takeoff, Bobby wished he had said more. The way he saw it, Jerry was the only person he had met since his arrest who had tried to help him. Yet he never asked for anything in return. In fact, there was nothing Bobby could give him. Jerry had gone out of his way for both Bobby and Anthony, two guys he didn't know and probably would never see again, two white guys from South Philly who managed to survive a week in jail because a young black guy decided to look out for them.

Federal authorities, not surprisingly, had a different perspective on the events leading up to the incident in Baltimore.

"We did all we could for those kids," said one Philadelphia-based FBI agent of Bobby and Tommy junior. "They just didn't want their father to testify. All they wanted was to go back to South Philadelphia. I mean, we moved Bobby to Baltimore. He's there twenty-four hours and he's arrested for murder. Jesus Christ, give me a break, will ya?"

But there would be no break. Like Tommy Del's earlier tryst with the prostitute, the murder of Stephen Hemerlein became an issue that defense attorneys tried to exploit.

Tommy Del had been scheduled to appear as a witness in the Salvatore Testa murder trial on Thursday, April 21. But Assistant District Attorney Barbara Christie had unexpectedly asked for a two-day recess. This gave DelGiorno the chance to go down to Baltimore and help bail Bobby out. But it also alerted reporters to the fact that something was up. It didn't take much probing to find out what.

By the time Tommy Del returned to Philadelphia and took the stand on Monday, April 25, the news had been headlined in all the papers and blared out over television and radio broadcasts.

"Mobster's son arrested in Baltimore slaying" was the gist of each news account. "Like father, like son" was the subtext. Defense attorneys hoped the jury would draw the same comparison.

The Testa murder trial was the first concrete example of the cooperative effort of law enforcement in attacking the Scarfo mob. The U.S. Attorney's Office had listed ten murders, including the killings of Salvie Testa and Frankie Flowers D'Alfonso, in the RICO indictment. But under the terms of an agreement reached in 1987, the Philadelphia District Attorney's Office was able to use the same evidence and testimony in bringing first-degree-murder charges against those involved in the two killings.

Christie, head of the DA's homicide unit, drew the Testa case. It was a plum, a high-profile assignment that she relished. The thin, dark-haired prosecutor with the raspy voice of a chain smoker had a well-earned reputation as an aggressive, no-holds-barred litigator. "She's got more balls than a lot of defense attorneys in this town," one investigator said admiringly. But many of her high-profile convictions did not stand, a fact supported by a series of stunning appellate court reversals of murder convictions due to prosecutorial misconduct.

In fact, the Testa trial was marred by a series of acrimonious disputes between Christie and the team of defense attorneys. The battles, which attracted widespread media attention, were a clash of both symbols and substance. Christie sat alone at the prosecution table. And across the aisle, dressed impeccably, were nine of the highest-priced and well-known criminal defense attorneys in the city. Beside them sat their nine scowling—and equally well-dressed—clients.

One woman against eighteen men.

The problem was that Christie turned the trial into more than a murder case. This was the DA's shot at taking down the Scarfo mob, so she tried to throw every bit of information into it. Testimony ran far afield. First Caramandi and then DelGiorno talked at length about La Cosa Nostra, their initiation rites, "doing work" and Scarfo's insatiable blood lust. The Testa murder and all the intrigue that surrounded it—the missed opportunities, Scarfo's complaints about not getting it done soon enough, the broken engagement with Chuckie Merlino's daughter, the threats to kill Joey Pungitore and his family if he didn't set his friend up—sounded like the script from a weekly soap opera. Was this *Dallas* or *The Godfather?*

Tommy Del, at his wiseguy best, offered chilling testimony about the inner workings of the organization. He detailed Scarfo's notorious reputation for violence within his own crime family and the cavalier fashion with which murders were carried out.

Two days earlier he had been sitting in a posh hotel room in Baltimore berating Bobby for his involvement in a senseless killing; now he was on the witness stand in Common Pleas Court in Philadelphia boldly outlining his own involvement in a series of equally senseless murders.

Some of it was humorous, like the time he said Nicky Crow Caramandi nearly shot mob underboss Chuckie Merlino's son, Joey, while they were testing out the silencers on two potential murder weapons in the cellar of a South Philadelphia row house.

"The Crow was, he was playing with it [the gun] and pointing it all over the place," Tommy Del said. "And I said to him, I asked him, 'What are you doing?' And he said, 'Don't worry, it's not loaded.' And he turned around and said, 'Look.' "

With that, DelGiorno said, Caramandi pointed the gun at some iron grating and pulled the trigger.

"And when he shot it, could you tell whether it was loaded?" DelGiorno was asked.

"Oh, it was loaded," he said.

He explained how the bullet had ricocheted around the tiny cellar and just missed Merlino's head.

"And did that cause you any concern?"

"Sure. I got scared. I said, 'Jesus Christ. You shoot this kid, how am I gonna explain to his father? He ain't gonna believe it is an accident.' "

Nearly everyone in the courtroom laughed at the story, a Philadelphia version of "The Gang that Couldn't Shoot Straight." But no one found any humor in DelGiorno's cold-blooded description of the celebration Scarfo organized at La Cucina, the swank South Street restaurant, several hours after Salvatore Testa was finally killed. This was the same restaurant where Scarfo staged his Christmas parties. Mob soldier Charlie Iannece, who had helped Caramandi dump Testa's corpse on a back road in New Jersey, was late arriving at the restaurant because of the problems they encountered in disposing of the stiff and bloated body. Once Iannece got to La Cucina, DelGiorno said he asked how it had gone.

"I was talking to Charlie at the bar," Tommy Del said. "He told me that when he got into the store [the sweet shop where Testa had been ambushed] it was a real mess, that there was blood all over; that his legs were stiff. He had to straighten them out. . . . While we were talking, I saw blood on his neck. I told him, 'You have blood on your neck, Charlie.' He said, 'I know. It was hard to get off.' So he went to the bathroom and washed it off."

After that, DelGiorno and Iannece picked up plates and

headed for the buffet table and the feast that Scarfo had ordered up to mark the occasion.

Testa, DelGiorno told the jury, should never have been killed. But that, he said, was the way Scarfo was. Deceit and deception were the marks of his organization. "We lived in a world of lies," he said.

Tommy Del, who was on the witness stand for four days, was asked at the end of his cross-examination if he felt any remorse for the murder of Salvatore Testa.

"You really liked the kid, didn't you?" a defense attorney asked.

"Yes, I liked him," DelGiorno said. "I don't know about how much remorse I had. I just thought that he got killed for no sensible reason. But I didn't have no remorse over it because a lot of guys that I know . . . the last five years got killed for no sensible reason."

"Tell me some sensible reason to go out and murder people," the defense attorney then asked sarcastically. "What is the most sensible killing you did?" Before DelGiorno could answer, Christie jumped up and raised an objection. The defense attorney then withdrew his question. Three-hundred-miles away, in Virginia Beach, Bobby DelGiorno would have liked to have heard the answer.

On May 10, after two days of deliberation, a Common Pleas Court jury, scared, confused and probably overwhelmed by a flood of information—but with enough reasonable doubt to walk away with clear consciences—came back with not guilty verdicts all around. The courtroom, crammed with family members, friends and supporters of the mobsters, cheered as Scarfo and the other defendants were led away in handcuffs to await a September trial in U.S. District Court on the Harvest Time RICO charges.

Bobby DelGiorno, sitting in Virginia waiting for an October date with the Circuit Court of Baltimore, could appreciate how the defendants felt. "You know, you see them on TV laughing and smiling while they're being taken out of the courthouse," Bobby said. "But I knew they weren't smiling and laughing on the inside. It was more anger, probably, and hurt and afraid. . . . I know the feeling. Nobody's happy to be in that position.

"After I got in trouble, I couldn't go nowhere. I was confined to the house. The FBI told me if I was to travel back to Philly they would revoke my bail and put me back in jail. They were just trying to scare me. But I was already pretty scared.

"They let me go to my brother's house in Lancaster. So I was up there. I stayed for two weeks one time, then visited a couple of other times. While I was there, me and Tommy would talk about my case and all our problems. He would tell me how he hated it up there. He said it ain't nothing like home. He said he moved away from Virginia Beach to get away from our father, but he said, 'Now me and Chrissy are here and there ain't nobody we know. . . . I really don't want to live like this. I want to be able to go home and see my mother every day, my friends.'

"I said, 'Tom, so would I. I can't believe I'm in this mess that I'm in. Now the FBI's really got me by the balls. I had the upper hand on them, now they got the upper hand.' So Tommy starts talking again about what he was gonna do before, testifying against our father. I was still confused, but he asked me what was gonna happen if I got found guilty. I said, 'Probably get a lot of time.' He said, 'What have you got to lose? If they got you by the balls now, they're really gonna have you by the balls after your trial's over. You ain't never gonna be allowed to go to Philly.'

"He was right. I didn't know what was gonna happen. I said, 'Tom, listen, I'll do anything you wanna do.' "

And so the plan to "rat out the rat," as the boys called it, was once again put in motion. Tommy junior told Bobby he would take care of everything. He would make contact with the defense attorneys in the RICO case and offer to testify, telling everything their father had been doing while living in protective custody, that he's nothing but a liar and that the FBI's been feeding things into his head, coaching him. In exchange, he and Bobby wanted assurances that they could return to South Philadelphia without any problems.

"All we want," Tommy junior said, "is to be left alone."

That summer, two months before the start of the RICO trial, Tommy junior called a lawyer in New Jersey who was a friend of his uncle's. The attorney served as the go-between, setting up the first face-to-face meeting between Tommy junior and Robert Simone, Nicky Scarfo's lawyer. By August, a month before the start of the RICO trial and two months before Bobby's scheduled appearance in Baltimore, an agreement had been worked out. Tommy junior would testify in open court for the defense in the RICO case provided Bobby's Baltimore murder case had been resolved.

"My brother said he didn't want the feds using his testimony to hurt me," Bobby said. "Simone told him they understood. He said nobody held anything against us and they would only use Tommy if my case was over. . . . In the meantime, I'm back in Virginia Beach trying to act like nothin's going on. I felt like a spy. And sometimes I felt bad because there were some agents trying to help me with my case. But to me that was only because they didn't want my problems to mess up their case."

Bobby, his father and two FBI agents drove up from Virginia Beach to Baltimore the night before the murder trial was to begin. They checked into rooms at Stouffer's Hotel a few blocks from the courthouse. By then, Tommy Del had finished testifying in the RICO trial in Philadelphia, which was already in its second month. On the stand for nearly a week, he had outlined the extortions, shakedowns, drug scams and killings that were the mark of the Scarfo organization. And he had coldly described his own involvement in a series of murders, including the brutal ambush of Johnny Calabrese that opened the door to his own initiation in the Mafia. Carrying out a mob hit, he matter-of-factly told the RICO jury, "gave you strength" within the organization.

"It's the difference between being in the major leagues and

the minor leagues as far as gangsters are concerned," Tommy Del had said.

Bobby and Anthony, clearly minor leaguers, were due to appear at 9:00 A.M. October 19 in Baltimore City Circuit Courtroom 226 for the start of their own murder trial. Tommy junior, back in Lancaster, was waiting for a phone call from his brother once the case was resolved. For weeks there had been talk of a plea bargain, word that the prosecution might be willing to reduce the charges against the two defendants. While there had been allegations at the bail hearing about a drug deal gone awry, attempted robbery and eyewitness testimony, the closer it came to a trial date the clearer it was that the prosecution had very little firsthand evidence other than the statements of Bobby and Anthony. Both continued to insist that the shooting was an accident, that Hemerlein had instigated the fight and that the gun had discharged as he tried to wrestle it away from Anthony Forline.

"We met at my lawyer's office before we went over to the courthouse," Bobby said. "One of the FBI agents went with me. My father stayed back at the hotel with the other agent. Anthony was there with his lawyer and my mother was there, too. She was waiting for my father to show up. She really wanted to chew him out. She was blaming him for all of this, which in a way was true, but in a way it wasn't."

Over in the courtroom Anthony's family and friends of his and Bobby's from the neighborhood sat waiting. They had all driven down from Philadelphia to offer moral support. Prior to the start of jury selection, however, the defense lawyers and the prosecutor went into the judge's chambers for a meeting.

It lasted more than two hours.

"My heart was thumping," Bobby said. "So was Anthony's. We were all out in the hallway, pacing up and down, wondering what was going on. I knew they might be talking about a plea bargain, but we didn't know what to expect. We felt we were innocent of murder."

But they also knew that Stephen Hemerlein was dead and that there would have to be a legal accounting.

"In our heart we knew it was an accident, but they didn't want to hear that," Bobby said of the prosecutor. "Somebody was dead and somebody's gotta pay the consequences."

Shortly before noon, the lawyers emerged from the judge's chambers. Bobby saw the prosecutor walk over and begin talking to members of Stephen Hemerlein's family, who had also turned out for the trial. Then Bobby's attorney called him aside.

"We've got to talk," he said. "Let's go back to my office."

While their friends headed to a restaurant for lunch, Bobby, Anthony and their parents walked across the street to the lawyer's office hoping for good news.

"It was me, Anthony, my mother and stepfather and Anthony's mother and father. We sit down in a conference room. The lawyer says the state wants to make a plea bargain. He says just listen. He said it was a good plea bargain, but that Anthony might have to do a little time.

"So Anthony just put his head down. And the lawyer says that we both have to take the plea bargain. He says the only way the state will agree is if we both agree. In other words, one of us can't take it and the other one can take. It had to be both of us.

"My lawyer says that they want me to plead to manslaughter. That I get ten years, but that the judge will knock off five years and give me the other five years as probation. He says to me that it's a good plea bargain and he's not telling me not to take it. But he also says he feels he can beat the case and that they have nothing to back the charges against me.

"Then Anthony's lawyer started talking. And the thing was, Anthony had to plead guilty to second-degree murder and have twenty years plus five years for the gun. Fifteen years would be suspended and the five and five would run concurrent. Anthony asks how much time he would have to do. His lawyer said probably eighteen months. And he said if you don't take this, the judge said it's a great deal and no matter what you get found guilty on, you're gonna do way more time than that. The gun alone was five years, even if we beat the murder charge.

"Anthony looked at his father and his father said, 'Ant, what do you want to do?' So I turned around to Anthony and said, 'I'll do anything you want to do. I'll plead guilty if it's for your benefit or I'll go to trial. Whatever you want.' Anthony says, 'What's eighteen months? I'll plead guilty. I don't want to go in there and roll the dice and get twenty years.' "

An hour later they were back in court in front of Judge Joseph I. Pines to withdraw their not-guilty pleas and accept the plea bargain outlined by their lawyers. First the prosecutor described the events leading up to the murder. He called Bobby and Anthony "two tough kids from Philly who came here and tried to play the role."

"I think DelGiorno tried to impress people," he later told a reporter, "and they aren't easily impressed here by his kind of talk."

Anthony's attorney said his client didn't even know what DelGiorno and Hemerlein were fighting about. "It was just a tragic confluence of alcohol and emotions," he said.

In less than an hour, the hearing was over. Bobby pleaded guilty to manslaughter. Anthony pleaded guilty to second-degree murder. Sentencing was set for the first week in January.

"Afterwards, my mother ran up and started hugging me," Bobby said. "She wanted to know when she would see me again. I asked her if Tommy had talked to her yet, and she said no but that she and Joe were supposed to go and see him in Lancaster. I said good, but I didn't tell her anything about what we were planning. I wanted my brother to be the one to tell her."

Bobby left with an FBI agent and headed back for the hotel where his father was waiting. Once again, he got a less than cordial reception.

"He didn't even ask how I felt," Bobby said. "He just said, 'Your ass got out of this one, but you better watch yourself from now on because these people ain't always gonna be here to help you.' I knew in my heart he was right, and I wished it had never happened, but it was like he was throwing it in my face."

Bobby ignored the taunts, however. He was more concerned with contacting his brother. But for the rest of the afternoon he was stuck in the hotel room with his father, unable to use the phone. Finally, that night as he, Tommy Del and the two FBI agents were having dinner in the hotel restaurant, he saw his chance to make the call. Excusing himself to go to the men's room, he headed instead to the hotel lobby and a bank of pay phones.

He called collect.

"I told Tommy they couldn't do anything to me now," Bobby said. "I told him the plea bargain was set. So I said it was okay for him to call Bobby Simone. I said, 'Tell him you're ready to testify.' "

Chapter Eighteen

Bobby returned to Virginia Beach with his father after the hearing in Baltimore. Three days later, Tommy junior called to say that the RICO trial in Philadelphia was dragging on and that the defense didn't plan to use him until the very end of the case. He said he would call again once he knew when he was going on the stand. At that point, Bobby was supposed to pack up and leave. Until then he had to sit tight.

Late in October Nicky Crow Caramandi took the witness stand at the RICO trial and corroborated the testimony of Tommy Del. Together the two mobsters were murdering their former gangland cohorts in open court. Federal prosecutors also had introduced hundreds of pieces of evidence, surveillance photos, wiretapped phone conversations, even a videotape of Scarfo, Leonetti, Caramandi and Iannece meeting on the Boardwalk in Atlantic City. All of it corroborated and solidified the testimony of the two gangster-informants. There were also dozens of other witnesses, ranging from FBI agents and state police detectives who had spent years tracking the mob to drug dealers, loan sharks and numbers writers who had been strong-armed and threatened by the defendants.

The case was unprecedented. Never before had the federal government so thoroughly peeled away the layers of fear, intimidation, lies and deceit to expose the workings of an American Mafia family. Never before had the mob's time-honored code of silence—*omerta*—been so completely shattered. Although no one realized it at the time, the RICO trial in Philadelphia was just the beginning. Over the next three years the federal government, taking its cue from the City of Brotherly Love, would begin building cases that reverberated throughout the American underworld. Tommy DelGiorno and Nick Caramandi started it all. In the end, John Gotti and the other top mob bosses in New York would be scrambling for cover as well.

None of that, however, meant anything to Bobby, his brother or his mother.

"I just wanted my boys home," Maryann said. "And I wanted their father dead. God help me, I wanted him dead."

Tommy junior had filled Maryann and Joe in on his plan to testify. They, like Bobby, were waiting for word. Each day Maryann would pick up the paper and follow the events of the trial. Throughout the city people were shocked, amazed and horrified by the testimony. Maryann had heard it all before. She had lived it. Now all she wanted was for it to end.

But even she couldn't believe the headlines that appeared on November 2. Mark Scarfo, the young, handsome, seventeen-year-old son of mob boss Nicodemo Scarfo, had tried to kill himself. He had been found by his mother hanging by the neck from a cord wrapped around a bathroom fixture in the office of Scarf Inc., an Atlantic City cement contracting company. He was rushed to the hospital in a coma. According to his friends, pressure brought on by more than a year of arrests, indictments and trials had taken a toll on the personable high school senior. Taunts and jeering from fellow students had pushed him over the edge.

The trial recessed early the next day so that Scarfo, in handcuffs and leg irons, could be taken to visit his son's bedside. Mark Scarfo, the youngest of Little Nicky's three sons, was truly one of the innocent.

Maryann grieved for the boy and for his mother, a woman she did not know but with whom she could empathize. Only another mother, she thought, could appreciate the suffering. Only another mother would understand the quiet rage and bitter helplessness. Even as she prayed for her own sons' safe return, Maryann was haunted by the image of Mark Scarfo hanging by the neck. And by the thought of his mother finding him and screaming in anguish as she rushed to save him. [At this writing, five years later, Mark Scarfo remains comatose in a nursing facility.]

A week after the tragic headlines about Mark Scarfo rocked Philadelphia, Bobby got the call that he and his mother had been waiting for.

"It was Tommy. He said he was gonna testify. He said he was supposed to be in court in two days and for me to get away as soon as I could. He told me to make it look like I had run away again, that way all the focus would be on me and he could slip into Philadelphia and testify.

"The next morning, when I got up, my father was sittin' at the kitchen table drinking coffee, all dressed up to go play golf. He was supposed to meet two agents on the golf course. Roe was still sleeping and Danny and Michael were at school. So I says to him, 'What time are you comin' back?' He said about five o'clock. Then he said, 'What do you wanna know for? You're not planning to have no party over here?' I got real serious. 'No. I ain't havin' no party.' Then I went over and picked up his golf bag. 'I'll carry this out to the car for you,' I said.

"Once he left, I started packing. I just threw all my clothes into two big bags. Emptied all my drawers. I made two or three trips out to my car, loaded as much as I could into it and then I was gone. I couldn't believe it. For the first time I was packing for some place that I wanted to go to. This was gonna be the last move for the rest of my life. I was going home to Philadelphia.

"The last stop I made was to close out my account at the bank in Virginia Beach. I had about fifteen thousand dollars. Then I went to a pay phone and called Lancaster. Chrissy answered. She said Tommy was at their bank, closing their accounts. 'We're trying to tie up all the loose ends so we'll be ready,' she said. This was on a Monday or a Tuesday. Tommy was gonna testify in a day or two. I told Chrissy, 'Tell Tommy I'm on the road, that I'm heading for grandpop's house. I'll see you when you get there.'

"That six-hour drive was one of the longest of my life. Every hour that went by I thought, 'I'm one hour closer to starting my life over.' I had to find out who I was. I couldn't go through life moving from place to place, using one phony name after another. I had to be me again, whoever that was."

Early that night, Bobby pulled up in front of his grandmother's house, a tidy brick row house on Snyder Avenue near Second Street. On the inside door, blocked from view on the street, was a sign that read WELCOME HOME. Inside, Bobby's grandparents, his mother and his stepfather sat impatiently waiting. When Bobby walked in they all jumped up and began hugging him and one another.

Bobby was home. This time for good.

"The FBI called my mother that night and said they were tired of chasing after me," Bobby said. "They said they were done with me. They couldn't believe I would run away again and cause more problems after what they had done for me, helping me out of that case in Baltimore. They said they were coming to get my car the next day. My mother just hung up."

The next morning, Wednesday, November 9, Tommy and Chrissy arrived from Lancaster. The same WELCOME HOME sign and welcoming committee were there to meet them. There were hugs and kisses and then Tommy went upstairs to change. He was due in court. One of the defense attorneys was sending a car to pick him up.

After Tommy left for the RICO trial, there was a knock on the door. Two FBI agents were there looking for Bobby. They said they weren't there to talk him into coming back, but they wanted the keys to his government-leased car and his license and other forms of identification. They considered Bobby's leaving a security breach. Now his father, Roe, Danny and Michael would have to be relocated again and given yet another false set of names and identifications. Bobby handed over the keys to the car and a sealed envelope containing his identification cards.

"Bob, we have to talk," one of the agents said as Bobby was about to close the door. "This could mean life or death."

Bobby swung the door back open wide.

"What is that supposed to mean?" he said.

"You're no match for the mob, Bob," the agent said. "They're killers."

"I'm not trying to be their match," Bobby answered. "I just want to live a normal life, here, where I belong. . . . This is my father's mess. He got himself into this and you guys just made it worse for me and my three brothers. You wanna make things right? Put my father in jail. Don't let him testify no more. Then maybe we could all live in peace."

Bobby closed the door.

"You'll be dead in a week," he heard the agent say.

———————

The appearance of Tommy DelGiorno, Jr., as a witness for the defense was one of the dramatic high points of the RICO trial, even though it proved to have very little impact on the outcome of the case.

He arrived in court that morning dressed in a black and white sweater and dark slacks. When his name was called out as a witness, a murmur spread through the courtroom. Some spectators thought Tommy Del was being called back to the stand. Others, friends and family members of some of the defendants who had been tipped off about the surprise witness, nodded in approval. This would be the defense's last and best chance to discredit the government's chief witness.

Tommy junior's testimony, coming at the end of a two-month trial, was relatively brief. He was on the stand for a little more than an hour. Under direct questioning from Bobby Simone he recounted life in protective custody, told how his father had made him keep a gun hidden from the FBI in case he had to "go back to the old ways" and alleged that his father was told what to say on the witness stand.

During debriefing sessions, he said, FBI agents would go over the same incidents again and again. "They would come back at him and ask, 'Well, couldn't it have happened this way?' and my father would say, 'Well, yeah, it could have,' and by the time they were done. . . . my father was telling the story that they wanted him to tell."

He also testified about the tens of thousands of dollars his father had already received—the rent money for the house he owned, the monthly payments for utility bills, the weekly allowance for household and living expenses. And he said his father had boasted about a government promise of tens of thousands more once he had finished testifying at all the trials.

His father's life in protective custody, Tommy junior added, was really life on a very long and untended federal leash. When he wasn't testifying, Tommy Del came and went just about as he pleased, his son said. He spent much of his free time on the golf course. And after testifying, he usually returned home drunk.

Under cross-examination by a government prosecutor, Tommy junior admitted that he had called his father "a fuckin' rat" and that he blamed him for the fact that he and his brother were forced to leave South Philadelphia. He also acknowledged that he had said he would do almost anything to be able to come back home. "But I never said I would lie," he told the jury.

Asked on redirect why he was testifying, Tommy looked straight ahead and said, "I want to come home and live with my family, just live my own life. I don't want to walk down the street, if these people are convicted, and run into their family, friends or relatives and they point their finger at me like I'm the bad guy.

"I want to clear the record so that I can have a clear conscience so that I can walk down the street and have nobody talking about me under their breath, you know, about my father."

The defense rested its case shortly after Tommy junior stepped down from the witness stand. In rebuttal, over the next day and a half, the federal government called nearly a dozen witnesses, FBI agents and state police detectives, to counter the testimony of Tommy junior. One law enforcement officer after the other testified about Tommy Del and his debriefing sessions, about how there was no attempt to influence or fashion his testimony. Again and again, the witnesses repeated, the only deal Tommy Del had was a promise that the government would speak in his behalf at his own sentencing provided he testified honestly and truthfully in court.

None of it mattered, however, back on Gladstone Street. Regardless of what the jury decided, for Maryann the verdict was already in. Her boys were home.

"No matter how this turns out, our clients appreciate what you did," one of the defense attorneys told Tommy as he was driven back to South Philadelphia after his stint on the witness stand. Tommy was dropped off at his grandparents' home on Snyder Avenue where Bobby and Chrissy were waiting. He was cheered as he walked in the door and bombarded with questions. Then the phone rang. It was Maryann.

"Come on over the house," she said. "There are some people here waiting to see you."

In less than five minutes the boys and Chrissy pulled up in front of the familiar brick row house on Gladstone Street. Outside, telephone poles and railings were covered with yellow ribbons. In the window was a gigantic sign. WELCOME HOME BOYS it said for everyone to see.

"Everybody who loved and cared about us was there," Bobby said. "Everybody was smiling and laughing. I think that's when it finally hit me. We were back home and nothing would ever make us leave."

Maryann stood in the living room where it had all started. She was crying again. But for the first time in longer than she could remember, they were tears of joy and happiness rather than frustration and despair. It was November 9, 1988, almost two years to the day from when Bobby and Tommy junior showed up and told her they would have to go into hiding with their father.

"I thought I had lost my babies," Maryann said. "I thought their father had won. . . ."

———

Shortly before 8:00 P.M. on Saturday, November 19, the jury in the RICO trial returned its verdict: guilty on all counts.

Between 1980, with the shooting of Angelo Bruno, and 1985, with the murder of Frankie D'Alfonso, twenty-eight mob members and associates of the Philadelphia crime family, including an entire generation of mob leadership, had been killed. With the verdict in the RICO case, seventeen major Mafia figures, including the entire hierarchy of the Scarfo organization, had been convicted. All faced prison sentences of from thirty to fifty-five years. No other Mafia family in America had ever been dealt such a staggering blow. La Cosa Nostra in Philadelphia was now a shambles, bankrupt, decimated. And still the prosecutions kept coming.

In April of 1989, a Commons Pleas Court jury in Philadelphia found Scarfo and seven codefendants guilty in the D'Alfonso killing. Little Nicky Scarfo became the first American Mafia boss ever convicted of first-degree murder. He and the others were sentenced to life in prison. For Scarfo, then sixty years old, the sentence almost didn't matter. His life term would not begin until after he had completed a fourteen-year sentence for his conspiracy conviction in the Penns Landing extortion scam and a fifty-five-year sentence he received in the RICO case. As a result, when an Appellate Court in 1992 granted the defendants a new trial in the D'Alfonso case on procedural grounds, it was a hollow victory for the humiliated mob boss. No matter what the outcome of that new trial [still pending at this writing], Nicodemo Scarfo is destined to spend the rest of his life behind bars.

What's more, his reputation as a hotheaded, vainglorious and incompetent Mafia chief has been solidified in both law enforcement and underworld circles. Scarfo's penchant for violence and his heavy-handed leadership style were the key factors in the demise of his organization. DelGiorno and Caramandi turned to the government because they knew there was no way to reason with their mob boss, no way to get out from under the senseless murder sentence that he imposed for even the slightest infraction. That they were able to testify again and again with impunity started a trend that spread first through the Philadelphia organization and then throughout the American Mafia. Today *omerta* has been shattered, broken into so many pieces that it's unlikely the once sacrosanct code of silence will ever again be an effective shield against law enforcement.

Following the RICO convictions, mob soldier Gino Milano agreed to testify for the government and became the star witness in the D'Alfonso murder trial. Following his conviction in the D'Alfonso trial and prior to sentencing for his RICO conviction, Lawrence Merlino contacted federal authorities and agreed to cooperate. And just a month after being sentenced to forty-five years in jail for his conviction in the RICO case, Philip Leonetti, Scarfo's nephew and underboss, turned government informant. In less than three years, five made members of the Philadelphia mob, including the underboss and two former capos—DelGiorno and Merlino—had become government stool pigeons. A sixth, George Fresolone, who was associated with the Newark, New Jersey, branch of the Scarfo family, added to the embarrassment by working undercover for the New Jersey State Police for more than a year in 1990, capping his stint as an informant by tape-recording his own mob initiation ceremony.

Throughout the underworld, the Scarfo family was mocked and ridiculed. Wiseguys and law enforcement investigators alike started to joke about Scarfo and his "South Philadelphia Boys Choir." Everybody, it seemed, was singing. But the joke turned sour when mobsters saw the impact of what happened in Philadelphia begin to spread. In 1991 Alfonse D'Arco, the acting boss of the Lucchese crime family, Peter Chiodo, a capo in the Lucchese organization and Salvatore "Sammy the Bull" Gravano, the underboss of the Gambino crime family, turned to the government and took to the witness stand. While D'Arco and Chiodo were important witnesses, they were quickly over-shadowed by Gravano, who cut his deal while sitting in jail awaiting trial on racketeering and murder charges with his longtime friend and mob boss, celebrity gangster John Gotti.

There are several explanations for why Gravano "flipped." Despite his bravado, Sammy the Bull, authorities said, was soft and feared a lifetime in jail. The FBI and the U.S. Attorney's Office in Brooklyn had put together a staggering case based on hundreds of hours of bugged conversations in Gotti's mob clubhouses. What's more, the feds had Philip Leonetti. The Philadelphia songbird, who had begun cooperating in 1989, could link Gravano to the 1981 murder of Frank Stillitano, the Trenton gangster Scarfo had ordered killed as a favor to the Gambino organization. In fact, by the time Gravano cut his deal, Leonetti had already appeared before a federal grand jury in New York and told the story of his meetings with Sammy the Bull at Bally's Park Place casino, where the Stillitano murder plot was set in motion. Leonetti had also testified about meet-ings in Staten Island that he and Scarfo had attended, meetings where Gotti and Gravano boasted about their role in the De-cember 1985 shooting of Paul Castellano, the Gambino family boss whom Gotti succeeded.

Leonetti was a key domino. When he fell, Gravano felt

tremendous pressure. He then "flipped" and fingered his own mob boss from the witness stand. Like Scarfo, Gotti was convicted of racketeering and murder charges in a highly publicized RICO case that ended in the spring of 1992.

As 1993 began, both Scarfo and Gotti—mob bosses who shared management styles and temperaments—were sharing the same federal penitentiary in Marion, Illinois, the toughest maximum-security prison in the country. Both were serving what amounted to life terms. Leonetti and Gravano, meanwhile, continued to make appearances in court and before grand juries, helping federal authorities in a multipronged attack that will forever change the face of the American Mafia. Like DelGiorno and Caramandi, they were trading their information for light prison sentences. Leonetti, who admitted to his own involvement in ten gangland killings, had his forty-five-year prison sentence reduced to six and a half years. Today he is free, living with his mother, girlfriend, and teenaged son in hiding under the Federal Witness Protection Program. Gravano, who confessed to nineteen mob murders, faces a maximum twenty-year sentence under the terms of his plea bargain. But he is likely to receive much less.

It's a trade-off the government is happy to make. In order to convict men like Scarfo and Gotti, other men like DelGiorno, Caramandi, Leonetti and Gravano get a free pass. They get to walk away from their crimes, wipe the slate clean and, defense attorneys would have you believe, get to do it all over again somewhere in Middle America. That's the deal. "Swans don't swim in sewers."

But along the way, some people get trampled.

Maryann Fisher had her life turned upside down and nearly killed herself. Bobby DelGiorno and his brother, Tommy, were forced to live in hiding for two years, even though they had been accused of no crime. Anthony Forline, sucked into the turmoil, ended up in jail. Stephen Hemerlein ended up dead.

"All my life I was taught not to rat," Bobby said one day as he drove down the street a few blocks from his home in

South Philadelphia. "These guys, as soon as they get in trouble, what do they do? Rat. They were big shot gangsters, they did the crimes, but when it was time to face the music, they turned and ran.

"What my father did shouldn't be allowed. You shouldn't be able to testify like he did and get off free, get all that money, live in luxury. If he wanted to testify, all right, fine, that's his choice. But he shoulda gone to jail for what he did. What about the people he killed? What about their families? What's the government say about that?"

Epilogue

On June 8, 1989, in a courtroom on the seventeenth floor of the federal courthouse in Philadelphia, Thomas DelGiorno appeared for sentencing before U.S. District Court Judge Louis C. Bechtle.

The hearing went on for more than an hour. FBI agents, Justice Department attorneys, state troopers and prosecutors from New Jersey and Pennsylvania stood up to speak in Tommy Del's behalf. It was pointed out that DelGiorno's co-operation had been without precedent, that he had testified at a dozen trials and that, as a result, fifty-three mob members and associates had been convicted and sentenced to lengthy prison terms.

Tommy Del, facing a maximum twenty-year sentence under the terms of the plea bargain he had entered into two years earlier, got five years. This, defense attorneys were quick to point out, amounted to twelve months for each of the five murders in which he played a role. In fact, with credit for the time he spent living in protective custody with the New Jersey State Police and the FBI, Tommy Del was paroled from prison in less than a year. By the spring of 1990 he joined his wife and sons Danny and Michael in the Federal Witness Protection Program.

Six months earlier, Bobby and Anthony had been sentenced in Baltimore for their guilty pleas in the Hemerlein killing. Bobby got a five-year suspended sentence and was placed on five years probation. Anthony got twenty years, with all but five years suspended.

So it was that Anthony Forline, who only wanted to help his friend, ended up with the same five-year prison sentence as Tommy Del, who only wanted to help himself. What's more, Forline would spend more than three years behind bars before earning parole. It would be 1992 before he was released from jail.

Meanwhile, the remnants of the Scarfo crime family continued the internecine struggle that "Little Nicky" had set in motion. Street violence, which had subsided in the late 1980s after Scarfo's arrest and convictions, flared up again as different factions moved to fill the leadership void in the organization. The turmoil rivaled that of the Scarfo years as younger members of the mob—some of them Bobby's contemporaries—emerged as major players and as targets.

John Stanfa, the Sicilian-born mob associate who drove Angelo Bruno home on the night he was killed in 1980, was identified in 1991 as the new boss of the Philadelphia family, according to local and federal law enforcement authorities.

Stanfa's ties to both the Gambino family in New York and the Sicilian Mafia in his native Palermo were most troubling to investigators who considered the new Philadelphia don a possible prototype of the American mob boss of the future. Low-keyed and schooled in the traditions of *omerta,* Stanfa, said the Pennsylvania Crime Commission, "has national and international organized crime connections" and might be ushering in a new era in the American underworld. In a sense, authorities said, Stanfa's rise signaled a return to the old ways and a rejection of the "Americanization" of La Cosa Nostra that was epitomized by the flash and glitter of mob bosses like Scarfo and Gotti.

"The metamorphosis in the Philadelphia Family may represent the future of La Cosa Nostra," the commission reported, going on to predict that "the Sicilian Mafia, which maintains the older values and traditions in organized crime, will regenerate an ailing American La Cosa Nostra."

Either by design or indifference, Stanfa did little to curb the violence that rocked the Philadelphia underworld in the early 1990s.

Six mob figures were killed during his first two years in power, including one mob informant, Mario "Sonny" Riccobene. Riccobene, the half brother of imprisoned mob soldier and Scarfo rival Harry Riccobene, had ignored the warnings of federal authorities and returned to the Philadelphia area in 1992. He was, however, a persona non grata in the underworld because he had testified for the government in two major 1984 mob trials. After moving around the fringes of the mob for several months, Sonny Riccobene grew comfortable and complacent, investigators said, mistakenly believing that he might be able to return to his old haunts. On January 28, 1993, several months after leaving the Federal Witness Protection Program and relocating to South Jersey, Mario Riccobene was gunned down in the parking lot of a Brooklawn, New Jersey, diner. His murder was seen as a message to Tommy Del, Nick Caramandi, Philip Leonetti and all the other informants.

"The mob doesn't forgive," said one investigator. "And it never forgets."

Even more troubling, from Maryann's perspective, was a series of botched mob hits aimed at the sons of prominent Philadelphia mobsters. It was not hard for her to imagine that her Bobby could have been in the line of fire.

In October of 1989, Nicky Scarfo, Jr., who was just twenty-six years old, was shot as he ate dinner in a South Philadelphia restaurant. Miraculously, the young mob figure survived despite taking seven bullets to the body. Three years later, Joey and Michael Ciancaglini, the young sons of imprisoned mob capo Joseph "Chickie" Ciancaglini, were targeted in what authorities believe was an ongoing internal power struggle.

In March of 1992 Michael Ciancaglini, then twenty-nine, managed to outrun two shotgun-wielding hit men. He barely made it through the front door of his South Philadelphia row house as his would-be assassins blasted away.

A year later, his brother, Joey, thirty-four, wasn't as lucky. Shortly after 6:00 A.M. on a Tuesday early in March of 1993, a man wearing a ski mask and carrying a high caliber pistol walked into Joey Ciancaglini's South Philadelphia luncheonette and pumped five bullets into his head and body. Joey, in critical condition for weeks, survived. But authorities say the shooting has left him scarred—both physically and mentally—for the rest of his life.

"You gotta wonder about some of these kids," said a Philadelphia police detective who has tracked the mob for twenty years. "Their fathers and brothers are dead or in jail. You think they would learn. Instead, they're out there doing the same stuff."

The lesson, however, has not been lost on Gladstone Street.

A few months after Bobby returned home, he went out on a date with a girl named Dee, who lived around the corner. When Bobby left South Philadelphia in 1986, she had been the kid sister of a guy from the neighborhood. Within a year of his return, she was his fiancée. Bobby and Dee were formally engaged on Christmas Eve of 1989. It was the best present Maryann got that year.

The following September, Tommy junior and Chrissy were married in Our Lady of Mount Carmel Church. Bobby was the best man. A year later, Tommy junior returned the favor, holding the ring and offering the toast when Bobby and Dee walked down the aisle. Tommy junior and Chrissy now live a few blocks from Maryann. Bobby and Dee live even closer, literally around the corner. Most mornings Bobby stops by his mother's kitchen for a cup of coffee before going to work.

The boys have started several small businesses, including a construction company that buys, renovates and resells row houses. Tommy and Bobby do most of the work themselves. It is hard, clean, and satisfying.

"Tommy's got a lot of plans," Bobby says proudly. "He's always thinkin'. When we were away and Tommy would complain that we wanted to go home, my father used to tell him, 'You'll never make it back there without me to give you money.' I think Tommy wants to show him he was wrong."

Neither Bobby nor Tommy junior has spoken with their father since they left Virginia Beach. Neither regrets the estrangement, but both brothers say they miss Danny and Michael, their young half brothers.

"I know what they're going through," Bobby says. "That's no way to live. I think they'd be happier back here, too, unless my father's got them brainwashed.

"All my life I wanted to be just like my father. And in the beginning you really don't see how many people he hurt, how he got up there, killing, extortion, bringing drugs in. Even when I found out what he did, I still wanted to be like him. It was the greed, the money. Seeing what he had and what he was able to do drove me. . . . You see money, you don't think of the consequences. You just want the money. The bottom line, you want to be rich, you want to be popular, you want everybody to think you're a big shot. That's what I wanted.

"Now I look back and I say, 'I can't believe it. That's what I wanted? I wanted to kill people? Over money? Over being a bigshot gangster?' Now I look down on them guys rather than look up at them. All my life I had looked up to them guys, thought they were like God, that they could never do no wrong. But all they do is use people. That's what they do . . . they take.

"I look at my stepfather. He never had nothin'. Worked as a longshoreman, worked hard. And I would always say I don't want to be like him. I want to have something. I want to have money. I want to live the easy life.

"Now, I look at him and what he's got, that's what I want. A good job, a family, a house. Come home each night and not have to worry about looking over my shoulder, worry about some bullet to the back of the head. Now I understand and I respect him for what he has, for what he's done. . . . People in the mob, my father, Nicky Crow, Scarfo, all them guys, they thought it was never gonna end. But when you go around hurtin' people, it always comes back in your face. It always comes back, no matter what you do."

As Bobby spoke, Maryann sat at her kitchen table on Gladstone Street drinking a cup of coffee.

When he finished, she smiled.

Mobfather—
Twelve Years Later

ommy Del made two trips back to Philadelphia after testifying in the big mob trials that brought down the Scarfo organization. Neither could be considered a triumphant return.

He first came back in January of 1997 to testify in the retrial of the Frankie Flowers murder case. The original 1989 convictions of Scarfo and his codefendants had been overturned by an appellate court panel. Prosecutorial misconduct and trial judge error had unduly influenced the jury in the case, the panel ruled. It was one of several setbacks for the Philadelphia District Attorney's Office, whose record in prosecuting the Scarfo crime family was abysmal.

By the time the retrial began, a lot had changed in Tommy Del's life and in the Philadelphia underworld. Some of it ended up on display in the Common Pleas Courtroom, which was packed each day with family members and friends of the defendants.

For many of them, it was a rare chance to see the defendants, who had been doing their time in federal prisons far from Philadelphia. Scarfo, Salvatore Merlino, Frank Iannarella, Phil and Frank Narducci, and Joe Ligambi all ended up back in town to face murder and murder conspiracy charges. Lawrence Merlino, who had pleaded guilty to a third-degree murder charge as part of his cooperating agreement, was no longer a part of the case. Neither was Nicky Milano, who was severed from the trial as a concession by the District Attorney's Office to make sure that his brother, Gino, would testify again.

Salvatore Merlino's son, "Skinny Joey," was at the trial most days, along with a group of young mobsters who now were major players in the crime family. The younger Merlino was the underboss and the focus of lots of law enforcement attention. He had taken on celebrity status in the city. A young, John Gotti–like figure, his criminal activities were front-page news, and his nighttime comings and goings were chronicled in the gossip columns.

Young, handsome, and with an arrogant swagger that drove the feds nuts, Skinny Joey had become the new face of the Philadelphia mob. He was the antithesis of the late Angelo Bruno, who had spent his whole career operating in the shadows. Bruno's philosophy—make money, not headlines—had brought twenty-one years of success and stability to the organization. Merlino, who had a higher profile and a much smaller bank account than the old Don, loved the limelight. The Generation-X underboss became a habitué of the city's trendy restaurants, bars, and nightclubs, usually accompanied by an entourage of young wiseguys, whose fancy clothes and expensive cars signaled a new era in the underworld. Their attitude was typical South Philly street corner: What's the point of being a gangster if nobody knows who you are.

Joey and his group of sycophants and wannabes added extra color to the high-profile trial. One of his top lieutenants, George Borgesi, also was a regular in the courtroom. Borgesi's uncle, Joe Ligambi, was the accused hitman in the case. The wives, mothers, daughters, and sisters of the defendants filled the other seats on one side of the third-floor courtroom. Across the aisle sat Frankie D'Alfonso's widow and their three adult children, a son and two daughters. On most days, they were accompanied by someone from law enforcement.

Tommy Del was the leadoff witness and spent two days on the stand. His hair was grayer. He had gained weight; his face was rounder and fuller than when he had testified in the first trial. There were age lines fanning out around his eyes and creeping across his forehead. But when he opened his mouth, it was like stepping back in time.

He again told the tale of the murder plot and tied all the defendants to the case. And in that same self-deprecating, matter-of-fact style, he admitted to his own life of crime—to the gambling, the loansharking, and the murders on behalf of the Mafia. What was missing, however, was the edge. Tommy Del didn't seem to have his heart in it. He appeared bored; tired, it seemed, of telling the same old story. When he was asked about his mob initiation—usually a point of high drama in an organized-crime case—he acted as if it were no big deal. Mario Puzo built a literary genre around the code of *omerta* that is at the heart of the making ceremony: the pricking of the trigger finger, blood spilled on a piece of paper, the paper set on fire as it is cupped in the hands of a mobster who swears to live and die for "the family." Tommy made passing reference to the pin and the paper and then said, "You go around the room shakin' hands and kissin' everybody. Then you kiss the boss and you're made."

It was hardly a Godfather moment.

There were, however, flashes of the old Tommy. When a prosecutor quizzed him about his dealings with D'Alfonso, Tommy told of how they had been in the bookmaking business together, but that he had opted out of the partnership.

Asked why, he replied, "I didn't feel he was countin' right."

Asked what he meant, Tommy said, "He was cheatin' me."

He also bristled when asked about the loyalty oath he had taken to the mob. Defense attorneys wondered how that squared with his decision to cooperate, which they said was a clear act of betrayal. "They tried to kill me," Tommy said angrily. "Who betrayed who?"

DelGiorno's credibility, of course, became the real focus of the cross-examination. Scarfo's lawyer, Norris Gelman, pointing to the five gangland slayings in which Tommy Del had admitted playing a role, called him "almost a serial killer" and said his testimony was purchased through "amnesty, immunity . . . and money."

It was a theme that came up again and again. And this time the defense had numbers to back up the allegations. In all, the state of New Jersey and the federal government had spent about $750,000 on DelGiorno and his family during his years of cooperation.

Some of that had been brought up at the first trial, but never in the detail that came out this time. Among other things, Tommy admitted that he had received a $125,000 loan from the state to go into business after he was relocated. The business, he said, "failed." And hardly any of the money had been repaid. This squared with rumors that began circulating around South Philadelphia shortly after he was released from prison. The word was that Tommy Del had opened a restaurant somewhere near St. Louis. The wags downtown laughed and joked about how he had run the business into the ground and scammed the state out of its money.

The D'Alfonso retrial took a month. The jury deliberated for less than two hours, including a lunch break. On February 20, 1997, the panel came back with its decision: Not guilty. All defendants. All counts. Although it was a setback and, certainly, an embarrassment for the District Attorney's Office, it had minimal impact on the lives of the defendants. All but Ligambi were serving lengthy federal sentences for racketeering. At this writing, everyone except Ligambi is still in jail.

Tommy Del's next known appearance in Philadelphia occurred on May 9, 2000. He came back to give a deposition in one of the most unusual civil suits ever filed in the Common Pleas Court of the city. DelGiorno and his wife, Roseanne, were suing a corporation Raymond "Long John" Martorano had set up to buy out Tommy's interest in Cous' Little Italy back in 1982.

Once a hangout for wiseguys—and made infamous because it was where Angelo Bruno ate his last meal—the restaurant had fallen on hard times. Different owners, a fire, and a changing neighborhood had contributed to its demise. But now things were turning back the other way. Yuppies had discovered South Philadelphia and the Cous' site was being eyed as a location for upscale, half-million-dollar townhouses.

Martorano was now looking to cash in.

He was on something of a roll. His murder conviction in the McCullough case had been overturned. Again, an appellate court ruled prosecutorial misconduct. But instead of ordering a retrial, that panel said the jury and the public had been so tainted that the only remedy was the immediate release of Martorano and Albert Daidone, his codefendant. They were sprung in 1999.

It was another stunning setback for the Philadelphia District Attorney's Office. The DA had lost the Salvie Testa murder trial outright. It had charged and convicted the wrong man in the Stevie Bouras hit. And now it had had both the D'Alfonso and McCullough convictions overturned.

Al Daidone, happy to be out from under a potential life sentence, wanted nothing more to do with the rackets and headed for the Jersey Shore where, by most recent accounts, he is running a restaurant.

Martorano, however, returned to South Philadelphia and sought to reestablish himself in the underworld. Among other things, he was looking to sell the Cous' site to a developer, a move that was expected to generate some serious cash. The problem was, there was an outstanding mortgage on the property, one that Tommy Del said he had forgotten all about when he disappeared into the witness protection program.

Long story short, Martorano needed Tommy Del to sign a release freeing up the property. Tommy, hearing the request through a third party, balked. Then he got an attorney and filed suit.

"The litigation," the lawyer later said, "is rather unusual."

Rather, indeed.

Tommy claimed that he held a $125,000 mortgage on Cous' as part of the sale of the property to Martorano. He said the deal was struck shortly before Long John was jailed for the McCullough hit, and, at the time, Scarfo told him to not to press the issue.

"He said, 'How can we bother him,'" DelGiorno said of a conversation he had with Scarfo about the mortgage payments that were due. "He said we had made all kinds of money with him from the drugs and he had killed two people for us. So he said, 'Leave him alone. Later, when he gets on his feet, he'll pay you.'"

Tommy Del figured "later" had arrived. In the suit, he asked for $386,000. This was the principal, plus interest, which had gone uncollected for eight years. Tommy's lawyers estimated that the interest was accruing at forty-one dollars a day.

Asked by Martorano's lawyer at the deposition why he had waited so long to pursue the issue, Tommy Del said, "When Scarfo tells you to leave somebody alone, you let them alone. . . . I had no choice. It was either leave him alone or get killed. So I let him alone. Now I have a choice."

Ever the pragmatist, Tommy said he was willing to negotiate. "All he has to do is pay me," he said. "I'm willing to settle."

Four months after giving his deposition, Tommy Del did just that. In September, his lawyers filed a one-page notice with the Prothonotary's Office noting that the case had been "settled, discontinued and ended." No other details were provided. Neither side would comment. But the word on the street was that Tommy Del had walked away with considerably less than he sought. Maybe fifty grand. Maybe less. Still, he came out better than Martorano, who never got a chance to cash in on the real-estate boom.

On January 17, 2002, Raymond Martorano walked out of his home near Sixth and Fitzwater Streets in South Philadelphia and got into his car. Already wearing a pacemaker, he was on his way to an appointment with his heart doctor that afternoon. He never made it.

Two gunmen ran up and opened fired. Long John took a series of shots to the body, but managed to drive away from his assailants. In fact, he drove six blocks before crashing his

Lincoln Town Car into a fire hydrant in front of Pennsylvania Hospital, where his doctor's office was located. Martorano, seventy-four, had been shot in the arm, leg, and stomach. He lingered in a hospital intensive-care unit for three weeks before dying. No one has been charged with the crime, but law enforcement authorities have tried to link it to the current leadership of the crime family.

The organization, they say, is now headed by Joe Ligambi, the only mobster to win release in the Frankie Flowers retrial.

Bobby DelGiorno watched it all play out from his old neighborhood.

He's had no contact with his dad since he fled protective custody back in 1988, but the retrial and the lawsuit were reminders of the way things used to be. Today, it is clear to Bobby that his father is from another world, one that Bobby has happily left behind.

Bobby and his brother Tommy now live in side-by-side townhouses, which they built themselves a few blocks from where they grew up. Each home is worth in the mid–six figures, part of that same real-estate boom that Long John was looking to cash in on. Tommy has three kids. Bobby has one. They have done well. Both are in business for themselves. Tommy, as always, is reluctant to discuss specifics. Bobby, on the other hand, just puts it out there.

There have been some bumps along the way, but life overall is good.

His mother, Maryann, divides her time between her trailer home down near the shore and South Philadelphia, enjoying life as a grandmother. Sadly, Bobby says, she and Joe split up.

For a while, Bobby ran a bar down on Second Street. For the first eight years after he came home, in fact, that was his primary source of income. It was a neighborhood joint, not unlike the places his dad used to own.

"But it got to be a headache," Bobby said. "There's too much drugs out there today. I wasn't into that, but I knew I couldn't control it. I couldn't keep it out. And I knew eventually somebody was gonna get locked up and [the authorities] ain't gonna believe that I had nothing to do with it."

He and Tommy Jr. also got involved in real estate, renovating old properties and flipping them at a profit. One led to another and then to another. Bobby figures a couple dozen passed through their hands. Each time they walked away with cash, and each time they reinvested.

Bobby sold off the last of his properties a few years ago, but still holds some mortgage notes. He's now lending money to guys who are doing what he and his brother were doing eight years ago. He understands the game and usually holds "first position" as a lender in six-figure deals that continue to generate income. He watches CNBC, follows the stock market, and talks about securing an economic future for his wife, Dee, and their daughter, Nicole, the same way he used to talk about the bookmaking business. He's factored the odds, the risk, and the gamble.

"I would never put my money in the stock market," he says, rolling his eyes as he expounds about the corporate bandits who have run their companies into the ground and left their stockholders broke and demoralized.

"You don't know what companies are legit and what companies aren't. These guys are more ruthless than mobsters. At least with the mob, when they take a bet and you win, you get paid. These guys had people investing and they just took the money. . . . Every day I see another guy on CNBC being taken out of his office in handcuffs."

It's about respect, Bobby says.

"If somebody hands you money, you're not gonna respect it. That's the way my father was. That's the way I was. Now I respect what I've earned. The hardest thing is keeping it and making it make money for you."

Those are some of the things Bobby's learned since he came back to Philadelphia looking for his life. He has no second thoughts about that decision. And though he has had no contact with his father, in a strange way he thinks Tommy Del would be "proud" of what he's accomplished.

"I think I had more money by the time I reached thirty than my dad had when he was a mobster," Bobby says. "And I made it legitimately. He might of spent more than I have, but I think when you work hard, you protect your money. At least that's the way I am. Dee's always kidding me about how I am, about how I'm always saving for that rainy day."

Bobby doesn't think much about what has happened to the other young guys in the mob, guys like Joey Merlino and Georgie Borgesi and Nicky Scarfo Jr., guys who were his contemporaries and who have spent the last decade dodging bullets and trying to duck federal prosecutions. Merlino and Borgesi are currently serving fourteen-year sentences on racketeering charges. Scarfo, who was nearly killed in 1989, has done two stints in prison since then on mob-related gambling and racketeering charges.

Bobby says that's another world, one in which he has no interest.

As he talks, sipping an iced tea in the modern kitchen of his stylish three-story townhouse, it is hard to picture Bobby up an alley in Baltimore with a gun in his hand and a dead man at his feet. That was, he said, another time, another place—and the kid in the alley was, in so many ways, another person.

They say there are no second acts in life, but Bobby puts the lie to that proposition. He has gotten a second chance, and he has grabbed it with both hands. He's always been an entrepreneur, a self-starter, a true believer in the American dream. Now he's channeling this energy in a legitimate direction.

And it's paying off. Big time.

"You just gotta work hard, every day," he says. "I think sometimes, if I had gone to school. . . ."

Bobby doesn't finish the thought, but what might have been sits there as he talks about the past and plans for the future.

"You only get so many opportunities. . . . I think my father, he never thought I would amount to much. I only went to the tenth grade. Sometimes I wonder if I had had an education, I'd be in the corporate world. I've got that push."

Eventually, he says, he would like to spend six months each year in Florida and six months in the Philadelphia area. But that's after his daughter, who is seven years old, is in college. For now, he wants to keep working. He has started another business and is deciding whether to expand it, to take on workers, or to continue "busting his ass" on his own.

The one-time wannabe wiseguy is in the exterminating business. How's that for irony? He's got his own company and a growing list of clients. A friend turned him on to the business. He went to school, learned how to apply the chemicals, what to look for on a job, how to bid on a contract. Now he makes calls, three or four a day, sometimes more. The money's good. The hours are decent. He runs the company out of his house. Dee works the phones.

"You'd be surprised how much money you can make," he says. "But you gotta work hard. You gotta go out and get the customers. You gotta show up and do the work."

The mob is just a distant memory. So are his concerns about coming back to South Philadelphia. It has all worked out well. He and his brother have been left alone. They've stayed down around Second Street, surrounded by friends whose loyalty is unquestioned.

"I'll tell ya, right now," he says. "I fear for my life more going into some of those pest control jobs than I do about the mob. Some of the contracts I get are in really bad neighborhoods."

Bobby, shaking his head as if he himself is amazed at what has happened, says he's now a member of Town Watch and the Second Street Irish Society, a local group that raises money for needy causes. Many of the other members, he says with a laugh, are in "law enforcement."

Coming back to Philadelphia, marrying Dee, and having a daughter have "stabilized" his life. Now, he says, he sees some of the ridiculous risks he took as a kid for what they were. And he has no intention of going back there.

"I've got too much to lose," he says.

So he'll keep working, because that's what he knows how to do and because it's who he is.

"I can't ever let my guard down," Bobby DelGiorno said. "Whether I had money or didn't have money, I think I'd still live my life the same way. I want to be judged not for what I have, but for who I am."

GLOSSARY OF MAJOR PLAYERS

Angelo Bruno
Philadelphia mob boss from 1959 until his shotgun assassination on March 21, 1980. His murder was the catalyst for a five-year internecine struggle that left nearly thirty mob members and associates dead.

John "Johnny" Calabrese
Mob associate involved in gambling, drug dealing and burglary. Gunned down by Tommy DelGiorno and Frank Iannarella in October 1981.

Antonio "Tony Bananas" Caponigro
Plotted the Bruno murder while serving as crime family consiglière. Later found brutally beaten and shot to death in New York City.

Nicholas "Nicky Crow" Caramandi
Mob family soldier who joined Tommy DelGiorno on the witness stand to take down the Scarfo mob.

Joseph "Chickie" Ciancaglini

Mob family capo and former driver/bodyguard of Frank Sindone. Became Tommy Del's partner in Cous' Little Italy restaurant after Sindone was found murdered.

Edward "Broadway Eddie" Colcher

A South Philadelphia bon vivant who was the gambling partner of Frank D'Alfonso and who became a good friend of Maryann, Bobby and Tommy Junior.

Frank "Frankie Flowers" D'Alfonso

A major South Philadelphia bookmaker and gambler, he was a close friend of Angelo Bruno and was Tommy DelGiorno's first mob mentor. Gunned down a block from his Ninth Street home in July of 1985.

A. Thomas "Tommy Del" DelGiorno

Philadelphia mob family capo who became a government witness and brought down the Scarfo crime family.

Robert "Bobby Del" DelGiorno

The youngest of Tommy Del and Maryann DelGiorno Fisher's two sons.

Daniel and Michael DelGiorno

Sons of Tommy and Roseanne DelGiorno, half brothers to Bobby and Tommy Junior.

Roseanne DelGiorno

Tommy Del's second wife. The mother of Danny and Michael.

Thomas G. "Tommy Junior" DelGiorno

Bobby's older brother by seventeen months.

Joe Fisher

Maryann DelGiorno's husband and the stepfather of Bobby and Tommy Junior.

Maryann DelGiorno Fisher

Tommy Del's first wife. The mother of Bobby and Tommy Junior.

Anthony Forline

Bobby's best friend and Gladstone Street neighbor. He was charged along with Bobby in the 1988 murder of Stephen Hemerlein.

Frank "J.R."Forline

The uncle of Anthony Forline, he was a loan shark and mob associate found murdered in February of 1985.

Salvatore Grande

Mob soldier and hit man in the Salvatore Testa murder.

Stephen Hemerlein

Baltimore man shot to death during a dispute with Bobby DelGiorno and Anthony Forline in April of 1988.

Frank "Faffy" Iannarella

Mob capo who worked with Tommy DelGiorno throughout the 1980s. They were initiated into the mob after murdering Johnny Calabrese in 1981.

Philip Leonetti

Scarfo's nephew and underboss. He became a government witness after being sentenced to fifty-five years in prison for a 1988 racketeering conviction. Currently in the Witness Protection Program.

Joseph "Joey" McGreal

Tough-as-nails Philadelphia teamster who befriended Tommy Del in the early 1970s. Found murdered in New Jersey in 1973 in an apparent dispute over control of the Camden County bartenders union.

John McCullough

Philadelphia roofers union boss gunned down in December of 1980 after ignoring mob warning to stay out of Atlantic City union activities.

Nicholas "Nicky Whip" Milano

Young mob soldier and hit man, he was a protégé of Tommy Del.

Frank "Chickie" Narducci

Ran gambling operations for Bruno crime family. Shot to death in 1982 in retribution for the murder of Phil Testa.

Nicodemo "Little Nicky" Scarfo

Philadelphia mob boss from 1981 until 1991. His brutal and bloody reign ended with a series of arrests and prosecutions that destroyed his crime family. Currently serving two lengthy federal prison sentences.

Frank Sindone

Top mob loan shark, he became Tommy Del's business partner. Murdered in 1980 because of his suspected involvement in the plot to kill Angelo Bruno.

Pasquale "Pat the Cat" Spirito

Getaway driver for DelGiorno and Iannarella in Calabrese killing. Gunned down in April of 1983 after falling out of favor with Scarfo and others.

John Stanfa

Sicilian-born mob figure who drove Bruno home on the night he was killed. Emerged as Philadelphia mob boss in 1991. Strong ties to both the Gambino crime family in New York and to Mafia figures in Palermo.

Philip "Chicken Man" Testa

Mob boss who succeeded Angelo Bruno. Killed in March of 1981 when a remote control bomb planted under his porch was detonated.

Salvatore "Salvie" Testa

Son of Phil Testa, became a capo in the Scarfo organization. Murdered on Scarfo's orders in September of 1984.

Index